Lani's Story

Lani's Story
Not a victim. A survivor.

Lani Brennan with Hazel Flynn

HarperCollins*Publishers*

HarperCollinsPublishers

First published in Australia in 2013
by HarperCollinsPublishers Australia Pty Limited
ABN 36 009 913 517
harpercollins.com.au

Copyright © Lani Brennan 2013

The right of Lani Brennan to be identified as the author of
this work has been asserted by her under the *Copyright Amendment
(Moral Rights) Act 2000.*

This work is copyright. Apart from any use as permitted under the
Copyright Act 1968, no part may be reproduced, copied, scanned, stored
in a retrieval system, recorded, or transmitted, in any form or by any
means, without the prior written permission of the publisher.

HarperCollinsPublishers
Level 13, 201 Elizabeth Street, Sydney NSW 2000, Australia
31 View Road, Glenfield, Auckland 0627, New Zealand
A 53, Sector 57, Noida, UP, India
77–85 Fulham Palace Road, London W6 8JB, United Kingdom
2 Bloor Street East, 20th floor, Toronto, Ontario M4W 1A8, Canada
10 East 53rd Street, New York NY 10022, USA

National Library of Australia Cataloguing-in-Publication data:

Brennan, Lani.
  Lani's story/Lani Brennan
  978 0 7322 9348 2 (pbk.)
  978 0 7304 9510 9 (ebook)
  Brennan, Lani.
  Women—Violence against—Australia
  Abused women—Australia—Biography
  Indigenous women—Violence against—Australia—Biography
  Family violence—Australia
  Victims of family violence—Australia
  Women, Aboriginal Australian—Social Conditions
  Women, Aboriginal Australian—Australia—crimes against
362.82920994

Cover design by Matt Stanton, HarperCollins Design Studio
Cover image by Mark Rogers
Typeset in 11.5/15.5pt Adobe Caslon by Kirby Jones

This book is dedicated to the memory of all those who lost their lives through domestic violence, to all the other survivors out there, and to those dedicated workers who spend their days reaching out to people in their time of greatest need.

I would like to acknowledge the traditional custodians of this land. I would also like to pay respect to the elders both past and present.

Prologue

Somewhere in the distance I can hear a strange, high sound. It doesn't quite sound human. Whatever's making it is broken and barely alive, crying out in pain and fear. There's defeat in there too. Whatever is making that noise doesn't have long to go. I'm trying to figure it out. If I can just understand where it's coming from, maybe I can help, but my thoughts are so heavy and slow. I have the urge to shake my head to help clear it but I can't; for some reason I can't seem to move. Slowly I start to work it out. There's something stopping me moving, something pinning me down. I need to breathe. I can't breathe. Why can't I breathe?

All at once my eyes open and I understand. I can't move because he is on top of me, he's raping me. I can't breathe because he has his hands around my neck. No, that's not right—not his hands, something else. I can see the end of it out of the corner of my eye. What is that thing? If only I could think. I know, it's an electrical cord, a bright orange one and, oh god, he's pulling it tighter around my throat. I'm going to die. But I can't die. I have to get out. I have to help the poor creature that's making that awful noise. Then just before I pass out again it comes to me. It's me. That inhuman sound is coming from me.

I've done terrible things in my life, things I am deeply ashamed of. I've had far, far more terrible things done to me. I've suffered violence and abuse and degradation that no human being should suffer. But I am not a victim. I am a survivor.

When I was at my lowest point, thirteen years ago, if you'd told me what my life would be like today I would have thought you were making a sick joke. Me, safe and happy, loved and loving, respected and worthy of respect? There's no way that was possible. I believed the only way the torture would stop would be for me to die. I prayed to die. But I didn't die. I survived.

My life has changed so much that when I look back it's almost as though those things happened to someone else. But everything I've been through is woven into my soul. Knowing I had the strength, somehow, to survive all that, and to fight for justice—that's the steel deep within me. And being able to love, not to be consumed by hate; being able to show my daughters how to grow strong and free from fear—that's what gives shape to my life. Being able to help other people see that there is a way out of their misery—that's my purpose on this earth.

My name is Lani, and this is my story.

Chapter One

Scientists are still arguing about what causes alcoholism and how big a role genes might play in it. Well, whether it is genetic or not, it runs through generations on both sides of my family.

My mother, Kathy, is a Maori woman who moved to Sydney from New Zealand when she was nineteen. She met my dad, Rory, in a pub at Bondi, both of them no doubt with a drink in hand. My dad had been through hell as a kid. His mum, my beloved nan, was a lifeline to me over and over again during the bad times, but she'd been a desperate alcoholic when he was growing up.

My nan, Maureen, was white and was working as a barmaid at a Sydney pub, a waterside early opener, when she met my dad's father, who was a Murri Aboriginal man originally from Cunnamulla in Queensland. He was already married with kids, but that didn't stop him hooking up with Maureen. She got pregnant, and he wanted nothing more to do with her.

My dad is dark-skinned, and given how much casual racism I still face on the streets now, I can't imagine what it would have been like for a white woman to have a son to an Aboriginal man back in the fifties. Pretty soon Maureen was permanently drunk, with periodic visits to Sydney's Callan Park Mental Hospital to receive electroshock treatment. She and Rory lived in a crowded flat along with her mother, Kathleen, and brother Fred. Maureen was drowning in alcohol and was often horrifically violent towards her son.

I guess it's no wonder Rory ran off the rails early and stayed off them for many years. By the time he met young Kathy in Bondi in the late 1970s he was already a drunk, too. I still feel resentful about the damage Rory's father, my grandfather in name only, did to him by abandoning his child before birth—and doing it again, years later.

(When I was about twelve, Rory called on the services of Link-Up, the great organisation that has helped so many Aboriginal people from the Stolen Generations reunite with their families. Through Link-Up, Dad got hold of his father, and arranged to go and see him. It turned out my grandfather lived in Sydney, just half an hour's drive away. Not long after he'd made contact, Dad took me and my sister along to meet him. We stayed in the car while Dad went into the club where his father was waiting. Rory told his father he had brought us along and that we wanted to meet him. Our grandfather came out to the car, asked us if we wanted a soft drink, brought us out one, and then told my dad to go away and never contact him again. So as well as rejecting his own son, he rejected his grandchildren too.)

Before they became parents, Rory and Kathy drank and partied hard. In fact, Dad says that Mum used to be able to drink him under the table; she says that's not really the way it was. But when she got pregnant with me, their first child, she just put down the bottle and never picked it up again. Knowing what I know now about how hard it is to stop, I think that's an amazing effort.

Dad was a different matter. He just kept right on drinking, and drinking, and drinking. I came along in January 1981 and just under a year later my sister, Koorine, arrived, but he kept going. I remember seeing a photo of Mum and Dad with either me or Koorine as a toddler: a baby girl up on Dad's shoulders, while the pram they're pushing is full of beer cans.

It was terrible for my mum, and not just because of Dad's unreliability and the money that was spent. Alcohol inflamed Rory and his anger flared up out of control. As he's said himself, 'There was nothing I liked better than getting fully charged up and having a fight.' That was bad enough when it was with another (probably drunk) man, but he also took his anger out at home, sometimes hitting Kathy. Occasionally she would try to defend herself, in one incident hitting him on the head with a heavy metal ashtray, but mostly it was classic domestic violence with the woman in the firing line.

I really don't remember much about this period at all, partly because I was so young when everything changed for the better, and partly because I think kids in those situations tend to block out the memories. I do know there were parties non-stop at the house, with rivers of grog. And I remember one night Dad came home, drunk of course, and we were trying to open the front door for him and somehow he got it off its hinges and it fell on top of us. But that's about it for my memories of very early childhood.

Maureen, Dad's mother, was living with us too by this time, and she had stopped drinking. She used to take care of us when Mum was at work. As we were growing up, Nan, or Wha Wha, as we always called her, would tell us stories about her life as a young woman. We would listen, fascinated, as she painted incredible pictures of her time as a showgirl visiting Vietnam, dancing to entertain the troops. She told us she and John Wayne became fast friends and she told us they were both so desperate for a drink they used to risk their lives by running through the jungle from one camp to another. We lapped it all up.

To me, Wha Wha, in the photos from her showgirl days, looked like Marilyn Monroe with blonde, wavy hair, blue eyes and an hourglass figure. In my childhood she looked the way Marilyn might have looked if she hadn't died so young. Wha Wha held herself very well and always presented herself nicely, even though, like my parents, she dressed from op shops. She'd put together a nice outfit and always wear a little brooch or another piece of jewellery.

Having sobered up, she was a completely different person from the violent figure of my father's childhood. Everyone used to ring her up for advice and she had a really caring and gentle nature. She loved us to death, we knew. It was mutual: she was, without doubt, my favourite family member when I was a child. I loved her to the moon and back. When we were children, even if we were in the wrong, doing something naughty, she was on our side, always defending us. A few years later I would really put that forgiveness to the test, but the well of her kindness never ran dry.

When I was around six, Dad did something wonderful: he followed his mother and wife's lead and got sober with the help of Alcoholics Anonymous. He used to go to regular AA meetings in Redfern, the centre of Sydney's Aboriginal community, and he would take Koorine and me along. The meetings were in what had once been the Rachel Forster Hospital complex, but everyone just called it 'the roundhouse'. We'd sit under the table and draw pictures for all the members. We used to love going along and meeting those people, but at the same time I used to think, 'They're crackers!' I'd hear their life stories and think, 'I hope I never turn out like them.' Little did I know …

After he got sober, Dad was terrific. He used to take Koorine and me out to parks and beaches all the time. It was as if he was making up for lost time. I think he felt a lot of guilt about the way he had been when we were younger, and he worked very hard at becoming a really good family man.

Because other people close to me often have a different perspective on things, I've asked some of them how they recall events, starting with my mum.

> KATHY BRENNAN: I was only about eighteen when I first came to Australia. I wasn't such a big drinker; it was mainly Rory. I sort of tried to keep up with him when he did drink but I wasn't the one that had the drinking problem. I suppose I did outdrink him a couple of times, but it wasn't for me. The domestic violence in our relationship happened while the drinking was on. It stopped when the drinking stopped.

Those years were really happy ones. We moved around a lot, from one rented house to another around the La Perouse area, but that didn't worry us kids. At the time, Dad was working as a garbo and a gravedigger at Botany Cemetery and my sister and I used to go there a lot when he was working and help him, carrying bricks down while he was digging graves. Wherever we were, we'd find our own fun.

La Perouse was a beautiful community to grow up in. It was a real neighbourhood—you could leave all your doors open at night, everyone knew each other and looked out for one another. We kids could play all through the streets safely. The rule was that when the streetlights came on it was time for everyone to get home, otherwise we were free to roam and have adventures together, swimming or walking along the beach and around the sandhills, catching lizards or just singing and making up games as we went along.

A local church group based down on the Aboriginal mission (or the Mish, as it was universally known among the locals) used to organise holiday camps and fun get-togethers. We weren't especially religious, but that didn't matter, it was more a community gathering spot than anything else.

There was plenty of socialising between families. I remember a lot of backyard cricket, impromptu parties and barbecues. It felt like everyone knew everyone, and everyone was equally accepted.

Sport became really important to Koorine and me, and Dad was a big part of that. His work kept him really fit and he liked to look good—people always used to comment on it (I tease him even now about having tickets on himself)—and Mum was in great shape too; she still is. We were a fit, sporty family. I used to play representative netball, with Dad there cheering me on, and he arranged for us to get involved with Nippers, the junior lifesaving organisation. There wasn't a Nippers at La Perouse then so he'd take my sister and me and other local kids all the way over to Cronulla Beach every Sunday morning so we could take part. He kept us really busy.

He had been a great runner when he was young. I was too, and he encouraged me in that. I loved running, although I did it differently from pretty much all the other kids. Everyone had spiked shoes and blocks to jump from and coaches and all those kinds of things. I was a barefoot runner. I'd just turn up, kick off my thongs and run. I loved it and I was really good at it too. People who knew about that kind of thing used to say I had a real talent—I even remember people talking about me as a future champion if I kept it up.

Koorine and I went to La Perouse Public School, and it was a great environment. The community was always involved in school activities—aunties, uncles, grandparents, parents. It was less like a school and more like a family. I never encountered any racism. We didn't think about people as white or Koori or Asian. We were all just people. There were a lot of different nationalities and everyone got along.

At some point in my primary school years Dad bought a caravan which was parked at Bundeena, technically a suburb of Sydney but in effect a village, isolated by its position in the Royal National Park that occupies much of the land between Sydney and Wollongong. He used to take us there on weekends to enjoy its peaceful beauty, but then, when I was about ten, Mum and Dad decided we would move to Bundeena full-time. They'd been offered a house in the Mish, but it was one that didn't suit their needs so they knocked it back, saying, 'Oh no, we're going to go bush instead.' I think they ended up regarding it as one of the worst decisions they ever made—well, I did, anyway!

It was at Bundeena that I first remember encountering racism. Mum says we did really well there, but Koorine and I were the only Aboriginal kids at the local school and it felt like ours was the only non-white family in the area. Even though we were both really good at sport, winning ribbons all the time, we used to get taunted with insults like 'charcoal chicken'. I was also horribly teased because I started developing early, a humiliating experience that made me so angry.

We were so tied up with our own concerns that we didn't think about what the change must have been like for Mum and Dad, but it can't have been easy. They too had enjoyed a big support network and lots of friends in La Perouse; now they were just as cut off as we were. But it must have been especially hard for Mum because she had a new baby (my brother Garri) and soon another on the way (Darryl).

Then we moved again, to Grays Point in the Sutherland Shire. It was a bit closer to the city but still a fair way from our old stomping ground. Rather than move us to yet another school, Mum re-enrolled us at La Perouse and made round trips of an hour or more twice a day to take us there and pick us up. Back in our old community with our old friends we were soon happy again. I wasn't good at schoolwork except for maths, but I was a model student, never in trouble and always easygoing.

It wasn't too much longer before we moved back into the La Perouse area. I kept up my interest in dance, which had started with lessons at Bundeena, but shifted from ballet and modern dance to indigenous dance. La Perouse School had an indigenous dance group which Koorine and I joined. We had Torres Strait Islander and Aboriginal dancing, with the boys on their didgeridoos. People would contact the school and invite us to play all over the place—at the airport to welcome dignitaries, at other schools and all sorts of places.

When I was in Year 5 we competed in the Sydney Rock Eisteddfod, a huge event sponsored by the state government where children from schools all around New South Wales could get up and perform, using music and dance to tell a story. It was a real institution, and taking part in it was a great opportunity for us. We didn't even care that we were so different from the kids from most of the other schools with their professional-looking costumes and props, while all we had were black leotards and hand-painted tights. To our amazement, our piece, which was a mixture of traditional and contemporary dancing, took out first prize! We were absolutely thrilled. To add to the excitement, we won computers, which the school didn't have then. The whole community was stoked.

If only things could have stayed this way, with us kids happy and active within a stable family. But my parents' marriage was breaking up and everything was about to go horribly wrong.

> RORY BRENNAN: I did have it hard when I was young, with all the violence and the drama. When she was in her eighties and had dementia, my mother, Maureen, told me about her life. I was shocked. She'd had a rough life herself. She'd been sexually assaulted as a young girl of fourteen or so when she was travelling around with a circus. She'd gotten pregnant and gone back home. In those days abortions were all illegal backyard ones, and her parents forced her to go through that. She turned to the drink. She was an alcoholic when I was growing up. She'd been in Callan Park, she'd had suicide attempts, electroshock treatment, she'd been in straitjackets.

She'd drink brandy by choice, some kind of cheap hospital brandy. She'd have it by her bed. I didn't have a bedroom—I slept on the sofa—and I remember she'd be in her bed, she'd have the bottle next to her and when she woke up she'd reach for it. I'd hear the noise of the cork coming out. She used to beat me with a belt with the brass buckle on it. Or she'd be going out the door, telling me that I was worthless, I was no good, I was the reason all this shit had happened, and she was going to put me in a home. She'd be going to walk out the door, saying all this stuff to me, and I'd be there trying to hold the door closed. That was a daily thing when I was eight or nine.

I didn't know who my father was. She wouldn't tell me anything about him. When you're growing up you want to know your father's name. You end up making up stories because you feel so embarrassed.

I didn't have friends over much because of the way we lived, but if I did ever bring anyone back with me she might be lying on the floor passed out and they'd have to step over her. They'd say, 'What's wrong with your mum?' I didn't really know for a long while, but around the age of twelve I started to realise it was the alcohol, and then I started really resenting and hating her.

By thirteen or fourteen I was rebelling—drinking and mucking up. I turned from being a kid full of fear and anxiety and worry to somebody who had a chip on my shoulder, wanted to take on the world, wouldn't back down from no one. When I was about fourteen, fifteen and just getting into drinking heavily, that was when Mum got sober.

I really started running off the rails. I wasn't mixing with or looking up to people who were doing decent things. The ones I was mixing with were six, seven years older than me when I was fifteen or sixteen; they were drinking every day. They were violent people, been in jail, from broken homes. They did all the opposite things of what a normal person does. I fitted into all of it, I was off and running.

I became a regular at a pub in Bondi called the Astra. There'd always be some drama, some fight, some violence—that was all part of it. I met Kathryn there. She could put a few away then, and we met up and were together. You just hooked up.

It wasn't very long at all before we had Lani, but nothing really changed for me. It changed for Kathryn—she stopped drinking completely—but I just kept on going. I had mates over all the time. There were always people around. I'd have mates who'd come and stay for weeks at a time. There was always drinking, partying—it was open house. I worked here and there, bits and pieces, but a lot of the time I'd be home with the girls while Kathryn was working. She'd come home and I'd take off with my mates down the pub and that's the way it was, day after day. Kathryn was having to cope with it all. She and my mum became very close. Mum was very staunch and fantastic with the girls.

For some reason, when I was in my early thirties my mother finally came out with my father's name. That blew me out of the sky because in all those years she'd never said anything. At first I didn't believe her, but Link-Up tracked him down and I went and met him. I wrote him a letter; I think it was a pretty big shock to him. We ended up meeting in a club in Balmain. I was a dark secret—he already had a woman and kids when he had the fling with my mother, so I was like the ghost that turned up from the past. That's what he said to me; he said, 'Not after all this time.' That was a shattering thing for me because you're abandoned, you get rejected, then you get rejected again thirty years later. I sprung the kids on him. I thought maybe it would soften him. The look on his face when I turned up wasn't a look of happiness, it was a look of surprise: 'Not him again.' That was the only time the girls saw him.

After I got sober I became much more involved with the girls. I used to do all sorts of things with them: I'd take them to the beach, spend the day at the pool, I'd take them over to Nippers. Lani was a happy-go-lucky kid, good at whatever sport she tried, and outgoing. We became a normal type of family.

It wasn't fair on Kathryn, though, because I wasn't really there for a lot of it. I probably hadn't understood her needs. I'd just been doing my thing and being with the girls, and she'd been taking care of a lot of things that needed taking care of. That took its toll on the marriage.

I know for a lot of people memory runs smoothly, like a film. When they think back to themselves at, say, fifteen, they can picture the class they were in at school, their friends and their family home. They can recall what a typical day or a typical week was like back then. Tapping into a memory is like selecting a movie scene on a DVD: it flows on from what came before and it leads into what comes after. It's all part of a story that fits together and makes sense. My memories aren't like that.

Because I started drinking heavily and using drugs at such a young age, my memory is shot. It's not just vague, like 'Where did I leave those car keys?', it has big holes in it. Huge holes. In fact, for a lot of the time between when I was about fourteen and eighteen, drifting along on the tide of whatever was on offer, there's more gap than there is memory.

When I set out to remember that time in my life, instead of memories unreeling smoothly it's more like I'm driving through pea-soup fog, hunched over the steering wheel as I inch forward, trying to make sense of the dim shapes off to the side. Every now and then, something looms suddenly into view out of the grey. Then it's gone again. Something else, unconnected, looms out, then it too disappears back into the fog. I remember moments, scenes, images. I know it's my own life, but it almost feels as if I'm catching glimpses of what happened to someone else.

The parts before and after are much clearer. My childhood memories are clear. The part of my life when I was being tortured physically and mentally, fearing death, is all too horribly clear. And the sober years since, when I have built up everything that matters to me, that's all clear too. But of my teenage years, only fragments remain. In some ways it's just as well.

When we moved back to La Perouse, Garri and Darryl were still babies; I would have only been about eleven and the two boys were under two years old. Looking back, things must have been hard for both Mum and Dad, not that I saw it that way at the time. When we first moved back we lived with close family friends at Phillip Bay in La Perouse. Their place had a backyard with a big shed that served as another living space; we kids thought it was a fantastic arrangement. They had three daughters who were around the same age as me and Koorine and we had heaps of fun all living together, tumbling and running around everywhere and hurling ourselves off the old half-tyre swings in the yard.

We moved from there into our own place but things weren't going well. Even though Dad had been sober for five years or more, a lot of damage had been done to his relationship with Mum in the years before that. They'd only been teenagers when they got together. Mum had had to cope with young kids and a violent, unpredictable husband and it left its scars. The cracks in their relationship got deeper and they started arguing more and more. I've got to give them both credit, they really tried hard to keep the family together. And even when they realised they weren't going to stay together forever, they put the final split off as long as possible, because my brothers were still so little.

In fact, I remember that Mum went back to New Zealand for a while when the boys were still toddlers. She said it was to help out her family back there, and I'm sure it was, but I can also see now that it probably was a chance for my parents to have a break from one another because they weren't yet ready to call it a day on their marriage. Koorine and I were typical kids, too busy complaining about the extra workload of helping Dad and our nan, Wha Wha, who was still living with us, to think about things from the adults' point of view.

By now I was almost at the end of Year 6. I'd turned eleven at the start of the year and my unravelling was about to begin.

I had my first drink of alcohol and my first smoke of marijuana on the same day. Now that I have my own kids of that age, it seems like a very big deal to be delving into harmful substances so very young—only eleven! I thought I knew what I was doing, though. I sought it out.

It wasn't exactly hard to get hold of booze and drugs. No planning was required. There were always kids around the neighbourhood who were drinking and drugging on weekends, and high school kids who'd come onto the primary school grounds after school. Everyone knew what they were up to.

They'd sit behind one of the buildings, right out of sight. They'd throw their bikes down and sit around in a circle, six or seven of them, and drink and smoke. Even though we younger kids often played on the grounds, we stayed away from that area—why go there since all they were doing was writing themselves off?

But one day at the start of the summer holidays following the end of Year 6, I decided I was going to join them. It was a warm afternoon and daylight saving had started so we were allowed to stay out later. I headed for the school grounds knowing I wanted to get drunk. Even though I'd sat at my dad's feet through so many hours of AA meetings and listened to all those stories about the slide to rock bottom on booze and drugs, I didn't hesitate. I told myself I just wanted to be numb for a while and not have to think about anything, especially my fears about Mum and Dad splitting.

I walked up to the group and sat down. I knew the kids who were there, some more than others. They were the older brothers and sisters of kids I was at school with, or just teenagers I knew from the community. They were fine with me coming and joining them—everyone was welcome to party.

I think that first time I drank it was Passion Pop: cheap, sweet, bubbly wine that smelled good and tasted good. It passed around from one person to the next, all of us swigging out of the bottle.

There was moselle too, and then someone handed me a bong made out of an old Orchy juice bottle and I took a hit of that.

Unfortunately, my little experiment didn't make me feel sick or scared or ashamed, as it does for some people, who end up with the world spinning around them, just wanting it to be over. No, I loved it from the very first time. There is a lot of alcoholism and addiction in my family tree, and I'd just taken my first step along the same dark path.

I can't remember going home that night, or how I hid my state from my family. I probably just said I was feeling sick and went straight to my room. I'd be doing a lot of that from now on.

Things between Mum and Dad got worse and worse. Around the time I turned twelve and started high school, they stopped being a couple. But they arranged it so that Dad could stay around to help look after us kids—the boys especially, since they were so young. Dad had a mate called Tommy who'd gone through AA with him. Together they converted a shed in the backyard into a flat and Dad moved out there.

Even though things were pretty rocky, it wasn't Mum's choice for them to split. Looking back, I reckon Dad was going through some kind of early midlife crisis. I think everything caught up with him. He'd been through his drinking stage, he'd got sober, he done the family thing with all of us kids and my mum, trying to make it up to her, and he'd looked after his mother as she was getting older. Maybe one day he just looked at the way things were and thought, 'What have I done in my life? I haven't really seen the world, I haven't branched out.' I think he decided, 'Well, I'm going to give it a go and start fresh with a new life.' So he got a new girlfriend, told Mum it was over, and in his own mind moved on.

Having him around while all this was going on must have been really hard for Mum. She didn't know what was happening at first, and I think that for a while, even after she found out, she was hoping it wasn't really finished. She'd done all those hard yards with him in his drinking years and stuck by him as he got sober—she would have hoped that they'd be together to enjoy the good years after all that. It was pretty hard for her to take. I remember once when Dad was out and the phone in the flat, which had a separate line to the one in the house, started ringing. Mum ran out and grabbed it and yes, as she'd suspected, it was another woman calling. Mum was really angry. In fact, I think if I hadn't grabbed Dad's TV, she'd have smashed it up—quite a few other things got chucked at the wall that day.

Carol Simon is one of our oldest family friends, always known to us as 'Aunty Carol'.

> CAROL SIMON: I met Lani's mum, Kathy, at an Al-Anon meeting in Maroubra, twenty-seven or twenty-eight years ago. She was the only Maori lady in the room, and I was the only Aboriginal person. We just started talking. Her husband at the time, Lani's dad, Rory, was an alcoholic; my husband was an alcoholic and we used to just comfort each other.
>
> The reason you go to Al-Anon is so you can talk to other people who have similar issues and problems with the addicts in their lives, and it's like AA in that you're just on a first-name basis. For years it was like that, but because we both lived in the area we would run into each other, and we'd talk. Lani and Koorine would have only been

five and four when we met. Eventually we started getting together outside the meetings and I'd go to their house.

Kathy had it pretty rough when the girls were little. She's a very proud lady, isolated because there were no other family members to call on. She did have Rory's mum, Maureen; they were very good friends. The children were clearly well cared for, smiling little girls. But when you're in that situation, you present a front. I know we did—everyone thought we were the perfect family. No one knows what's really going on in your home when the door's closed.

Then Rory stopped drinking. When they give up drinking or drugs, it's called the 'isms': they still have alcoholism. You stop drinking but you're still an alcoholic and the issues are still there. But things would have settled down. When that happens you think, 'Oh this is good.' But the behaviour is still there; they have to replace the drink. (A lot of people replace it with gambling, and if that happens you still haven't recovered from drinking. You might have given up drinking but you've taken on something else.)

The marriage broke up. Rory had an affair that was going on for a long time before Kath found out. Yet Kath never complained, she never ran him down. When he left she was devastated. She went home to New Zealand for a few weeks to be with her nan, who raised her.

During all this, Wha Wha was our constant. If she wasn't at an AA meeting, she was home—she was a real homebody. I loved having her there, but I hated what was happening to my family. I found it all pretty hard to cope with, and it was around this time that I started hitting the alcohol and drugs a lot harder. I just loved the effect of it. I loved the person it made me, at least back then. I loved feeling untouchable. A few drinks or cones in and it was like no one could hurt me, no one could do anything. I felt on top of the world.

I'd felt for years and years that I was hiding behind some kind of mask. When I was younger, people used to say I was very outgoing, but I felt like it was all just a front. I always had a smile stuck on my face so no one would be able to see what was really going on. Even as a child I found it very hard to cry. I couldn't get a handle on emotions. I hated having feelings and I hated showing my feelings—except anger. When something happened that would leave most kids upset or tearful, I got angry instead. I couldn't explain it to myself, let alone anyone else, so I just hid my confusion.

Inside I felt like a very shy, withdrawn kid, although no one who knew me then would ever have believed it. Maybe Koorine was the only one who really understood. Deep down I was terrified of everything. But I was very, very good at hiding how I felt.

Chapter Two

That place behind the school shed where I'd gone for my first drink and smoke now became my regular haunt. I used to go back there all the time, bonging. It didn't matter who I was with, or who I was around, I was just interested in changing the way I felt. At first I liked the bong best and I was smoking more than drinking. But it didn't take long before I really didn't care if I was drunk or on drugs, I just wanted to be numb. And then I started preferring alcohol, because it wiped me out better. I knew I could drink and quickly get totally off my face. It let me block everything out and hide my feelings, even from myself.

People who haven't been there themselves often think, 'Oh, that's just a cop-out.' But people who use drugs and drinking the way I did do it for a reason. It seems to solve something inside them—though as we all know, it actually just leads to more problems—but it's what the addiction experts call 'self-medicating'. You're trying to use it to fix something you feel is broken.

Of course I didn't know this at the time—and let's be honest, it wouldn't have changed things if I had, because consequences are so hard to grasp when you're that age—but there has been some really worrying scientific research about the effect alcohol and drugs can have on developing brains. Alcohol especially.

Researchers have found that alcohol doesn't affect teenagers and their developing brains the same way it does adults; it's not such a sedative for younger people. Teenagers' motor skills don't get as badly affected—that means that they don't get the same degree of slurring and staggering that adults do and it doesn't make them as sleepy. Unfortunately, this means they can just keep drinking and drinking, without realising how much they are affected.

Alcohol also changes the way your brain actually develops. Teenagers who feel the way I did drink because they are 'stressed'—there's a heap of stuff that they feel bad about. They get upset or angry, and drink to change their mood. But there's another kind of stress too, a physical kind that releases certain chemicals into your brain. When teenagers drink a lot of alcohol it seems that it changes the way those chemicals work, and this also makes these kids want to drink more.

The other thing scientists have found out about the way alcohol affects the brain is that if you drink too much during those developing years it causes permanent damage to your memory, stopping you from being able to form some kinds of memories in the way you would have done otherwise. Unfortunately, I could have told them that for free!

Dad had moved out of the shed and settled into a relationship with his girlfriend, and when we kids met her we liked her. Even Mum eventually accepted it—after all, it was obvious they had moved in different directions with their lives, and they were never going to go back to the way things had been. Everyone was moving on except me. Somehow, even though I couldn't do anything about it, I just couldn't accept all the changes.

Wha Wha was still living with us, helping Mum with Garri and Darryl. Koorine and I weren't helping at all. I moved myself into the backyard flat, where I did what I liked. Koorine had followed me down the path of booze and drugs. In fact, I'd made her take her first hit of a bong when she was about twelve. She has the same addictive personality as me, and she's had her own long struggles with substance abuse. Plenty of times along that rocky road she's reminded me that I was the one who led her there. Years later, when I first got sober and she was still addicted, she would bitterly say to me, 'Look at you, straight now, and look at me, I'm a pot addict. I can't get off it.' To this day I feel guilty about my role in her addiction.

At the time, of course, we saw things very differently. Back then there was nothing either of us wanted more than to escape through grog and drugs. Our behaviour at home became, well, hectic would be a nice way to describe it. We were out of control, in a rage and drunk or stoned (or both) pretty much all the time.

We were verbally abusive and threatening to Mum, completely disrespecting her and the rules she tried to set for us, and I can see now we must have made life hell. At the time, we thought *she* was the problem. When things got really bad, my dad's mate Tommy arranged for Koorine and me to come and stay with him for a while. Another time, his parents went away for a short holiday and he let us stay at their place while they were away.

But things just got worse at home, and then something happened that hit me like a ton of bricks: Mum and Tommy started a relationship, and I lost the plot. I just couldn't handle it. I hated it. I thought it was the worst possible thing my mother could do. How could she get together with a bloke I knew as Dad's close mate and a friend to the whole family?

Growing up, I have to admit I'd been a 'daddy's girl'. I always took his side, I don't know why. And now, even though Dad had a new life with his girlfriend and was fine with the whole thing between Mum and Tommy, some kind of warped loyalty made me hate Tommy. I hated the fact that he was white. I hated the fact that he'd been so close to our family before my folks split. I was seeing things in such a twisted way, I started thinking, 'Oh, he was just pretending to be my dad's friend. He had his eye on her from the beginning. He was just waiting for everyone to split up so he could make his move on her.'

Then came one more blow, and it was this one that really sent me over the edge. My parents sat us down one day and announced that they were splitting us kids up. Mum was moving to a house in Hillsdale, a couple of suburbs away. Tommy was going to be on the scene all the time. The boys were going with her—that made sense, because they were so young—and so was I. But Koorine wasn't. Koorine was going to go and live with Dad and our grandmother in the house she'd got at Daceyville, another nearby suburb.

They didn't ask us about this new arrangement; they told us. We were stunned and upset and angry. At that point in our lives, Koorine and I were inseparable. We were true soul sisters, we felt like it was us against the world. We'd always had each other to lean on and now, it seemed to us, we were being ripped apart. As well as that, I was losing my nan. That was a huge change in itself because Wha Wha had lived with us almost my whole life. I was reeling.

Koorine wasn't happy about it, but I was really furious. I felt like I'd been rejected. I'd been singled out. Over and over the thoughts ran through my head: 'Why are Dad and Wha Wha leaving me behind? Why are they splitting me and my sister up? Why am I the black sheep? Why me? Why me? Why me?'

Now I can see it more from my parents' point of view. I think they thought that by separating us girls we'd both calm down. They hoped that without each other to egg the other one on, we'd make new friends and stop running so wild.

KATHY BRENNAN: I'm family-oriented and I didn't want our family to split. That's one thing I didn't want at all, but Rory had moved on and there was no chance of getting back together. The girls had already started to get a bit wild before the split. After Rory moved out I had them both with me, as well as the boys. But it got to the point where we just had to separate Lani and Koorine. It wasn't a good feeling at all, but we hoped it might help them settle down a bit.

RORY BRENNAN: Lani had started mucking up before the split. When she first started going onto the drink and drugs, I think I knew pretty quickly what was happening. Koorine was doing it too and with me going, Kathryn had to put up with both of them running amok. She said she couldn't take it any more, she couldn't handle both of them. So my mother got a houso commission place down in Daceyville and Koorine went there while Lani stayed with Kathryn.

Even now it's hard for me to see it from my parents' perspective. I have to really force myself because the patterns of my resentment were so strongly ingrained. I was so furious with Mum. I felt like she'd chosen her boyfriend over us, like she'd betrayed us. But it wasn't just her I resented, it was everyone—including Koorine. I thought she'd have it better with Dad and our grandmother (although Dad was often not there anyway, staying with his girlfriend instead) than I would with Mum. I was even angry with Wha Wha for letting it all happen. In my mind, I was cut off from everyone. No one cared about me, I thought, and I didn't care about them. If they'd all dropped dead right then in front of me I'd have thought it served them right.

And Tommy! Well, Tommy could do no right in my eyes. I was in a permanent rage and I saw everything he did through a filter of hate and suspicion. Instead of seeing that he made Mum happy and was helping her out with the boys, I just thought he was trying to control us. My attitude was a full-on 'How dare he tell me what to do, this is *my* house.'

CAROL SIMON: I've had to say to Lani, 'Hang on, you don't know what happened to your mother,' because she and Koorine have sort of put their dad on a pedestal. They blame Kath, and yet Kath's the one that was there, the one who stood by them. She had no money, she still had to pay rent. She was doing homecare and cleaning.

And then her friendship with Tommy developed into something more and I saw that they were good together. He was there all the time for them. In the meantime, Rory wasn't around, although he's close to the kids now. But when they speak about that time, they talk about Rory; they don't talk about their mum, and what she went through. Tommy was very good to Kathy financially; she would have probably lost everything without him. He was very good to the boys.

The girls started to play up, not come home. They started drinking and hanging around at Lapa [La Perouse]. Koorine sort of tagged along with Lani. They ran away and stayed out. I'd see Lani with her friends and she was always drunk or looked as if she had been drinking. I didn't know about the pot and drugs until much later.

She'd get very angry and very violent. She was violent towards her mum, violent towards Tommy, violent towards Rory, violent towards everyone. She hit Tommy and gave him an awful hiding; police were called. It's a wonder she never hurt anyone really badly, put them in hospital. She was like a volcano walking around. Kath was really scared. I went around there and slept over a couple of times, to support her.

When Lani got in trouble with the police, she would have been thirteen or fourteen. I was working with Juvenile Justice at the time. Kathy rang me, and I went and picked them up and went with them, because they'd never been to court before. From then on, I'd meet them either at court or the police station, wherever Kath wanted me. We'd go to court, and the solicitor would talk to Lani, and she'd say, 'Yes, I'm going to do this, and I'll do that.' And she'd get out, she always got out.

The combination of my anger and hate plus booze and drugs created a really bad self-perpetuating cycle. The more anger I felt, the more I drank and drugged. And the more I drank and drugged, the more I hated. I remember how clearly the thought came to me that Tommy had wrecked my family and that in retaliation I would kill him one day. Years later, Tommy would help me out when I most needed it, but my thinking was so screwed up in those early teenage years that I couldn't see what was right in front of my face. If he'd said the sky was blue I'd have thought it was some kind of trick he was trying to pull on us, and I was the only one who could see through it.

Things were no better at school. At the end of my last year of primary school, my parents had told me they were sending me to Randwick Girls High. I hated the idea. I remember sitting there going, 'Are you fucking serious? You're going to send me to a girls school?' Everyone else I knew from school was going to Matraville High, which was nearby. Instead, I was going to have to make my way over to Randwick where I'd be with a whole lot of people I didn't know and wouldn't have anything in common with. Back then I didn't like new things. I didn't like meeting new people and having to cope with new situations.

But they wouldn't change their minds. Now I realise they must have been reaching out for anything that seemed like it might change the path I was on. Instead of sending me to the local school, where all the kids I was drinking and drugging with were going, they were trying to put me in a new environment where maybe I'd see things differently. I was only thirteen; I could change. Randwick was and is a white-collar, middle-class area where people had good jobs and thought education was really important. Mum and Dad were hoping some of those attitudes might rub off on me. It wasn't to be. In fact, my downhill spiral was about to accelerate.

At Randwick Girls I felt like I really stuck out. Not because of being Aboriginal—there were a few Koori kids, but no one really focused on race or nationality. No, the reason I felt out of place was because we were a battling family, just getting by without much money to spare. Pretty much everyone else at school was doing better than that, and some of them were actually rich.

At least it wasn't like in America, where you wear normal clothes to school so kids with lots of money can put on a real fashion show. But even wearing a uniform there are differences in your backpack and your shoes and where you go on the weekend. One simple little example was the fact that most of the other girls in my year had money every day for the canteen, but my family couldn't afford that.

I'd started growing a chip on my shoulder even before high school, but now it was gigantic. Looking back all these years later, I can see that it was really all about my own feelings of being worthless, being less important than other people, and being ashamed of my family's situation. At the time, it was just more fuel for my anger: 'Why should those bitches have more than me? Why should they think they are better than us? Yeah, well I'll show them.'

So I turned into a standover merchant. I acted and felt tough. I wasn't going to take crap from anyone, and I made sure everyone knew it. I had a bad reputation and I made use of it. I wasn't big or tall, but I didn't need to be. I was strong and fit, but it wasn't really about being physically intimidating. I just let people know that I didn't care what happened. I was ready to fight with anyone, no matter how big they were, and the fact that people knew that meant I rarely if ever had to get physical.

Kids would bring me smokes or give me money, not because I did something bad to them but because they were scared I might. When you bully people in this way, it's surprising how little you have to do—most of the work is done by them, in their own minds. Because they're already intimidated or scared they'll bend over backwards to avoid any problems with you.

The kids who just wanted to fit in were easy to take advantage of. There's one girl in particular I feel really bad about, now that I'm able to see things clearly. Her name was Jackie and she was a nice girl who just wanted to make friends. Her parents had a shop in Bondi, so she had access to a whole lot of things I wanted. Every day she used to bring me stuff that she must have stolen from the shop. She wasn't the kind of girl who would normally steal, only when someone like me put her up to it. Day in, day out she used to bring me cigarettes and money for lunch. I didn't know and didn't care what would happen when her parents eventually caught her. I wasn't able to think too much beyond myself and my wants.

Even so, I got along with pretty much all the different crowds at school. There were the squareheads, the brainy ones; they were no threat so I could get along okay with them. There were the ones that acted like me, the knockabouts, although a lot of them had money and they were just playing at it. Then there was the heavy metal/grunge crowd—they were all right too, basically harmless. But the ones I really loved running with were the other wild kids, the ones who were really like me, who just didn't care what happened to them.

I never felt pretty, but I didn't feel ugly either. I just didn't spend time thinking about it. Like most of the girls, I had long hair and a short skirt. Unlike a lot of them I didn't worry about makeup or any of that: I had my ciggies in my skirt pocket or tucked into my bra and I was ready to go.

In the classroom I was struggling with pretty much every subject, except maths—I could always pass maths without doing any study. But I didn't care about failing. I looked at school as a social club where I could show up or not, as I pleased.

I was really running amok now. I was supposed to be living at Mum's new place but I made it impossible for anyone to keep tabs on me. I started truanting more and more. I was smoking a lot of pot, often in the backyard shed that I'd more or less claimed as my own. I had my first cone of the day as soon I could get out of bed and into the shed. One of the few peaceful memories I have of being with my mother and Tommy at that time was staying home from school, getting stoned in the shed and then going in and helping them paint the house. Just eating hamburgers and working alongside each other painting.

I occasionally used to worry about how much I was using. So many times I'd heard my father say, 'If you smoke marijuana, it won't stay at marijuana. It will lead to other things, other drugs.' And I thought, 'Yeah, whatever. That's just bullshit.' But inside I used to be a bit scared because I loved the pot so much, and I wondered if it really would lead me to other drugs, especially heroin. But I always found a way to push down the fear and laugh at Dad's concern. I used to justify it to myself by saying, 'Well, pot's grown naturally, it comes from a plant, so that's sweet.' Users are world champions at self-justification.

At lunchtime on those days when I did bother to go to school, I headed down to the back field or to a nearby park to smoke some more pot. (As well as the cash and cigarettes, Jackie would bring me a box of sweet Creme Eggs most days, because being stoned gave me the munchies.) I was angry with everyone, all the time. My solution was to do what I wanted to do, and only what I wanted to do. Fuck everyone else.

Things got worse and worse. I was suspended a few times in

Year 7 for swearing at teachers and jigging school. When I moved into Year 8, Koorine started in Year 7. Being together again from Monday mornings now that we were living apart felt pretty weird; we couldn't always find our way straight back into the close relationship we'd had. Soon, though, something happened that stopped even that contact. I got expelled.

Schools will work hard to stop a kid from being expelled. It's a drastic step and generally it's only taken in the most dire of circumstances. Well, I made it easy for them; they had no choice. I was angry about something—I don't even remember what, because any little thing could set me off—and I got into a confrontation with one of my teachers, who was trying to get me to control my behaviour. Without thinking twice, I picked up a chair and hit her on the head with it. I didn't think about the damage I could do to her, or the consequences for myself; I just lashed out. Now I'm ashamed of having been responsible for this kind of violence, but at the time I felt nothing except maybe a bit of extra swagger and pride that everyone would know how tough I was; they'd all see that I couldn't be messed with.

My expulsion was immediate. Because I was only fourteen and not yet of school-leaving age, the Education Department was obliged to find me another school to go to, but I was in no hurry to start. I couldn't see a future for myself that involved school or education.

Eventually I started at Maroubra High. It was okay. A lot of the friends that I'd grown up with were going there, and it was co-ed, which suited me better than an all-girls school, but it didn't improve my behaviour. I continued to run amok, doing whatever I wanted to do. I was using drugs and drinking more than ever, and all my interest in sport had gone out the window. I was even more of a standover merchant than I had been at Randwick Girls, targeting the vulnerable kids and assaulting them if they didn't do what I wanted, and sometimes even when they did.

I'd also started spending time down at The Block, the now demolished part of Redfern that was infamous for the open way drugs were dealt and used on the street, and the rife alcohol abuse and violence there. A few of us girls used to get together and go down there, meeting up with a few of the boys we knew to drink and take drugs. Sometimes Koorine and I would meet up and go together or I'd run into her there; sometimes not. Sometimes I barely noticed. By now, exactly the thing that Dad had warned us against was happening: I was taking anything I could get my hands on, as long as it didn't have to be injected. Speed, cocaine—whatever was on offer. It gives me a shudder to think what would have become of me if the drug ice (methamphetamine) had been around in those days, given how addictive and destructive it is.

I loved it down at The Block. Everyone was doing what I was doing, drinking and drugging. I wasn't interested in anything else and down there neither was anyone else. We were all just chasing the feeling of not caring, chasing oblivion. Don't get me wrong, I'm not blaming peer pressure for my choices. It wasn't about being a follower for me. I wanted to be doing what I was doing. I knew the effect it was going to have on me, and I wanted it.

I think even back then I knew I was an alcoholic and addict. I knew I didn't drink the way I'd seen other teenagers at school drinking. I'd seen plenty of that sort of indulging where people would have a few and say, 'Oh, I'm so tipsy, that's enough,' or even, 'Last time I wiped myself out. I won't do that again.' But it was different for me. I'd go totally overboard. It seemed like I just couldn't stop until there was no grog left. It got worse and worse. At the start, I was always the life of the party. But then I'd just drink more and more and lash out at someone. It got to the point where nobody wanted to invite me along because they'd just spend the whole night worrying about when I was going to turn violent or do something stupid.

Technically, I was still living with my mother and the boys. Mum had said I could stay there if I followed the rules, otherwise I could go and find somewhere else to live. I mostly dealt with this by keeping out of the way: either crashing at a friend's house instead of coming home at all, or just keeping to the shed when I was there, coming and going as I pleased. Tommy tried to support Mum in getting me to behave in a reasonable manner, but I didn't like rules, didn't like anyone telling me what to do and didn't like curfews, so I just fought all the time, spitting out, 'You're not my father, you don't tell me what to do!' I was spinning more and more out of control.

My alcoholic blackouts were becoming more frequent. This didn't mean I became unconscious, unfortunately—these were blackouts where I would still be on my feet, running my mouth and swinging my fists, but the next day I couldn't remember a thing about it. I didn't even have little glimpses that needed to be filled in—it was all just one big blank. I knew I was capable of doing some bad stuff and I used to hate waking up in the morning seeing my fist busted up and not knowing what I'd done, how much I'd hurt someone the night before.

But none of that was enough to make me change things for the better. For most of my life I've been a determined, strong-minded person. When that determination was focused on drink and drugs, nothing could stop me. I was sick of everyone telling me not to do it. It didn't matter to me that they were only doing it because they cared about me. The more people told me not to do it, the more I wanted to do it. And every time I used and drank, the anger would come out of me.

Sometimes I would get so off my face on drugs I'd think, 'Oh, what am I turning into?', but by that stage I couldn't seem to stop. It was as if drinking and drugging were my oxygen, the only way I could survive. For all that I acted tough and terrorised other people, I didn't like a lot of the places I found myself in. But I kept on chasing the high and chasing the adrenaline. I hated the square approach to life. Getting up, going to school or work, going home, playing by the rules—I didn't understand the appeal. Why would anyone live like that when they could live on the edge?

Stealing cars, for instance. For me and the people I hung with, stealing cars was just something you did. I got in my first stolen car right around the time I had my first drink and smoke, before I was even a teenager. Hotties, we called them. By the time I left home, I was an old hand. In fact, that's how I learned to drive—in hotties. My friends and I would steal them, or we'd get them passed on to us after someone we knew had finished with one. We didn't have a plan, we weren't stealing them to sell them for car rebirthing or anything as organised as that. We just stole them for thrills. We'd take them, drive around for a while, then dump them. I used to love it. I never gave a thought to the people who owned them. These days, if someone stole my car I'd be off my head, knowing how hard I have to work to get the money for the repayments. But back then I never thought about how it might affect someone's ability to travel to their job, or their debts. Me and my mates were out to have fun, and that was it.

I continued at Maroubra High as I'd started, with violence and intimidation. I stabbed one of my classmates in the forehead with a pencil, I assaulted another in music class, and I tried to burn the place down with a Bunsen burner in science. There was plenty more like that too. The school counsellors and principal tried to get through to me, and so did Mum, but I hated rules and regulations. I saw them as a personal attack on me and I set out to break them at every opportunity. Before long I'd pushed everyone to their limits and I got expelled from Maroubra High too.

The one thing I didn't sabotage was the job I had. Even though there were always plenty of people around willing to share their drugs and grog, living the way I was living at the age of fourteen and fifteen was expensive. So I'd got myself a night job at the Reject Shop at the Eastgardens shopping centre, a short bus ride from Mum's place, stacking shelves.

I can see now it's surprising that I was able to get a job, let alone keep it. But even when I was at my lowest in terms of addiction and my most out of control in all other ways, I've pretty much always worked. And I've always been able to put up a good front, making sure I was showered and my hair and teeth were brushed. More importantly, I was always able to present myself in a convincing way as someone you could trust to do a good job. Unfortunately I generally repaid that trust by stealing from my employer, a pattern that started right back in that first shelf-stacking job. I had the addict's view of the world: I was the only one that mattered, I had to do whatever it took to meet my needs, and they all owed me anyhow. Somehow, then or later, I never got caught.

Not surprisingly, things got even worse at home. Mum and I argued all the time now. The fights turned physical too. Sometimes when people find this out I can see the shock in their faces, but I have to say that it didn't seem such a big step at the time. There was a lot of physicality in my world, always had been. Growing up, I saw adults fight when they were drunk, and we kids loved a bit of rough play with one another, wrestling and footy tackling and tumbling around together. I'd already been using my body as a weapon, so when I struck out it really just seemed like a continuation of the verbal abuse I threw at Mum all the time.

It never happened with Dad. We argued plenty, and in my time I've called him every name under the sun, but no matter how furious I was I always drew a line with him, and not just because I was closer to him than Mum when I was a kid. It was because I felt like hitting Dad wouldn't be fair on him—being a man, he couldn't hit me back. I really didn't know much at all at this point about the violence that had gone on between Mum and Dad when he was drinking, but even if I had, I would have felt safe. He was a man, sober and in control of himself, and real men didn't hit women. That's what I thought was true back then.

Anyway, I had no such qualms about hitting Mum. Now that I'm sober and mellowing as I get older, I can see things more from my mum's point of view, and I feel closer to her than I ever have before. But my emotions are still tangled, and there are lingering resentments. As much as I'm now aware that she had a hard life herself, and was trying to do the best for her family, I still sometimes wish it had all been handled differently. Then I think about my own kids and what I'd do to protect them, and I can understand the dilemma she faced.

My parents' plan to get Koorine and me back on track by separating us hadn't worked out at all. She was also running wild, and had followed my lead and been kicked out of Randwick Girls High. My dad was mostly living with his new girlfriend rather than at the place he'd set up with Wha Wha and Koorine, although he was supporting them financially. My grandmother did her best but, like me, Koorine was determined to do what she wanted, no matter what anyone said.

Koorine ended up at J J Cahill High School in Mascot, so there was a period there when we hardly saw one another. I didn't really care; I was still angry with her, too. Every time I thought of Dad, I thought, 'You arsehole. You don't love me, you took Koorine instead of me and you took away my grandmother, the best person in my life. Why did you just leave me?' When I thought about Koorine, I thought, 'She's always been the favourite. Why should she get everything she wants?' And I even hated Wha Wha for letting it all happen. I felt alone and abandoned, with no one to answer to and nothing left to lose.

So when Mum made it clear I couldn't stay with her and my brothers if I kept on the way I was, I just didn't care. I didn't really have anywhere to go, but so what? What I did care about was *why* she was doing it. I was sure it was Tommy who was putting her up to it. I could easily imagine him saying to her over and over again, 'You don't have to put up with this, you can kick her out.' Now I can look back and see that, in reality, Mum had undoubtedly just had enough of it on her own account. She'd dealt with my father in his drinking years and she probably just thought, 'I'm not going to go through this again.' Tommy had fought his own battles: he'd been through AA and he was sober and he wanted a happy life, a chance to stick to the straight and narrow, and not to risk seeing all that derailed by the chaos I was bringing into their world.

Garri and Darryl were still so young—still preschoolers—and now I can understand that Mum had to think of their safety and security. Now, as I'm a mother myself, I know she must have been in a horrible position. On the one hand she had Koorine and me, her daughters who she loved and wanted to help. On the other hand, she had my brothers to protect. I was violent. I was drinking and drugging. I was hardly ever home anyway, and when I did crash into their lives I'd do what my dad had done all those years before: I'd bring the violence home.

As a mother, I'd like to think that I'd do as much as I could for a child of mine and I'd never turn them away, never refuse them a home. In the years that followed my being kicked out, I often thought bitterly that if Mum had just stopped hounding me about my behaviour, if she'd let me bong on in the house and do what I wanted to do, I would have stayed there and behaved better than I did. But maybe I was kidding myself.

Anyway, I didn't see any of that at the time. All I could focus on was my idea that Tommy had given Mum an ultimatum: Lani or me. I was her daughter. She should have chosen her flesh and blood every time, she should have protected me and told him to get stuffed. That was the thought that ran around and around in my head, carving such a deep groove of resentment that I still haven't been able to fully erase it.

KATHY BRENNAN: Lani was hostile but I had no idea at first that she'd started drinking and using drugs. Tommy and I got together and I'd moved into the place I'm still in, at Hillsdale. That was a new stepping stone. Too many bad, old memories in the other place—I had to move on, move away from the area. It was the best thing I've ever done. Tommy was good for Lani, too. She really had everything here, a roof over her head, everything. But she was very resentful to Tommy. I don't know why, I really don't. He took on a big thing being with me and we ended up being together for ten years.

I was working, just trying to make ends meet. All I wanted was to come home to a peaceful place. But she just went off the rails. She didn't like the discipline, didn't like the rules. She didn't know what she really wanted. She said, 'I'm leaving, I'm moving out.' And I thought, 'Whatever.' I thought she might come back, but she didn't.

When I did finally move out it didn't happen the way it does in daytime movies, with the mother going off her head over some particular thing then the daughter going off her head in return, packing a bag and delivering lots of dialogue while she's doing it. Our disintegration was more or less mutual. Mum said something like, 'If you're not going to go by my rules, get out.' I said something like, 'Well, I'm fucking not, so see you later.' It just sort of happened. We'd had that kind of confrontation before, and I would continue to drift in and out. But this time days and weeks passed, and I didn't go back. That's how we both knew I wasn't living there any more.

Chapter Three

I didn't move in anywhere else, as such. I just drifted. I'd stay at Wha Wha's place for a couple of nights, then crash at my best friend Rachel's house (we'd been close since the end of primary school), at some random acquaintance's place, at a youth hostel, a cheap motel or a backpacker hostel. I guess I was technically homeless, but I never thought of myself that way because I never slept rough. I hated the thought of sleeping on the street and somehow I'd always find a place to stay.

Other than Koorine and Rachel, I liked hanging around blokes more than girls. I was more on their wavelength. I know that a lot of teenage girls who are in a similar position trade sex for shelter or for booze or drugs, because often they feel like they have no other choice. But I never did that. I wasn't romantically interested in any of the boys or men I was spending my days with—I just didn't have those feelings at all. And they didn't see me in that light because I was basically one of the boys.

Sometimes they'd muck around when we were drunk, starting with the 'You're so beautiful' stuff. I just told them to fuck off and shut up. I was as violent as any of them, and I could pour as much alcohol down my throat as they could, if not more. If any of them had ever taken it any further after I told them to stop I would most likely have knocked them out. The few other girls who were regularly on the scene tended to be the same as me. Otherwise they moved on fairly quickly.

I was earning a bit of money from my job, but mostly I paid for what I needed by rorting: stealing things from shops and selling them, breaking into houses and robbing them, mugging people on the street. From the first time I did those things, I loved the adrenaline rush.

I was with three boys driving round at night in Sydney's eastern suburbs the first time we decided to go rob a place. I thought, 'Yeah, why not?' We drove down a few streets, checking out prospects, then pulled up just out of sight of a two-storey house where it looked like no one was home.

I went up and knocked on the door. If anyone answered I had my line ready: I was going to say I was looking for my friend's house but must have got the street number wrong. But no one was home. I ran down the street and gave the boys the signal. They pulled up in front, jumped out and it was on.

We had a bunch of gloves with us—dishwashing gloves, woollen gloves, whatever—and we all grabbed some and put them on. My heart was already racing, but when one of my mates smashed a side window and we all jumped inside I thought my chest might burst. Were the cops going to turn up? Were the people who lived there going to come home? It was pure excitement.

I can't remember what we took that first time, but it became a regular event. I'd go up looking harmless and if no one answered we'd be inside ransacking the place within minutes. We each just grabbed whatever we could, whatever took our fancy. There were VCR players in those days and we always searched for jewellery and cash. Good sports shoes like new Nikes were a score. Sometimes we found drugs. We'd grab pillowcases or sheets to wrap things up in if we weren't wearing backpacks. I took things the boys never thought to grab: a picture frame I liked, clothes, shoes, perfume.

Sometimes we did have to run for it, but we never got caught. We'd keep what we wanted and sell the rest to a dodgy pawnshop we knew where you didn't have to fill in the proper forms or to people we knew around the place, or our dealer would take it in exchange for drugs.

I was seeing Koorine a lot more now, either at my grandmother's or we'd catch up down at Bondi, where we'd both started spending a lot of time. Just above the Bondi beachfront there is a long row of beach huts, separate little structures that each have a roof and are partitioned by dividing walls into four spaces, with a picnic table and benches in each space, and no external walls. The way they are divided up means that even if there's a cold wind blowing, there's always at least one of the four spaces in each hut that's sheltered from the cold.

For years the huts have acted like a magnet for people whose days revolve around drink and drugs. They offer a little bit of privacy, but most important they are public facilities in a public space, available twenty-four hours a day, with toilets and taps nearby and shops and pubs just across the road. You can pretty much get as smashed as you like without being moved on, and you can always find like-minded lost souls to get blind with. Like hundreds of others before and since, the Bondi huts became my regular haunt.

Any time of the day or night you could just walk up to the huts and someone would be there, kids like me doing the same things I was doing, although most of them weren't getting wasted by themselves, like I was. There were runaways from time to time, but most of the kids there could go back to their family home when they wanted or needed to, and they could get money from their parents.

There was a mix of races, but it wasn't something that anyone paid attention to. As long as you were doing what everyone else was doing, you'd fit right in. You didn't need to know someone to walk up and join a group if your own crew wasn't there. You'd just go on up, say g'day and join in. I always had my backpack with me, and it had my bong in it and generally my grog, some pot and some clothes. There'd always be music pumping from a ghettoblaster someone had brought.

I wasn't scared going up to strangers, even when they were drunk and unpredictable. When I was drinking and drugging I wasn't really scared of anyone. Most of the time there was someone familiar around, one of the regular groups of girls or boys I knew from down there, and all of us always had each other's backs, no matter what, no questions asked, even if everyone was totally out of it.

But I didn't really need to be afraid anyway because Koorine and I were known as two of the worst in Bondi. Everyone used to say, 'Oh the Brennan sisters, they're psychos!' I had a loose group of friends and drinking buddies, but the pair of us and my old friend Rachel formed an inseparable trio. People used to reckon they could hear us coming from a mile away. We were quick to fight—we didn't put up with anyone's shit, that was the way we saw it. How we didn't end up seriously injured, I don't know. We'd fight with our fists or with whatever we could grab, it was all the same to us. I can see now how terrifying we must have been.

If I saw the girl I was then coming along the street now I'd think, 'God, who is this kid? She needs to go into a psych ward because she's so screwed up.' And if I saw the three of us as we were then coming towards me now, I'd feel very threatened, because those girls were capable of anything and there was no reasoning with them. In those days, if people did try to talk their way out of whatever we were threatening them with, I just thought they were easier victims; they were too scared to attack us so we should just go in even harder.

The reckless aggression had started a good while before. I have friends who knew me when I was still living with my mother who look back all these years later and laugh in a disbelieving way about how out of control I was even then, reminding me of the time I went crazy and started chasing them around with a big knife. But by the time I was hanging out at the Bondi huts, I was really gone as a result of all the drink and drugs.

Koorine and Rachel understood me, though. We got off our faces together, we roamed around causing havoc and we did whatever it took to survive. You'd think that just getting out of it every day would be easy. After all, it's the opposite of a straight life with all its boring chores and demanding responsibilities. Living just to indulge yourself should be a breeze, right?

In reality, it's hard. Ironically enough, in some ways it's harder work than having a real job, partly because it's so erratic. It's tough trying to get money every single day when you wake up without a clue where that money will come from. You need enough to support your habit, put a roof over your head and eat—usually in that order.

Stealing was part of our everyday lives. If we needed money to pay for a night at a motel or hostel, we'd rob someone on the street, steal from a shop and sell what we'd taken, or break into a house and burgle whatever we thought might make us a bit of cash. I remember once funding some pot by stealing freshwater pearl earrings from a shop and taking them to Wha Wha, who I knew liked pearls. I convinced her to give me twenty dollars for them so I could go and have a sesh.

You might think we'd quickly get banned from shops, or that we'd have been picked up by the police for shoplifting, but we hardly ever got caught. We weren't exactly subtle, either. I remember one time three of us walked into a Coles supermarket and each took one of the hot cooked chickens they have ready in those foil bags and stuffed them down our pants. Out we walked, with the chickens burning our legs and the hot oil dripping. A lot of other times we'd steal chocolate bars from corner shops and live on those for days. We regarded it as survival tactics: you do what you have to and that's all there is to it.

I remember the time I had my first acid trip. I took it down there at the beach and when I thought it hadn't worked I went back to the dealer and went off my head. He gave me another one, which I took straight away, and then the double dose hit me. I thought bombs were coming from the sky. Rachel and I ended up conning three backpackers into taking us back to their motel room. They'd never smoked pot, or yarndi, as we called it, before. We gave them cones and then, when they passed out, we robbed them, taking their money and credit cards. At no stage did we give a thought to the potential danger we'd put ourselves in by being in someone else's motel room, tripping and outnumbered.

We did have a few rules, though—some for safety and some that were more about our own moral code, such as it was. We didn't break into houses in the areas we usually hung out, because that would have been asking to get caught. And we didn't break into houso properties, because the people who lived there were like us, already struggling just to get by. We had no hesitation in robbing from people we saw as rich. We viewed ourselves as working on a kind of Robin Hood philosophy, except that the poor we were giving to were ourselves. We also had no qualms about stealing from shops because if we happened to think about it at all, we just figured they were insured, so they were going to get it all back anyway.

But I really didn't put much energy into thinking it through or justifying it to myself for the simple reason that I liked doing it; Koorine too. We saw ourselves as rebels, rejecting society's bullshit. We liked being streetwise, we liked criminal activity and the adrenaline that came with it. It was a thrill to break into a house and an even bigger thrill if we had to run from the scene to avoid getting caught. When I bashed someone it made me feel powerful.

I still get frustrated easily if I don't make a big effort not to, but back then when I got frustrated I'd black out in anger, and then I couldn't think of anything else: no consequences, no sense of what was going on around me—I'd just go in for the kill. I used to thrive on violence. I don't understand why, but it somehow made me feel better. Except sometimes it didn't.

I remember once attacking a girl with my stiletto shoe—who knows what she'd done to make me angry with her. I was so drunk she could have just looked in my direction and I'd have seen it as a personal insult. I couldn't stop—the anger flowed, white hot, and I just kept hitting. I was vaguely aware of people screaming at me, and trying to make me stop. But I couldn't control myself, I was frenzied. Finally I did stop and just walked away, without even looking back. I have no idea how badly she was hurt and no one made me pay for my actions.

I did get picked up a few times by the police for assault or trespassing or offensive language. And inevitably when they were attempting to arrest me I'd add 'assault on police' and 'resisting arrest' to the charges. But even then, I never really got in trouble. It felt like Koorine and I went to Children's Court every week for a while there, but over and over again we'd just get a slap on the wrist. Looking back, they were way too soft on me.

The two penalties we copped were community service hours and fines, mostly of fifty dollars here or a hundred dollars there. Then we'd be put on yet another good behaviour bond and off we'd go and do it all again. We didn't take the fines seriously. You were supposed to arrange to pay them off if, like us, you didn't have the money to pay them in full, but we never bothered. At the time we thought we'd just walked away, but the system was keeping track and to this day I hand over twenty dollars a fortnight, paying off state debt accumulated in those wild teenage years. It's like a lot of other things you bring on yourself when you're an addict: many years later when you sober up, you'll find the consequences sitting there, waiting for you.

Our rules weren't just about who we would or wouldn't rob, they were also about our drug use: it was fine to do 'fun' drugs, but we wouldn't use what we saw as harder drugs. In practice, this meant not injecting drugs. I hated needles and I hated the idea of injecting heroin, although I did smoke it occasionally by spotting it on marijuana.

Heroin is famously a downer—it suppresses your system, hence the semiconscious 'nodding' that's a giveaway sign of a user. But for whatever reason it had the opposite effect on me. Instead of going down, I was pumped up. I was kind of hyperactive on it. Even when I did use heroin, I saw myself as completely different to people shooting it up. I'd sat through all those AA meetings when I was a kid, I knew the mantra: you're not addicted to the drug, you're addicted to the needle. I wasn't like those pathetic junkies, not me.

It was only recently, well over a decade after getting sober, that I thought about the fact that even in the depths of the chaos of those addicted, alcoholic years, I kept to those self-imposed rules. But I think that's what everyone does, in their own way. There's always some personal line that an individual won't cross, no matter how low or degraded they might look to the outside world. As well as some kind of internal compass, the other thing that never left me was my work ethic. Somehow amid all the booze and drugs I could always pull it together, put up that good front and get hired. I'd gone from the night shelf-stacking job at the Reject Shop to a job selling women's clothes at Kmart. I could talk pleasantly to the customers in a way that probably would have amazed the people I terrorised at school or on the street. I could go in to work drunk and still function the way a normal person would. Only another drunk would be able to see through my act.

Even though I had left La Perouse behind when my parents split, I still saw people from that time around the place, especially at pubs and clubs. I was still years away from the legal drinking age of eighteen, but I never seemed to have any real problem getting in to those places. I'd see the old people or other people who'd known me since I was little; everyone could see how fast I was plummeting downhill, how angry I was and how deep into the clutches of alcohol. Every now and then someone would try to talk to me about it, to reach out to me, but I pushed them all away.

Other than Koorine, I was hardly seeing my family at all, except to bring more havoc into their lives. Every now and then Mum would have to come down to the school to see the principal about my latest outrage. And once a week, no matter what, I'd make sure they knew I was still alive. My brothers had started playing football—rugby league, of course. At the time, my idea of family loyalty was turning up to their Sunday games—come rain, hail or shine, booze or drugs, nothing would stop me. It was another one of my rules.

So week after week I would turn up blind drunk or out of it on drugs. I'm still a big mouth at the footy, cheering my team on, but back then you must have been able to hear me in the next suburb. I didn't care how abusive I was towards the ref or other players—everyone was going to hear what I thought. Garri and Darryl still look back on that time with a shudder and say, 'Oh my god, you embarrassed us so badly, you were so off your head.' When they saw me coming, my mum and whoever was with her used to race to the other side of the oval to get away from me. I didn't care. I thought, 'They're my brothers and I have a right to be here. I'm going to turn up every match whether you like it or not. Fuck youse all.'

> CAROL SIMON: Lani would turn up to her brothers' football games—they were only five or six, the boys—and she'd be drunk. Everybody could see. She loves those boys; she loves them like they're her own. She'd be

watching them, she wanted to be there with them, but she didn't know how to be. I'm getting emotional even now remembering the look on her face. She'd be standing there, and everyone would move away from her. She'd move towards us and we'd all just keep on moving away. Her anger was so much that she'd say something to her mother or to Tommy. The boys would be trying to play their football. They were shy, they had only just started to come out of their shell. When the game finished they'd stay close to their mother and she'd get them out of there straight away.

The other times my family would see me was when I'd work myself into a fury about all the things I thought had been denied me, and storm over to Mum's house. Often Koorine was with me. We'd gee each other up, telling ourselves we had a right to see our brothers. When we got there we'd bash on the door and, I can see now, terrorise the whole household. We'd be demanding to see the boys, who must have been petrified. We'd often ask for money, too, but the recurring theme of our anger was not being allowed in to see Garri and Darryl. I remember one instance when Mum refused to open the door (judging, quite rightly, that we were drunk and capable of anything), so I went to the front door and Koorine went to the back door and we tried to kick both doors in at once. The boys were still just kids—it must have been really traumatic for them.

It certainly was for Mum and Tommy, if he was there, since we were also trying to get inside in order to bash them both. Over and over again we'd scream at her that she was choosing her boyfriend over us, all the while trying to get inside. Then Mum or

Tommy would call the cops. And of course, when the police did show up I wouldn't go quietly. Instead, I'd fight the police too.

I could see it all so clearly: none of it was my fault. If Mum didn't give me a mouthful and slam the door in my face when I turned up, I would never have revved up. I had a right to just walk into my mother's house any time I wanted. If she'd been more understanding and said, 'Come in, sit down, see your brothers,' everything would have been all right. I only had my back up because of the way she'd acted. She bridged up at me, so I bridged back up.

That was my MO with everyone in those days: if you're going to come at me, it's going to be a lot worse for you than for me, I'll make sure of it.

The other thing that was clear to me was that my brothers had it much better than Koorine and me, when we were their age. They had more stability, the house they lived in was nicer because Mum and Tommy had fixed it up, there was no drinking in the house, Mum was always doing things for their school, they saw Dad on weekends—all of it was better. Their upbringing wasn't so chaotic, I told myself, ignoring the fact that I was a cyclone bringing chaos to their doorstep—they didn't have it tough like I did.

Mum and Tommy went to Bidura Children's Court to get an Apprehended Violence Order (AVO) taken out on us, saying they feared for their lives. Even so, I still find it hard to work my way through my tangle of feelings about all this. There are times when I return to feeling aggrieved and hard done by. As good as Tommy was to me when I needed a friend later on, I still feel the pull of the old resentments. And the idea that if they'd let me live the way I wanted to and stay at home I'd never have lost it—that idea loops around in my head, despite the fact that I know I *did* lose it when I was at home and running wild. But then I look at my own kids and imagine how I'd have felt in Mum and Tommy's shoes. I can understand how scared and upset I must have made my brothers.

So I can see that my mother got to the point where she felt like she had to let me go. It's a breaking point reached by many families of addicts—tough love, people used to call it. They feel they have to let you go, no matter how hard it is. I was so intent on doing myself harm that no one and nothing could have stopped it, and they could see that. Giving me money and other things I demanded would only have sped me on my way; they felt their hands were tied. But then up pops the thought they should have been there for me no matter what, and in my mind the cycle goes around again.

KATHY BRENNAN: Lani lashed out a few times with both Tommy and me. We reached a point where I had to get an AVO put on her. She and Koorine came around, both pretty charged up. They threatened Tommy, threatened to key my car and all the rest of it. We had to lock them out and I had to get the police around. The boys were only little. I never, ever wanted to stop her from seeing the boys, but I had to protect them because the girls were drinking.

It's the worst feeling ever to be scared of your own daughters, to have to call the police to come here and put my own children, intoxicated, in the back of the van. I think they [the girls] blame Tommy for that because he encouraged me, but I had to do it for me, not for him. I didn't want to get the police involved. I just wanted them to leave us alone. I thought, 'They're never going to leave us alone.' To tell you the truth, I don't really remember a lot of it. It's something you want to forget.

Even when professional help was offered, I wanted no part of it, though on some level I was desperately crying out for help. A few times I tried to kill myself, sometimes on the spur of the moment, sometimes with a bit more planning, usually involving prescription drugs. And there were plenty of near accidents when, drunk, I stepped into traffic without looking. Koorine just saved me from walking under a bus once, at Bondi. But it wasn't always an accident.

The voices in my head started around this time. The drugs and grog kicked them off, I have no doubt about that. I used to have them in there talking away continuously. I was paranoid, fearful of the unknown and not in my right mind. It felt like the voices were my friends, trying to protect me when all the world was against me. They'd say, 'Oh Lani, you shouldn't be doing that.' Or, 'Go and do this', 'Go and kill that person', and then I'd be answering them back, agreeing or arguing. I knew the voices weren't real, in a way, but I still felt they were there to help me.

With the voices' help, I drew up a list in my mind of all the people I was going to kill before I killed myself. And you can imagine, nearly everyone was on that list: Mum, Dad, Tommy, even Koorine, everyone. 'Friends' who I hated. Anyone I was really jealous of, or anyone who'd ever put me down.

About the only person who never made the list was my grandmother. I used to go to her house in Daceyville often. I wanted to go even more than I did, but I tried to resist the urge when I was under the influence, either drunk or on drugs, which was almost all the time. Experience had taught me I could flip out at any time: I knew that when I was using I was potentially a danger to anyone in my path. Wha Wha seemed so old and fragile to me; she hadn't been in good health for a long time. I didn't want to hurt her or scare her, though I know now sometimes I did.

Through it all, though, she never turned me away. There was always a room for me to crash in for a few hours and get some sleep or to stay overnight. I just couldn't move in. I asked her a few times to let me, but she said no. I never held it against her, though. I always saw her as the backbone of our family.

There were times when it all got to me and I felt I couldn't stand any of it any more. I'd think, 'Oh this is just too much all the time.' I knew I had problems. I figured I was mentally ill, that something was really seriously, permanently wrong with me, and I'd want to end it. That's when I walked out in front of cars deliberately. That's when I took handfuls of whatever prescription pills I could dig up, trying to overdose. Someone would find me, call an ambulance, and I'd get my stomach pumped out, and then back I'd go.

I remember saying at one stage, 'I just want to be free, I want to dive off a building,' but thank god I never tried that one because I wouldn't be here now. As much as I thought I wanted to die, I can see by where and how I made these attempts that, as close as I got, I really just wanted someone to help me, to save me from what my life had become.

The most memorable of these attempts was when I was about fifteen. I went over to my grandmother's house, threatening all and sundry as I usually did, and airing all the old grudges and resentments: all that 'poor me, poor me', 'you left me behind, I hate you all' sort of stuff. I was in a rage, drunk and drugged up. Poor Wha Wha, she must have called Mum and I must have been ranting long enough for Mum to get there.

I pulled out a great big carving knife I'd brought and threatened to slit my own throat right then and there in the yard. I was sure I was really going to do it, and I wanted the people who'd hurt me, especially my mum, to have to watch. I wanted them to see what they'd done to me. But Mum came flying across the grass and tackled me to get the knife off me. The next thing I was aware of there were police and an ambulance pulling up. They strapped me to a gurney and the police escorted me to the Kiloh Centre, part of the Prince of Wales Hospital in Randwick. It's a locked ward, an inpatient unit where they put you when you're a danger to yourself or others.

I was amazed by how much it was like the psych wards in the movies. We walked down corridors and everything was white—white walls, white floors, bright white lights, white coats on the doctors. There were locked doors all over the place and security guards. They took me to a room that was empty apart from a phone sitting on a little table, but because I was suicidal they took even that out. They made me take off my shoelaces and even my G-string, in case I used them to harm myself. I was freaking out at how weird it all was.

I had another waking blackout—I remember having a scuffle with someone, but I don't remember if it was a doctor, a nurse or a guard. I think I remember asking for a phone and being refused, then saying, 'I'm a juvenile, you can't do this!' But I can't remember much else. I don't even know how long I was in there, but after I got out I never did pick up a knife again as a weapon.

I was so sure by then that I didn't care about other people at all, and I certainly didn't care about myself, but soon something happened that showed me life could be better. It didn't start promisingly—I got kicked out of yet another school. Bye-bye Maroubra High, hello Randwick North. It was a school that took kids who had nowhere else to turn, kids who were still too young to legally leave school but who had been expelled multiple times and were running out of options. Kids like me.

I liked it. We didn't have to wear a uniform. Smoking cigarettes at school was tolerated. They even turned a blind eye to us nicking off to smoke bongs so long as we came back—at least we were getting some kind of education. There were lots of like-minded people there, including a kid who always had some yarndi to sell us. These were the kids who'd be up the back of the classroom mucking up in any other school, all gathered together. We'd walk out of class pretty much whenever we felt like it and go drinking or drugging. But we'd come back.

It was here that I hooked up with Lee, a Maori boy whose family lived in Bondi. I knew him from down in the beach huts. He drank and drugged too, but he had a home to go to. Still, his school record was bad enough that he ended up at Randwick North, and soon we were paired up. It was my first real boyfriend–girlfriend relationship and he was the first boy I slept with. The first time he said he loved me, I thought it was a joke.

Lee was a pothead more than a drinker, and he was a lot more quiet and gentle than many of the people I knew. He was never violent, he never raised his voice. He was genuine. He treated me really well, and in no time at all I moved in with him and his family. I was only fourteen but it seemed like a natural step, and his parents seemed to take it all in their stride and were very accepting. I got along well with them.

I liked being there; I didn't go mental at their house. Instead of flipping out, I found I could control myself. Theirs was a 'normal' household: mother, father, brother, a dog, cars, regular household meals, all of that. I wanted what he had, a real family unit where they'd do anything for him. I was happy to be there and there was just no point in going crazy when everyone was so nice.

We still drank, although I didn't drink to the extreme level that I had been doing. Instead, I smoked more pot. I was more mellow then, because it was the grog that pushed me into violence and mayhem. We did come home drunk regularly, but Lee's parents were calm and down to earth, and they seemed to pretty much understand where we were coming from. Sometimes I used to sit and have a couple of drinks with them and talk, just chilling. But mostly when Lee and I were home we used to hang out and bong in our bedroom. They were fine with it all.

Lee wasn't so much into thieving, but he dabbled in petty crime. His older brother, Shane, was a wild fella and the kids they hung around with were wild too. We occasionally stole cars and broke into houses. Sometimes the police would come by, but the boys' parents already knew their kids were no saints, so they were used to a certain level of attention. Unlike the way I'd treated my own family, I never really brought drama back to the house when I was living there.

Lee had a good friend named Simon and the three of us would travel to Randwick North High together. But I was only there for a couple of terms before I got kicked out for assaulting a teacher. Even though I felt a bit calmer in general when I was with Lee and his family, there were still times that terrible rage would overtake me. So again, I was expelled. I was pretty amazed about this because no one *ever* got kicked out of Randwick North; it was a tough school and not much could faze the teachers there. But once again I'd found the limits and pushed right through them.

The family handled it in their own ways. Lee's parents let me know they were disappointed in me, but they still welcomed me as part of their family. Lee and Simon and some other boys I knew reacted by going to the school one night and vandalising whatever they could get their hands on. They went berserk, demolishing everything they saw. What did that change? Nothing, of course, but at the time we saw that kind of 'revenge' as an act of loyalty.

Lee's family moved to Kingsgrove, an inland suburb about twenty kilometres from Bondi. Simon was living with us too, and it was a good time in my life. The family fed and clothed me, and more importantly they accepted me as I was. I felt more secure and stable than I had for a very long time. But after Lee and I had been together for almost two years, his family decided to leave Australia and go back home to New Zealand. Both Lee and his parents tried to convince me to come with them, but I made the decision to stay. There wasn't anything specially holding me in Sydney—other than Koorine and Wha Wha, I wasn't really seeing my family. But Australia was my home, and I felt I'd rather stick with what I knew.

We said our goodbyes and I headed back to Bondi, moving in with my friend Rachel, who was living in a kind of halfway house for teenagers who weren't living with their parents. Along with Koorine, we were soon drinking and drugging worse than ever: I was back to doing whatever it took to survive each day. It was often scary and there were quite a few times when I could easily have died or suffered permanent injury.

One frightening incident came about because of my addict's short-term, self-focused thinking. Somehow I had met people who were involved with a brothel in the inner-west suburb of Newtown. I used to steal clothes to order for the escorts—they'd describe the kind of thing they wanted and tell me their size and I'd go into boutiques around the place and shoplift things that fitted the bill, then I'd take the clothes to the escorts and they'd buy them from me at a price far below what they would have had to pay in the shops.

After a while the guy who ran the whole place got to know me and he asked if I'd be interested in selling pot for him. Of course I said yes. He gave me a whole heap and I took it—a mistake on both our parts because I just smoked my way through the lot; I didn't sell any of it. When he got sick of waiting for me to turn up with his money, the thousands of dollars I was supposed to have made from dealing, he sent his enforcers to hunt me down.

They knew where we lived and came around, determined to make me pay. I'd locked the door from the inside before they found out I was home, and then I hid in a cupboard. Thank god I did, because they kicked the door in and rampaged through the place looking for me. They tore the house up, but somehow they missed my hiding place. I think if they had found me there's a fair chance they would have killed or maimed me, as a warning to others who might get the same stupid idea. I steered clear of the house for a while after that, and kept well clear of Newtown. But I didn't forget the lesson I had learned: you can't rob powerful criminals without putting yourself in great danger.

Despite everything I'd been through, I was still a kid, only just sixteen. I went to stay with my dad for a while, and he and the caseworkers from the Department of Education who'd been assigned to keep track of me got Matraville High School to agree to take me on for Year 10. Technically, because of my age, I could legally have left school. But as mixed up as my thinking was, I knew I would need something on paper to show employers so I could find a full-time job. The NSW School Certificate doesn't exist any more, but at the time it was the qualification you got when you finished Year 10, the most basic school qualification given. Matraville was definitely, absolutely my last chance at any kind of education—if I blew it there, no one else would have me.

Chapter Four

I went to stay at Dad's for a while when I started Year 10 at Matraville High. I was trying to be a good girl, go to school, do the right thing and get my life back on the rails. But I was so easily sidetracked. I would leave Dad's place in Cronulla with every intention of getting to school, but too many times I'd make a detour. I'd see someone I knew and they'd say, 'Oh come on, let's go have a drink,' or there would be kids saying, 'We're going for a smoke, do you wanna come?' and that would be it for the day.

Then I told myself that it didn't matter anyway and that I hated school. I was so scattered. I really couldn't concentrate on the future, I just thought of the now. I lived in the moment all right, but not in a good way. I only thought far enough ahead to want to get off my face every day. School was just a sort of meeting ground. You knew that every day there'd be people hanging out nearby who also didn't want to go in and who you could take off with for the day.

People tried. My dad tried. I had teachers who encouraged me and told me I had heaps of potential. Looking back, I can see that

I was pretty smart back then, especially when it came to maths. I could pass all the maths quizzes in class and a lot of the written maths exams without even studying at all. I'd just rock up on days when I knew they were on, do the exam and go again. I just didn't care.

I was hardly ever making it to school and staying for the whole day, and as the year wore on it got to the point where it was obvious to everyone that it wasn't going to change for the better. My principal spoke to Dad and said, 'If Lani can get to school for the next few weeks and turn up for the exams, we'll pass her for Year 10.' So I went for a little while, picked up some pathetic version of a School Certificate—the only subject I passed was maths—and left school. I thought, 'Well, I've got my Year 10 papers, I can do what I want now.' And I went straight into work.

I walked right into a full-time job at the Aboriginal Cultural Centre in Darling Harbour, one of Sydney's tourist precincts. It was the same thing: no matter how out of control my life was, I could always land a job. And this was a beauty. I was doing everything: working on the floor selling artefacts, and doing light and sound work for dance performances—controlling microphones and speakers, sorting out backdrops, making the show announcements. Whatever had to be done, I could turn my hand to it.

You'd probably think that meant I'd cleaned up, but in fact my using increased massively while I was in that job. I've always been one to throw myself into work—I'm not one of those people that sits back and does nothing. I enjoy working. But at the same time, I used to be able to function at work blind drunk, and at that particular job I was drunk twenty-four seven. The people who were running the centre were white, and they didn't suspect a thing. I could sell $3000 paintings while I was blind without the customers or my bosses realising that I was drunk. I used chewing gum to cover the fumes on my breath and just talked. I used to talk really fast when I was drunk, so they must have just thought that was my personality—a bit excitable. I'd only ever start slurring my words towards the end of the night if we were having evening performances, and not always then. All the employees were blackfellas and a couple of them were on to me, but they had their own reasons for not giving me up.

By this stage, Rachel and I had a place together. She was still drinking and drugging too, but she was easing off, straightening her life out. She'd got a job first, and now that I had one she nudged me into getting a place of our own together. She had her head on much straighter than I did at the time. Being older, she was the one who applied for the private rental flat in Bondi that we chose, and she put her name on the lease—I wasn't quite seventeen and didn't have enough work history for any real estate agent's liking. Then Koorine and her boyfriend got their own flat around the corner from us. It felt great to be so independent. If you didn't know me too well, you'd think I was getting my life together beautifully.

I really did love my job. I loved being around all the Koori artworks and culture every day, and helping with the performances, but I loved the drink even more. So I stole from my employers. I stayed at the centre for about a year and there were some stages when I was stealing up to $1000 every day. That's a huge amount of money to go missing, but I never got caught. I ran a scam with a girl who worked in the office assisting the bookkeeper; let's call her Sue. I'd be on the floor selling artworks, but, unbeknownst to the customer and bosses, keeping the money for myself. The customer would walk out with their painting or sculpture and I'd pocket the money and split it with Sue.

My wages were enough to pay my weekly rent contribution and cover bills and food—not that I was eating much, anyway. I was skinny, like a lot of alcoholics. There was a kebab shop a couple of doors up from work where I'd get a kebab at lunchtime, and often that would be pretty much it for any real meals for the day. So the money I stole was all spent on drink and drugs, some for my co-workers to shut them up and keep them happy.

I had quickly realised that quite a few of the other staff were also ripping off the centre. Some were junkies, some just wanted money. They were stealing from the reception area and stealing from the office, while I was stealing from the till. Because we were all up to no good, we all more or less had each other's backs, but I thought it was better to be safe than sorry. So most days I'd go to a combined delicatessen/corner shop/bottle shop near work and buy grog and smokes for everyone, to keep them quiet. The people in the shop never asked for ID, and day after day I went there and bought cartons of cigarettes and bottles of spirits. I did buy beer too, sometimes, but spirits got you drunk more quickly, so it would usually be vodka or bourbon. I never had to bother about trying to organise a fake ID: no one ever checked.

I'd slip out just before the others finished, buy my supplies then I'd meet them on the waterfront of Darling Harbour and offer them whatever they wanted. From there we'd go to a pub in Leichhardt where we could drink until sun-up. A few pubs around the place had super-extended hours, but we liked this one best because of 'the blackout': Koori crews from all over, including a nearby Aboriginal refuge, would gather there, partying every night. I hooked up with a fella who worked there for a couple of months and we had a boyfriend–girlfriend relationship, except really it was just two drunks hanging out together and sometimes falling into bed.

Pretty much every night for the whole year or more that I worked at the centre I partied at the pub every night, often walking out into the morning light and going straight in to work. Luckily there were showers at work, and I kept a toothbrush and clean clothes there. I'd have a wash and spruce up a bit, then go out on the floor and start working.

As I said, my co-workers knew what I was up to, and how bad I was with the drink. When we'd have those big dance performance nights, where the rich people would come in and there would be trays of wine and food going around, they'd bring a tray of wine glasses back to the lighting and sound booth. The whole tray was just for me and I'd sit there and guzzle the lot while working. I used to feel like I was at the top of my game. Sometimes I'd slip up, saying 'Good morning' instead of 'Good evening' when I was doing the announcements, but no one said anything, and I never got pegged by management.

I was still having a good time and enjoying it, but as the year wore on even I could see things were getting out of hand. I couldn't deny to myself that I was a full-on alcoholic, because nobody my age (I wasn't yet eighteen) ever seemed to drink the way I did. Alcoholics often talk about the first drink of the day, and how for many people it creeps back so you're having it earlier and earlier. Well, my first drink of the day was happening just after midnight, but I didn't care. People used to say all the time, 'Jesus, you drink a lot. What are you doing? You're going to die.' I'd just laugh and say, 'When I die, put a bong in my coffin and a bottle of bourbon.' I just shrugged it off, again and again.

It wasn't just the booze, either. Because when you're doing that every night, day in and day out, you need something to keep you going, otherwise I wouldn't have been able to stay awake at work, let alone do my job. Uppers were my drugs of choice, cocaine and speed; my hatred of needles hadn't lessened, so I took anything I could snort. And I'd take acid trips too, if they were on offer. It was no harder to find whatever drug you wanted than it was to get into pubs underage. Wherever I went, there was a dealer around the place. The only thing that might stop you was not having the money, but I had the money.

Everything kept escalating: the more I stole, the more I drank; the more I drank, the more drugs I needed to keep me going; the more booze and drugs I consumed, the more money I needed to steal to pay for it all. It was the money I was stealing, not my wages, that kept me turning up to work. No matter how much I'd flushed away at the pub the night before, I knew that I could fill my pockets again that day. I started to get scared I was going to get caught stealing, but I kept going anyway.

The one thing I laid off was the violence. I saw myself as somehow more prim and proper, like I was growing up. And somehow, even though I was so out of it almost all the time and carrying lots of cash around, so vulnerable if someone had wanted to jump me the way me and my friends had jumped other people on the streets to get money when I was younger, I never got assaulted. Sometimes I'd be scared walking on my own in the early hours of the morning, coming down off everything and paranoid, constantly thinking, 'What's going on? Is that someone following me?' But I'd just brush it off.

I protected myself by never getting too close to people and telling myself I was ready for anything. Even though I seemed like the life of the party at the pub, and a friend to everyone at work—keeping all their secrets like they kept mine—in fact, I always kept a barrier around me, a protective wall. I decided that if I didn't let anyone in, other than Koorine and Rachel, no one could hurt me. I didn't trust many people. I often didn't understand what made them tick and I didn't want them to see into my soul and judge me. The way I looked at it back then, the fewer friends you had, the better off you were.

After about twelve months I left the job, just drifted out of it. Not long afterwards, I heard they'd gone broke. (There's a different Aboriginal cultural centre in Darling Harbour now.) They did some investigation and ended up charging Sue, the girl who had worked in the office and been in with me on the money scam, with fraud—but she didn't give me up so I never did get found out. I felt guilty over it, though, and I still do. The place probably went bankrupt because of my drinking habit and the drug habits of the junkies who were bleeding it dry along with me. We used that company and took people's hard-earned money just to support our habits.

Step nine of the Alcoholics Anonymous Twelve-Step Program is: 'Make direct amends to [people you have harmed] wherever possible, except when to do so would injure them or others.' Well, the Cultural Centre is one of the many examples in my life where it's just not possible to do this—I don't have any contact with any of those people any more. I don't even remember most of their names, let alone know where to find them. So my way of making amends is to have changed my life into something positive. I focus now on giving back, on working with kids who are headed down the same path as me and trying to help stop them before they go as far as I did. But I'm getting ahead of myself …

Not long after I'd left the job, Dad asked me to go to New Zealand for him. He'd met a Brazilian woman called Vera via the internet and they wanted to marry, but first Vera needed to get a visa for Australia, and the best place for her to do this was New Zealand. She didn't speak too much English (she and Dad had mostly communicated using a translation program) and she needed someone to help her. Dad had to stay in Sydney to work but I was at a loose end, so he asked me and I said yes. I was happy to have an adventure, and maybe I'd get the chance to meet Mum's side of the family while I was there.

Dad organised for me to get a passport, paid for my ticket and booked accommodation. I was still only seventeen and had never been on a plane before, and here I was flying off to another country on my own. I was terrified. Of course, my way of dealing with it at the time was to self-medicate. So when Dad came to Wha Wha's house to pick me up on the morning of the flight, I was drunk and stoned. I must have had a few more drinks on the plane, because by the time we landed in Auckland, I was totally off my face.

I was walking in circles in the baggage claim area long after all the other passengers had taken their things and gone. An old bloke called out, 'Bubby, are you okay?' I said, 'Yeah, I'm trying to find me luggage.' He said, 'You've walked past your luggage ten times.' I picked it up, stumbled my way into a taxi and went to the motel that Dad had booked for Vera and me.

She was already there waiting, and we met for the first time. I started as I meant to continue, pulling out the litre of vodka and litre of bourbon and the carton of cigarettes I'd bought duty-free. I didn't worry about the language gap between us, I just opened up the bottles and started drinking; there was no Coke or anything to have with it, so I just drank it straight. I kept urging her to have some, saying, 'It's cold over here, have a drink, it'll warm you up.' She'd never drunk spirits in her life and she'd never smoked, but I got her to do that too. I think she was doing it because she wanted to fit in. I was her boyfriend's daughter and she was trying to be nice. At one point I opened up my purse and found a twenty-dollar stick of yarndi that I'd accidentally smuggled in because I'd forgotten it was there, so I fired that up too. Vera ended up getting blind drunk that first night. I was a pretty bad influence on her.

Dad had organised everything down to the last detail (well, I suppose he knew what I was like). He'd given me a little book that had all the addresses and dates—where we needed to be when, and what we needed to do there, and he called me every day wherever we were staying to make sure I was getting it all done.

But my drinking was just as out of control there as it had been when I was working. We only stayed in the motel for a day or two, then Dad had arranged for us to move to a backpackers hostel. I met up with two other women there, one older, the other my age, who were just as big drinkers as I was and we partied pretty much all the time. There were also other drugs and lots of pot around, especially at the hostel where all the backpackers were on something, and everyone shared.

We'd head out each day and do what needed to be done, then I'd drop Vera back and take off, and when I turned up again I'd bring back my drink and whatever else I wanted. Vera didn't like it—we started having blues over it and Dad would tell me my behaviour was really worrying her. But I didn't really care. I stood over her in the way I had done with other kids at school, and forced her to put up with my ways. My attitude was, 'I don't really know you and I can do what I want. I've come here to help you out, I've come here to get you a visa, you should be grateful, not telling tales to Dad.'

RORY BRENNAN: At the time I asked Lani to go to New Zealand for me I knew she was drinking and all that but she didn't seem like she was too much off track. Not living with someone, it's hard to pick it. I thought I'd kill two birds with one stone. She could do me a favour and go try to help Vera out, and also she could hook up with her mother's family, who are from New Zealand. At first the reports that came back weren't too bad. Vera said, 'Gee, she's drinking and there's partying but she's a lot of fun.' But the drinking escalated and there was a fair bit of drama because of the grog.

The days rolled into weeks, and then it was time for me to go down to Gisborne and meet my family. Vera stayed in Auckland and I got on a coach for the meandering, all-stops, nine-hour bus ride. We seemed to stop at every tiny little town along the way, and everywhere we stopped I hopped off and had more to drink (I couldn't risk getting busted drinking on the coach itself). Of the whole day-long trip, the only clear memory I have is that Rotorua stank like rotten eggs.

I was going to stay with Alice, who had raised my mum and who I thought was my grandmother. She was there at the Gisborne bus depot to meet me, a little old lady who needed metal crutches to walk, but she was still driving. In fact, she was a lot tougher than she looked. She lived on her own and didn't wash using the hot water in the inside bathroom, but instead every day, sun, rain or hail, she'd walk all the way to a little tin shower arrangement down in the backyard and have a cold shower. She reckoned it helped her skin stay nice.

She welcomed me in. She must have known about my drinking, and heard how big a drunk I was, because even though I never saw her have a drink, when we arrived back at her place the fridge was full of beer for me. She didn't try to talk to me about it or get me to stop; maybe she just thought it was a stage I was going through. Instead she fed me from the meat and veggies boil-up she had going on the stove twenty-four hours a day—three o'clock in the morning you'd smell it, simmering away—and she introduced me to the rest of my family. One day when I was looking at some of her photos I asked her who the people were. Pointing at one lady she said, 'That's your grandmother.' That's how I found out Alice was really my great-grandmother—Mum had never said anything about it.

Alice, who I called Nana, was deeply into Maori culture; she talked the lingo and danced with the elders and spent a lot of time at the church, which was a real community hub for a small town (with a population of just over 30,000, Gisborne felt very small to me). I didn't feel Maori as such, but I loved the whole thing, I felt a spiritual connection straight away; I even tried to control myself while I was there and not get so drunk all the time. I went with Nana to meet the elders, played bingo with them and went to line-dancing and tried to pick up a bit of lingo—for a lot of the older people it was what they always spoke to each other and English was a second language.

Alice took me to the *marae*, the sacred place where Maori celebrate their culture and perform the old rituals. As we sat there, Nana started singing. At the first note I fell asleep and then at her last word I woke up. At first I felt terrible—I thought I'd been so rude and disrespectful, falling asleep like that. But the elders all explained that it was the power in the words she was singing. It was like I was a baby and she'd sung me to sleep.

I also spent time with some younger members of my family, especially my cousins. Pretty much all of them liked to smoke pot and hang out. They drank, too, but it never seemed to tip them over into aggression. I'd seen *Once Were Warriors*, the 1994 film that was a huge success around the world with its story of the domestic violence and other damage caused by a Maori man who was brutal when he was drunk, but I didn't see any hint of violence during my time in Gisborne.

While I was there I made a day trip to see Lee's family, which was a bit awkward because Lee's new girlfriend was pregnant and blowing up at him about his ex coming all the way from Australia, as if I was there to steal him back. That was so far off base. If I was really in love and wanted to spend the rest of my life with him, I would have gone with him when he asked me. But our relationship was more about being good friends, and the closeness I felt with his family. It was especially good to see his mum, Betty, because when he and I had been together she'd really looked after and mothered me. I stayed for dinner and we had a great catch-up, talking about the old days.

Soon, though, my time down south was finished and I headed back up to Auckland. I took care of some more visa things with Vera and then I headed back to Australia. (Vera had to remain a while longer, while her paperwork was processed.) I never felt tempted to stay. New Zealand is a beautiful country but it seemed to me at the time like not a lot happened there, and lots of the people I met said they were going to head to Australia to try to find work.

I'm really glad I had that opportunity to go and see it, to meet Nana and other family members and have those spiritual experiences. But I do regret having had the drunk goggles on. I wish I could see it again and get a clearer look at everything, but even if I do go back, I'll never have another chance to spend time with my great-grandmother because she has now passed away.

Chapter Five

When I flew back in to Sydney from New Zealand in 1999 I returned to no job and no fixed address. I floated along in a daze of drink and drugs, staying at my grandmother's or Dad's, or crashing with friends. Then I turned eighteen and was old enough to get unemployment benefits. The dole was hardly a fortune, but it bought my booze, especially since I wasn't paying rent.

Having registered for it, I was required to turn up to the Centrelink office every fortnight and show proof I had been actively trying to get work. The evidence was a form you filled in with the phone numbers of places you had unsuccessfully approached. I wasn't really looking for work and I didn't go to great lengths to fake it: I just looked out the office window across the road to where there was a hot bread shop and some other businesses and copied the numbers off their awnings, using the same numbers time after time. I guess there was meant to be some way the system picked up these dodgy forms, but if so, it failed with me. Once again, I didn't get caught.

After a while, though, a job did come along that I was genuinely interested in. I was sent along to the interview and was keen to do well. It was a full-time job as an assistant at the Murawina Child Care Centre, an indigenous-run centre which, at that time, was based in a terrace house on The Block in Redfern. I liked what I saw, and they must have done too, because they hired me. I was stoked, and everything about it lived up to my hopes. In fact, it was even better than I had imagined.

There was nothing glamorous about the job—it involved all the basics of daily life with young kids: changing nappies, cleaning up, helping them with their food, settling them for naps, playing with them and doing art and craft activities. But I loved it all. I loved the kids, and I loved the fact that in some ways it gave me permission to act like a kid, to muck around and have fun. My own childhood had been cut far too short and my time at Murawina was uncomplicated, rewarding and happy, at least at the start.

There was plenty to do, and fortunately throughout all my lost years my willingness to work hard (once I was in a job) had stayed strong. I knew a lot of the workers and a lot of the parents even before I started, and I got along well with them. I felt good about the fact that people trusted me to look after their children, and about the fact that my boss, Tonette Simpson, who ran the centre, gave me lots of positive feedback about how well I was doing.

I could see that the children's time at Murawina really made a difference in their lives, and it was great to be part of that. It felt like I was doing something with my own life, at last. My confidence and my self-esteem slowly started to build.

But I was still an addict. For all that the job was great, I was still dependent on alcohol and marijuana. In my other jobs I had found it easy to turn up drunk or stoned, but here it would have felt all wrong to do that. The responsibility of looking after tiny children was too serious. I had too much respect for the children, their parents and my fellow workers. But still, I used to look at the clock ticking towards knock-off time, hanging out for my chance to cut loose. I didn't indulge during my work hours, but at night time and especially at weekends I made up for it with a vengeance.

One of my regular haunts was a pub near Maroubra. At this particular pub you walked in off the street down a set of stairs to a dim, dark bar. I was eighteen now and could drink legally, but it wouldn't have mattered either way. You could get totally off your face down there and no one cared. It was a real favourite of the heavy-drinking crowd for that reason, and because the pub had cheap drink nights that made it so easy to get blind—two-dollar bourbon nights were one of the most popular.

I often hung out there with an old childhood friend from my La Perouse school days. We were great mates and on Friday nights we frequently made a beeline for this pub. Sometimes there was karaoke in the bar, other nights it was a DJ or the jukebox, but the entertainment wasn't the attraction. Everyone came for the cheap grog and the party atmosphere. It didn't take long for most people to get roaring drunk, and there were always plenty of shouts going round, so you wouldn't sit for long with an empty glass in front of you.

Murawina was an opportunity for me to turn my life around, and maybe, given enough time, I might have been able to do so. But who knows? As I came to view it much later, I was born with the disease of alcoholism. I was an addict waiting to happen—it was always just a matter of time. Unfortunately for me and those around me, I'd started down that path at such a young age and raced down it for so long that even with something good like Murawina in my life, I just couldn't stop.

Even though I was still a teenager, I seemed to have lived a lifetime and a half already. I thought I had experienced the lowest of the low (nearly cutting my own throat, robbing people in the street, losing years of my life to drink), but I was about to find out what hell really looks like. If I'd known then how bad things were going to get, I might not have had the strength to live through it. But I had no idea. For all my sense of myself as streetwise and tough, I was really just a kid, a naive, defenceless kid.

I was about to meet a man who would nearly kill me, who would leave deep and permanent scars on my body, mind and soul. He was an extreme case—a truly vicious and evil person—but it's no coincidence that I ended up in some kind of violent, dysfunctional relationship, since that's where my addiction had led me. I ended up with that type of man because that's who I spent most of my time with, other addicts and users who thought of their own needs before anyone else's. There was no chance of meeting a decent, loving man living the way I did in those years.

My friend and I were at the Maroubra pub on this particular night in October 1999 and so was her brother Joe. I knew him vaguely, just like I'd known all her family since I was tiny. He was three years older than us and I'd never got to know him well because he was always in and out of lock-up—first juvenile detention, then jail—so I'd never spent any real time around him. People in the community used to say, 'He's a bad one.' But out of loyalty to my friend I pretty much stayed out of those conversations.

When we were younger, he'd been in a relationship with a friend of mine, Lisa. I'd been really close to Lisa growing up—

we were in and out of each other's houses all the time. But we drifted apart when she got together with Joe Timbery. I didn't think much of it at the time, but now I look back on it in a whole other light. There were whispers and gossip about him hurting her, but it seemed that whenever anyone asked her outright she denied that he was the cause. People talked about how violent he was in general, but I never heard the details and I didn't pay much attention—I was wrapped up in my own dramas.

Anyway, when he turned up at the Maroubra pub one Friday night in October 1999, no introductions were needed. It was already late and we were playing the pokies when he arrived. I knew he'd got out of jail fairly recently; it wasn't so uncommon among that crowd. Everyone had been having a good time for hours and I was already blind drunk.

Even after he bought me a drink and made it clear he was interested in me, I didn't specially focus on him, just took in a general impression. He was wearing a tracksuit and had his hair shaved up on the sides, with a rat's tail. He looked rough, with terrible teeth and jail tattoos that were all but impossible to make out on his dark skin in the dim light. His eyes were an unusual green colour but nothing else about him physically stood out.

He was still muscly at that point, having bulked up in jail, but like me he was on the short side and shouldn't have posed much of a threat to anyone, really. Yet it was clear people were wary of him. From the moment he walked in, the other drinkers who knew him went out of their way not to draw his attention or antagonise him. They treated him like a ticking time bomb.

I wasn't impressed by this, or put off by it. I registered it but didn't think much more about it. My attention was on the drink in my hand. I could drink as much as he could—we drank together and then we were together, simple as that. It felt like he was claiming me.

It's hard to explain to anyone who hasn't been in the grip of addiction, but things work so differently when you're a drunk. There's a bit of general conversation, but no 'getting to know you' talk, no romantic banter, no 'Are you interested in going out with me?' Instead it's an unspoken agreement; suddenly you're hooked up. You've met, you've shared a few drinks and maybe a few bongs, and that's it, you're together for however long it lasts—the night, a couple of weeks or months, whatever it turns out to be. No one is thinking about the next day, let alone any further into the future.

There's another factor at work too. As well as the 'drunk goggles' affecting your ability to properly understand what's going on around you, there's also the way you feel inside. My new job had started to restore a little of my self-esteem, but it was like throwing handfuls of earth into a coal mine. For all my bravado, I felt just about worthless a lot of the time. A bloke like Timbery didn't have to make any great effort to woo me. He just assumed he could have me because he wanted me, and at the time that's how I saw it too. It didn't feel like I had a choice. Every now and then during the night I'd start to remember what I knew about his bad reputation, but everything was okay, we were all having fun, so I just pushed those thoughts back under the tide of beer and bourbon.

We all had more drinks, mingled with the other regulars, danced a bit to the karaoke, then it was closing time, and Joe, his sister and I headed off to their other sister's place a couple of kilometres away, a Housing Department flat at the bottom of a two-storey building. It was small, and his sister lived there with her partner and four kids, but it had three bedrooms and her younger sister often stayed there too. I'd been there heaps of times as a friend of both girls.

It was a fifteen-minute walk if you were sober, but more than half an hour in the state we were in, cutting across Coral Sea Park. We arrived, went straight into the end bedroom and had sex. Not surprisingly, I don't remember anything about it, since I was already just about passed out. Joe had been a heroin addict before he went to jail and he'd got straight back on it again as soon as he came out, but even though he was shooting up there was no thought of using a condom. He just didn't care, and I was beyond thinking that sensibly.

The next morning we got up and I thought, 'Shit, what have I done?' It didn't feel right because he was my friends' brother and because I was now in a better state to recall his reputation for being possessive and violent. But he was being okay to me and we went out to the kitchen where I started chatting to his sisters; it was all so normal and ordinary that I stopped worrying.

From then on, Joe Timbery and I were together. We headed off that morning to get drunk again, and that was what we did every day when I didn't have to work. There were no dates, no talking about a 'relationship', we were just together getting drunk, and together going home to his sister's flat or to their father's place.

Their dad lived on the Mish, the Aboriginal mission at La Perouse, in an old brick house on Murrong Place. The entrance had a front porch and opened straight into the lounge room with a connected dining room. The kitchen, and behind it the laundry, were off to one side. The dining room led to a hallway with three bedrooms and a bathroom coming off it. His father's bedroom was at the back, Joe's was in the middle and the large front bedroom was used by whoever was around at the time. The whole family were like gypsies. The elder of the two girls kept her own place, their dad stayed in his place (their mum had finally had enough and moved out not long before Joe and I got together), but Joe, his other sister and his two brothers drifted around. One of the brothers had a partner and young kids and the whole lot of them often stayed in the front room.

The house was dirty and neglected, with holes in the walls and old, worn furniture. Joe had a mattress in his room, but no bed—the mattress was just on the floor. Their mother had tried her best, and even came back and cleaned for a while after she moved out because nobody else was doing much. But the house reflected the lives that were being lived in it.

Joe's dad made and sold boomerangs. The extended Timbery family is one of the oldest and best known in the La Perouse Aboriginal community, with a story that goes back to the first encounters with white colonists at Botany Bay. There have been quite a few notable traditional craftspeople in the clan, and Sydney's Powerhouse Museum has in its collections some boomerangs made by an earlier Joe Timbery. Joe's father kept up the tradition, but he was also a drinker who liked to party, so his boomerangs were made to sell to the tourist trade down at The Rocks. They were still good work and he could make a lot of money if he put the effort in. He had his woodcarving and wood-burning tools at home, where he did his work. I liked him and we got along well.

Everything was sweet for the first few weeks. Joe and I just rolled along together, drinking and drugging. He was shooting up heroin and speed most days. I still had my deathly hate of needles so I stayed away from injecting, but I smoked pot and sniffed speed if it was on offer. I kept working at Murawina, and that meant I kept myself together during working hours, but Joe didn't have a job so every day was just a free-for-all for him.

It was only a couple of weeks before the verbal abuse started. We'd have been out somewhere drinking, at a pub or club, seeing other people and talking to them, then on the way home Joe would start coming out with a whole lot of jealous accusations. 'Why were you talking to that bloke, you slut?' 'You're just a cunt' (or 'a dog' or 'a ho'). He was always jealous—it didn't matter if the person I was saying hello to was male or female, nineteen or ninety. Joe wanted to control everything I did and every encounter I had. He'd say things like, 'You're my woman, what are you doing fucking talking to him? What, you fucking want him?'

When it started it seemed so stupid and unwarranted that I'd fight back, saying, 'What the fuck are you talking about?' No one who was supposed to be my friend or boyfriend had ever spoken to me like that. I used to talk to other people that way when I was younger, in the years when I was still at school. Back then I'd get drunk and sometimes treat people that way, like they were a piece of shit, running them down and acting like I was better than everyone. But I wasn't like that any more and I couldn't believe he was acting that way.

I thought I could make him see sense, so I'd get drawn into 'explaining myself'. Since there was nothing to hide, I'd try to explain that to him. But in my confusion at his behaviour, I'd get tongue-tied and the words would trip over one another. That made me feel as though I was acting guilty, as if there was something to be guilty about, and then I'd start to get really nervous and my words would get even more jammed up. Then the only path to take seemed to be to go off my head back at him. We'd have a verbal fight then everything would settle down, he'd say he was sorry and he could see he had no cause for jealousy and on we'd go till the next time.

But maybe a month after the verbal abuse started, things escalated and Joe hit me for the first time. Once again, we were drunk and walking back to his sister's flat after a night at the pub. He started up with the nasty talk, the usual jealous accusations. I was arguing back, telling him not to be stupid, as usual. We were walking our frequent route across Coral Sea Park, but this time he just got more and more worked up.

Then he got a look on his face that stopped me in my tracks. His expression changed into a mask of rage, the way I'd seen people change over the years when they were on the drink and seeing red. I was still trying to make my befuddled brain work out what I was seeing when he hit me, full across the face. It was an open-handed slap, but he put all his weight behind it, and my head snapped around.

I was so shocked; I simply hadn't seen it coming. The pain was bad enough, but it was the shock of it that really winded me. Part of my mind was still trying to take it in, while another was thinking, 'Oh my god, were all those rumours true? What kind of a man is this? And what is he going to do now?' I was suddenly frozen with fear. It was a pitch-black night, and we were alone in the middle of a deserted park. The thought of running flashed through my brain, but almost before it had formed it was gone because I knew he could run me down if he wanted to.

I tried to steady myself, and in my head frantically replayed the argument in the moments before he struck out. What had I said? What had I done to deserve this? I was no stranger to fighting, but only with other females—that was 'fair' because we were equally matched. It's why I lashed out at Mum but never physically at Dad—it wouldn't have been right because he was bigger and stronger and so could never have felt he could retaliate. (Somehow I pushed attacking Tommy to the back of my mind.)

If it had been another girl who'd hit me, I would have hit her back without even thinking about it. But in all the time I'd been drinking and drugging and surviving in that world, I'd never been hit by a man. In fact, I'd said many times I would never let it happen. Over the years plenty of women I'd known had experienced domestic violence. Sometimes they'd talk about it, and sometimes you looked at them and just knew. I'd always been staunch about it: if I ever saw one of my friends going through it, I'd say to her, 'What the hell are you doing? Don't let him do that. If he acts like that, he doesn't love you, no matter what he says.' But I was learning all too quickly that when you're in the situation yourself, it feels totally different.

I was in a shocked turmoil of emotions. I thought I was in love, and he'd said he loved me. He was supposed to take care of me, not hurt me. Maybe I deserved it, with my big mouth. I was suddenly so afraid. All of that—the jumble of thoughts and emotions and physical sensations—seemed to take ages, but really it was just moments. Suddenly he was full of apologies, reaching out tenderly and saying, 'I'm sorry, I'm so sorry. I didn't mean to do that. I love you. I'm not like that. It'll never happen again.'

I was still shaken, but I did what many, many women who experience violence from their partners do. I made excuses in my head for his behaviour. I rationalised it. I thought, 'It's just the grog. I must have run my mouth too hard and pushed him over the edge. He's said he's sorry, he's promised it won't happen again.' I wanted to believe him.

Paul Kelly captures it perfectly in his song 'Sweet Guy'. It's written from the perspective of a woman whose man turns on her for no reason, with no warning ('I was stitched by strangers'), but afterwards is remorseful and tender. Over and over again she asks herself, 'What makes such a sweet guy turn so mean?' So many women think the nice side they originally fell for is the 'real' him. Like I did, they tell themselves, 'He's really a sweet guy. That other side, the vicious side, that's not the real him.' That's what those men want you to believe. And often we want so much for it to be true that we make it easy for them to tell that lie to themselves and to us.

The other thing that we women do a lot, in normal relationships, not just violent ones, is think we can change our partners. In a good relationship, people do change a bit for each other. They don't change the core of their personality, but they might stop doing something the other person finds annoying, or maybe they'll develop an interest in a sport or hobby simply because the other person likes it. But hoping for change and thinking you're the one that can make it happen is unhealthy if the other person's behaviour is violent or addicted. By thinking you can change them, you take on responsibility for their behaviour. They never have to own up to themselves about what they're doing, and they never will change. To be worthy of you, they need to change first.

Well, I know all that now, but I didn't then. I was an addict with a low self-image and no real support network. I was easy pickings for such a manipulative, malicious man.

Eventually we started walking again, continuing to the flat. I felt some comfort in the fact that we were going there. I thought, 'He's said he's not ever going to do anything like that again, but even if something happens and he forgets his promise, his family won't let him do it ever again.' The seed of fear had been planted, though, and soon that fear would be fertilised every day, growing into a vine that choked and imprisoned me.

It wasn't long before he did hit me again, and then apologised for it—again he said he hadn't meant to do it, it was just that I'd provoked him. If only I could keep my mouth under control, he said, everything would be sweet. I still wanted to believe this, but every time he hit me it was harder and he was more out of control—he never used an open hand again after that first time in the park. It was always fists.

Each new degradation was shocking: the first time I had to go out in public with a black eye, then the first time with two black eyes. I soon realised that all the apologies and 'I won't do it again's were just lies. But somehow, somewhere deep down, I felt like maybe I did deserve it. Maybe everything in my life so far, at least since I had my first drink, had led me to this point, and this was my fate. I seemed to have no other place to go.

CAROL SIMON: I knew Joseph Timbery through his mum, who was a good friend of mine. He was a very quiet boy. If there was a group of kids, he wasn't the one that would cause trouble. In the house it would be his brothers and sisters that were loud and noisy. He'd be just sitting on the step in the room, he wasn't someone that you noticed. And yet, he was someone that you didn't feel at ease with. With his brothers, what you saw is what you got. They'd wave, and say hello. He was always quiet, but not an easy quiet. Even at a young age, he ran that house. The father reckons he did, but he didn't.

His mother was really worried about him. When he got into trouble, she rang me up and I took her to the

Children's Court. I had a lot to do with him because he was in and out of there. I didn't realise that he and Lani were together until the gossip went around Lapa, and people were saying, 'Get her away from him.' The people on the mission could see the violence that went on in the house. I remember ringing Kathy up and asking if it was true. She said, 'Yep,' and I said, 'Kathy, you're joking.'

After we had been together a couple of months, I took my brothers to the football. They were still so young—only about seven and eight—and they loved their footy, just like I did. My relationship with Mum had improved enough for her to agree to me taking the boys. I remember being really happy about it, thinking, 'I haven't seen my brothers in a while, I'm going to take them out and have a good time.'

Joe hadn't shown his full evil side yet, but he was openly possessive and jealous. Pretty much the only time we spent apart was when I was at work, and even that was a problem. I had to account for every minute I wasn't in his sight, so it was no surprise when he announced he was coming too. We went on the bus to pick up Garri and Darryl and I begged him the whole way, 'Please, no arguing, no fighting. Let's just have a nice time with them.'

It was a pre-season game with our team, South Sydney, at the stadium at Moore Park. I made one big mistake: I packed my backpack with grog to drink during the game. I knew that drinking grog meant there most likely would be some kind of drama, but I felt I couldn't get through those hours without it. We both drank throughout the game and the boys had a good time too, then it was time to get the bus home. We got on with lots of other footy fans right outside the stadium and the bus set off along Anzac Parade towards the southern suburbs. It didn't take long before Joe started up.

It was the usual thing: some random man on the bus looked in my direction, and to Joe that was the excuse for calling me all sorts of abusive names, drunkenly getting louder and louder. He started threatening me—'I'm gunna make you pay, slut'—and then followed up with all the rest of the vile poison that poured out of him at every opportunity.

I felt so humiliated. It was horrible enough that all the people on the bus were looking at us, some with hostility, some with concern and some with anxiety, but much, much worse were the looks on Garri and Darryl's faces. I felt so bad that their nice night out had turned into this nightmare, and so ashamed that they were seeing me this way. They were too upset to say much, but the look in their eyes said it all. They were terrified and couldn't understand what was happening. I quickly decided I had to get them off the bus because Joe was getting himself even more worked up and I thought he was going to start bashing me right there in front of everyone.

I pressed the stop button and rushed the boys off at the next bus stop; by that stage we were at Maroubra. Joe got off after us and followed along behind. I was so afraid of what might happen next. I didn't think he would hurt the boys, but I thought he might very well hurt me in front of them. I knew I had to ring Mum and get her to come and pick the boys up. Mobile phones were still fairly new then, and I didn't have one. So I went to a payphone and called her, attempting to keep the hysteria out of my voice.

I tried to downplay it, saying to Mum, 'Joe's flipping out, I can't bring the boys home. Can you come get them?' Much later

I found out she'd heard a few things around the community by then, things about Joe's temper, but I'd made sure she hadn't seen me with black eyes or any other signs of how bad it had all become already. She would never have let me take my brothers out if she'd known the truth of it.

Joe always was a coward, and when he heard me ringing Mum he took off. She came quickly and picked the boys up—I never took them out again when I was with Joe. After they'd gone he came back out of the shadows, circling round again. Together we got on another bus to head home. This time, I was blowing up right back at him. God, the scene we must have been making! In those days I still fought back verbally—even though I knew it meant I would cop it even worse later, I still had fight left in me and a sense of outrage about how I was being treated. Before long, even that would be beaten out of me.

Why didn't I go home with my mum when she came to get my brothers? Why didn't I head anywhere except back into Joe's orbit? How could I possibly get back on a bus with him by my own choice? If I had enough fight in me to yell back at him, why didn't I have enough to walk away for good?

It's that same thing again: unless you've been in that situation, it's impossible to explain. Or at least, impossible to explain in a way that makes sense. That's because when you're in that kind of abusive relationship, you're not thinking clearly. Every day acid is poured on your self-esteem so you start believing this is your doing, or it's what you deserve. You feel like you have no other choice. Obviously, if you look at the straight facts, I did have choices. I could have asked for help, tried to find refuge, realised that I was worth more than the life that was swallowing me. But I can only see that now, clean and sober, years later. At the time,

I was stupefied by alcohol and drugs. I thought I was useless and worthless. I simply did not believe there was any other path open to me.

The control that Joe had over my life and the degradation got worse and worse. The one good thing in my life was my job at Murawina, and he hated it for that reason. By then the beatings had become a very frequent occurrence, so I often had to go to work with black eyes. I would use makeup to try to disguise them, but I wasn't fooling anyone. The kids would say to me, 'Lani, Lani, what happened?' and the other workers would look at me sadly.

And Joe would ring me at the centre all the time, demanding to speak to me. Even though he knew exactly where I was, he needed to know my every move and to get inside my head, letting me know I was never free of him. He'd often be just a few blocks away, having come to Redfern to score. He would get me on the phone and start straight into the abuse, saying, 'What are you doing, you fucking slut?' I'd say, 'I'm just working, Joe.' He'd say, 'I want money. I haven't had me fucking shot. Just wait till after work, I'm gunna be waiting for ya, I'm gunna get you, dog.'

Other times, when he did have heroin or speed, he'd come and shoot up right outside the front of my work where he knew he'd be seen, and then he'd try to barge into the centre to harass me. If I stepped outside or tried to lead him up to the roof to get him out of sight of the kids, he'd slap or punch me.

If my injuries were too obvious or it was clear from when he woke up that he was even more out of control that day, I'd ring in sick. Tonette, my boss, was so understanding. She knew I wasn't sick, she could see what was happening, but she gave me support, letting me know she was there for me, and urging me to get help and get away from Joe. I hung in there for a couple of months, as things got worse and worse. But it got to the point where I knew I had to give up the job.

I had a meeting with Tonette and said to her, 'I can't do this any more. You know what I'm going through. I can't keep it up. I can't keep coming in to work beaten up; it's not fair on the kids.' She was very upset. She knew I was a good worker, she knew I loved the job. But she could understand that I was in an impossible situation. She was fuming at Joe for the damage he was doing to my life. Later on, she would tell the detective in charge of my case, 'Lani was a great worker and everyone loved her. But then she got together with him and went downhill really quickly.'

Once my tie to Murawina was gone, I was completely under Joe's control. We were together almost every minute of every day. He hated me trying to contact my family, and I had well and truly dropped out of touch with my friends. All we did from waking to passing out was drink and drug. The violence got worse and worse; it wasn't just fists any more. He'd smash me into walls or grab me by the hair and slam my head into a table. This was still only a few months into the relationship; I was now nineteen years old. Every time I thought it had reached a new low, I was proved wrong. There was always worse to come.

Around this time, I saved Joe's life. I thought bitterly of it afterwards, wishing I'd stood and watched him die, but at the time I just acted on instinct. He overdosed after shooting up and stopped breathing. He had no pulse. I called an ambulance and gave him CPR until it arrived. Once Joe was conscious again, the paramedic said to him, 'You know, you want to thank this girl who just saved your life. You were gone, and even if we had been able to bring you back you would have had brain damage if she hadn't saved you.' Expecting Joe to have a grain of gratitude or humility in him? The paramedic had no idea who he was talking to.

Chapter Six

My drinking and drug taking had escalated as I realised that the violence and abuse was only going to get worse and worse. When I opened my eyes each day I knew what I was in for, so the quicker I got off my face, the better. A day's consumption might be twelve beers and half a bottle of cheap vodka. As time went on, I even drank meths. It didn't lessen the beatings, but I didn't feel them quite as much. It dulled the physical pain and sent my mind to another place where I didn't have to be fully conscious of what I was suffering.

I stayed away from my family. I wanted to protect them from the knowledge of how bad things had become. Lots of people in the La Perouse community knew what was going on, though. By now the physical damage Joe was causing me was so severe and so constant, there was no covering it up.

Every now and then I would bump into an old friend on the street or in a pub or club, but I never spoke about what was happening. For a start, Joe was usually there, listening. But even if I'd had the opportunity to open up, I wouldn't have. Everyone I ran into seemed happier and had their lives more sorted out than me; I would have been ashamed to admit the true depths I'd sunk to. I couldn't shake the feeling that maybe there was some truth in what Joe said to me, that it was because of me he was like this. And I didn't think anyone could do anything to help me anyway.

He'd long since stopped apologising or pretending he wasn't really like that. He just continually said, 'It's your fault this is happening. If you could shut your big mouth, I wouldn't have to do this.' The other thing he said over and over and over was, 'You're my woman. I can do what I want to you.'

I could see him now for the monster he was, the monster I was chained to. It wasn't a love–hate relationship. By now I just hated him. But most of the time I was careful not to let that show, because it just fuelled the fire of his aggression. Sometimes I used to think my only hope was that he would get sick of me and move on to a new woman. That would have meant him torturing someone else, but it's a sign of the state I was in that, as awful as that would have been, I held a tiny sliver of hope it might happen. I'd given up any delusions about him changing.

When I look back on this time, I see myself as the walking dead. My lungs were breathing, my heart was pumping blood, but it all happened on automatic pilot. There was no spark of life in my soul. I began to find myself praying to die when the worst of the bashings were going on. There wasn't a moment when the fear and violence didn't dominate everything. I'd either just been beaten, or was about to be beaten, and always I was carrying the bruises and injuries from the most recent beatings. A good day was when I only copped a punch to the face or a full-on kick in the back. A bad day was when he really went to town on me.

He'd started using weapons as well as his fists and feet, picking up whatever was to hand and using it to cause maximum damage. He'd smash a bottle over my head, or pick up a golf club that was in his father's house and beat me with that. When I think back on it now, I can't believe I survived being hit in the head with a swung golf club even once, let alone repeatedly. If his father's boomerang-making gear was out he'd grab it, gouging me with the chisel and coming at me with the wood-burning craft tool. He kept a little baseball bat in his room, about the size of a police baton. That was a favourite of his; he'd hit me all over the body with it.

When I left the house now I covered myself in long pants, long-sleeved tops and jumpers even in hot weather, big sunglasses and heaps of makeup in an effort to hide the injuries. I was often limping or hunched in pain. We had no car, so anywhere we went had to be on foot or by public transport. I felt so conspicuous, like everyone was looking at me and judging me. And since Joe was almost always right there, breathing down my neck, they probably were looking at us. In my mind it reinforced how trapped I was: if all these people around us could see what was happening to me and they weren't stepping in to help, there was no possible chance anyone would be there for me even if I managed to leave Joe.

He made me go with him to where his mother worked, an Aboriginal centre in the city, on her paydays. He'd call her out of work and bully her into giving him some of her hard-earned money, then he'd want to pub crawl all the way back from the city to Maroubra, and pick up more alcohol to take home. I kept my head down, I couldn't look anyone in the eye.

I could never tell what might set him off. Alcohol often made his fury worse, but he was just as likely to lash out on those rare occasions when he was sober or straight (generally because he had to report to the police station over something or other; he was on two years parole for an assault he'd done just before I got together with him). From first waking up in the morning to just before he passed out, it could happen at any time. He'd get this look in his eyes just before it started. It made my blood freeze.

His viciousness seemed to have no end. One time at Murrong Place I tried to get away from him by running for the bedroom window. He caught me, bashed me, barricaded the door so I couldn't get out that way, took all my shoes and then smashed beer bottles all over the ground outside, within jumping distance of the window, so that I couldn't escape that way, either.

He'd often try to cover up the noise of what he was doing by turning the radio in his room way up—it was always on a country music station, so that would be blaring out. But it didn't really mask the sound and he just didn't care that the rest of his family could hear everything that was going on. They tried to intervene a few times, all of them. His father was too old and often too unwell to take him on, and we all knew Joe had laid into him, too. But his sisters and even his married brother would yell at him when they saw the damage he'd caused me, saying, 'What are you doing? This is wrong, leave her alone.'

Domestic violence was nothing new in that house, but this was way beyond anything any of them had been part of. One time the brother even jumped on Joe and started hitting him until Joe let me go and ran out of the house. But mostly Joe would just go off his head at them and intimidate them into shutting up.

His father's bedroom shared a wall with Joe's, and sometimes when I was screaming in pain or begging Joe to stop, his father would be banging on the wall, calling out, 'What are you doing to that poor girl? Stop it, you're going to kill her!' Joe was so controlling I was hardly ever out of his sight, but if he did leave the room for a minute when his family was there, or if he'd gone out of the house to score drugs or buy grog, they would say to me, 'Lani, what are you doing? Get out of here.' At various points his father, his mother, his sisters—all of them—said to me: 'What are you doing with Joe? He's going to kill you. Go, run.' I'd say, 'You don't understand, it's not that easy to leave.' But they did understand because they were scared of him, too.

A lot of people were: people on the street, on buses, people living on the mission. He used to walk around the Mish carrying a machete, saying he owned La Perouse because it had belonged to his ancestors and he could do whatever he liked there. He acted totally out of control. He didn't have any friends. He had drug buddies and there were some far-gone cases who would grog on with him, but a lot of people didn't like drinking with him and would go out of their way to avoid it because they knew he was likely to go off his head at some point. The thing is, though, he wasn't really out of control—he had rat cunning and he was very careful to pick his targets. He only attacked people who were smaller and weaker than he was.

Once or twice when we were drinking with other people and there were blokes there I knew, fellas I'd known from school or through my family, and Joe started verbally abusing me, they stepped in and tried to stop it. I always dreaded this because I knew it meant I would cop it much worse later. In fact I used to get angry at them for trying to intervene, knowing it would just make him more violent and it would be me he'd take it out on. He'd snarl back at them, but if it ever looked like a big bloke might take him on, he'd be out of there quick smart, dragging me behind him. It was the same with the violence—he didn't hesitate to bash me in a public place, but only if he thought no one would step in and only when there was no police or security around.

Once we ran into my father when we were on the street. Dad saw us from a distance and made a beeline for us. Joe, the big man when he was beating up someone weaker than him, showed his true colours and took off down the road. He knew what Dad would have done to him. Dad tried to persuade me to come with him to safety, but I was too afraid not to follow Joe.

We spent most of our time at his father's place, but sometimes even his father would have had enough and he'd kick Joe out for bashing me or hitting other family members. Then we'd go and stay at his sister's flat until his father relented and let him back. After a while, his mother arranged for a caravan to be parked outside the house. Joe claimed it for himself, while still keeping the middle bedroom. Inside the house was bad enough, but in the caravan he went completely berserk. He bashed me, he tore the place up. There was no stopping him.

The neighbours at Murrong Place knew exactly what was going on—they could hear everything. Sometimes even now I get a flush of shame thinking about what it must have been like for them and knowing they've seen me at my absolute lowest.

Some of them tried to help. They'd ring my dad on his mobile when they heard things get really bad, and tell him I was screaming for help. They'd call the police too, anonymously. I can understand why none of them confronted Joe, though. It's such a small community and they couldn't leave. That was their home, they had to stay there, and they were thinking about the repercussions that might happen. Like me, in a way, they were terrorised.

The police were there very often in response to these calls, but I didn't turn to them for help either. Part of it was my own distrust of authority, built up in my teenage years, but much more than that was the fear of what would happen to me after they'd left. They would mostly question me in front of Joe or at least within his earshot. I may as well have been wearing a gag. There was no way I could be honest about what he'd done while he was listening. Sometimes I was hostile to them, sometimes I barely spoke. I always denied everything. I understand that the training on how to handle domestic violence has changed a lot since then, at least in New South Wales. Police need to realise that it's just not on to ask a terrorised woman to open up about what has just happened to her in front of the person who's done it. They need to find a way to make the woman safe enough to feel like she can tell them what really happened, in her own time.

Ambulances came often, too. The paramedics would patch or stitch me up and unsuccessfully try to persuade me to leave.

Sometimes, if Dad got one of the calls from the neighbours, he'd make the half-hour drive from Cronulla to La Perouse. But when he got there, I'd hide from him. I'd hear him banging on the door, calling out to me, but I'd be too scared of what Joe would do afterwards, and too humiliated to open up. Sometimes I was so badly bashed I couldn't even get on my feet to get to the door. Joe would taunt me about it. After threatening me with 'Shut the fuck up, or else', he'd say, 'Your father's a Johnny-come-lately.' He'd picked that phrase up from a Steve Earle song about a Vietnam war vet, though he had no idea what it really meant. He used it as a way of saying that Dad wasn't going to be in time to save me—he would crow, 'He's going to come too late. You'll be dead.'

When I did hear Dad at the door, or sometimes Mum and Tommy or Koorine, I'd be silently praying. Sometimes I'd pray for them to leave quickly and sometimes I would pray that they would kick the door in, see what was happening and stop it. Then I'd hear them walk away and I'd want to cry. I felt so alone.

I was nineteen years old and I'd been with Joe for less than six months.

A couple of times in those months I did run to Mum. It happened when Joe was bashing me as we were leaving a club or walking between pubs and there was a taxi nearby. I'd jump in and go to Mum's house. I was blind drunk and in such a mess I would just lash out when I got there, the way a dog that's been kicked and beaten and left cowering in a corner will attack the next person who comes along, even if they are reaching out a gentle hand wanting to help.

I'd turn up yelling, demanding money, upset and incoherent. Mum and Tommy tried their best, wanting to call the police so I could press charges against Joe. I'd just get more revved up and turn aggressive. I felt like everything was closing in on me, everyone was telling me to do things I couldn't possibly do. I was backed into a corner and the only response was to fight everyone. When the police did come, I was scared to say anything to them because I had no trust in the law; my only experiences of it had always been on the wrong side. So I'd turn on Mum and Tommy, and they'd tell me I had to go.

Garri and Darryl would be in their bedrooms, where they'd been sent, crying out, 'Are you okay?' I remember them once making holes in the flyscreens on their windows, trying to pass money and a phone to me. Mum, too, sometimes slipped me money. She didn't want to, because she knew that I would just spend it on grog and drugs. Tommy felt that it was just enabling my addictions and worsening the problem, and Mum agreed—but I was her daughter, and she desperately wanted to help me somehow. So she'd slide a twenty- or fifty-dollar note out her window for me before I stormed off into the night.

Each time, I went back to Joe. Women's refuges exist for people in exactly the situation I was in, but I didn't really know anything about them. I couldn't go to friends—I'd shut them all out of my life—and while my family tried to help, and I wanted to reach out to them, I tried hard to stay away for their own safety. Joe often told me that if I ever left him he was going to kill my brothers and my grandmother. By then I knew what he was capable of doing, how evil he was. He knew which primary school the boys went to and sometimes he'd go there and hang around out the front at the end of the school day. He'd say, 'Do you think your brothers won't leave with me? They will.'

The thought that this was all my fault, that I'd got myself into this situation, weighed down on me like concrete. I thought the chances of me dying at Joe's hands were high, but at least I could try to keep my family safe. Why should they have to suffer because of my actions? That was how I looked at it. I didn't want to die, but if he killed me I felt it would have happened because I'd put myself within his grasp.

There was one more thing he was doing to me that no one knew about, the worst weapon yet in his campaign to completely break me down mentally. He was repeatedly raping me.

The first time it happened, I was so confused. At the very beginning of our relationship when he was still pretending to be a nice guy, we had lots of consensual sex like most people do in the early days of a romance. He seemed to want it all the time.

When he started to show his true colours, but the violence was still intermittent, there were times in between when we could have normal sexual relations. Then when I saw what he was really like, there were often times when I didn't want to be anywhere near him, but I just went along with sex, hoping it might make things easier.

But then one day we were in his room and he had just bashed me, then he started to touch me and try to undress me. I didn't want any part of it—he'd just been beating me, for god's sake. But he kept on going, forcing himself on me. I told him no, but he just kept going. I thought rape was something that a stranger did to you, not your partner. I still believed it when he said that the woman had to put out whenever the man wanted it. But even so, a little voice deep in my head was saying this wasn't right. I was so shocked I said, 'Do you know what this is? It's rape. You're raping me.' He just kept on going. Then I realised it wasn't just that he didn't care, he was actually getting off on it. He was enjoying forcing me to have sex against my will immediately after bashing me, the sick bastard.

Then, like he had with the scale of the violence, he got worse and worse. It became a pattern that he would rape me after bashing me. Then he began to bash me *while* he was raping me. He'd punch me with a closed fist, or pick up his wooden bat and lay into me with that. Before long, I had nearly permanent bruises on my thighs from him smashing the bat into me to force me to open my legs.

At first it was vaginal rape and forced oral sex, but then he anally raped me, too. I begged him not to, told him he was a dog for what he was doing, asked him in despair what was wrong with him that he would do this, but none of it made any difference; he just kept going. The vaginal rapes hurt and left me feeling dirty and disgusted, but the anal rapes were so far beyond anything I could imagine. I'd never had anal sex in my life and found the thought of it horrible, so to be raped that way was such a violation. It made me feel sick with shame and horror. I couldn't bear the thought of anyone finding out about it.

Once he started with the rapes, he didn't stop. Any time he wanted sex, he took it. Even if I went along with vaginal sex in the hope that would be enough, he would make it clear he wanted anal sex as well. I'd say no, and he would just anally rape me. It felt like I was his possession, of less value than a rag, there for him to do whatever he wanted.

One time we were walking back from Matraville where we'd been drinking. It was starting to get dark and we had an hour's walk home all the way along Bunnerong Road, a multi-lane roadway that was busy in the daytime with trucks and through traffic. It has houses and flats along the first half of it, but then there's a huge stretch leading to La Perouse where there is just open land or industrial estates on either side. As we left the club where we'd been, Joe punched me in the face, without warning. It was the usual rant—someone in the club had stopped to say hello to me. How dare I speak to anyone else? And on he went.

He dragged me down the street and when I had trouble keeping up, he turned back to me and snarled, 'Hurry up! If you don't, I'll fuck you right here and show everyone how much of a slut you really are.' He kept hitting and kicking me as we walked along, sometimes shoving me over low walls out the front of flats, then dragging me back onto the path again. I was crying, begging him to stop. When we got to the long dark stretch beyond the houses, I was so afraid. It seemed to take forever until we reached the lights of La Perouse. There was no one on the street and the cars that passed were just headlights zooming by, oblivious to what was going on metres away.

He kept bashing me as we walked through the Mish and into his father's house. When we got into his bedroom he spun me around and threw me on the bed, saying, 'You won't be leaving me. The only way you'll be leaving is in a coffin.' Then he started to rape me, saying in that horrible taunting voice, 'Lay back and make out like you're enjoying it.'

And then Joe found one more thing he could do to degrade and horrify me: he started shooting me up against my will. I would pass out, either from drink or from a bashing, and wake up with a syringe hanging out of my arm. The first time it happened it took me a few seconds to accept that what I was seeing was real, not part of some nightmare where I was only dreaming I'd woken. Had he really done this to me? I hated needles, I'd always stayed away from them. That's part of why he did it, because he knew it was one part of myself I'd kept separate from him. He shot up all the time, but I didn't. So he decided to see to it that I did.

The other reason he would do it was to bring me back to consciousness so he could attack me again. I'd come to with a jolt, suddenly wide awake with the syringe still in my vein—it must have been speed he used—then he would bash me or rape me or both. I was awake all right, living a nightmare that never ended.

When I was younger, I'd felt that I hated the world and all the people in it. Now I was full of a different kind of hate. I hated Joe, but I also hated myself so much. All the things that I thought were true and strong about myself had been broken. I'd always thought that no one would ever mistreat me—I wouldn't allow it. I'd never let anyone hit or abuse me. Now here I was, permanently drunk and drugged, being bashed and raped over and over. How had I come to this?

I'd seen myself as a strong person, someone who could look after herself. But the drugs and alcohol had shaped me into a person I didn't want to be. I couldn't control any part of my life. Every day I woke to a new hell with no possible escape. I was vulnerable and so afraid all the time. I'd gone from being the life of the party, staunch and fearless, to a shivering wreck, fearing every shadow, every word.

I was so full of guilt and shame, and sick with dread at the thought that my family and old friends might see how far down I had fallen. I thought I was a dirty, worthless failure and tried to end it all many times; I thought since I was likely to die soon anyway, it should be at my own hands. That would be a release, a way out of this torture. I gathered whatever pills I could get hold of in the house—prescription pills Joe's father or sisters had, or painkillers. I did it on a couple of different occasions, getting all that I could find down my throat. For all I know they were just antibiotics or something equally harmless. Anyway, they made me feel sick, but nothing more. I was still here.

I'd always been a loudmouth, but now I felt like I had lost my voice. I just stayed silent much of the time when Joe was enraged, because I knew if I opened my mouth I was going to suffer more. He would say to me, 'You're damaged goods. No one else will ever want to touch you.' And, 'I'll leave scars all over your body, you'll never forget me. Every time you look in the mirror you'll see what I done to you. You can never get away from me.'

Dad and Vera were still together, and they had decided to get married. I was happy for them, and their wedding was too big an occasion to miss, though I dreaded people seeing me. Joe knew he couldn't keep me away from it, and he would never have dared to show his own face there. Some old friends of the family, John and Delly Duckett, arranged with Dad to pick me up and get me there safely. I made myself look as presentable as possible, but when they saw me at the door, I could tell how upset they were. I was wearing clothes that covered up a lot of the bruises, but I had two black eyes. Delly got John to stop at a pharmacy on the way to the wedding. She went in and bought foundation and concealer and powder and eye makeup, and did her best in the car to fix me up so I could show my face.

Someone said to me recently, 'It's so lucky you didn't get pregnant to Joe.' I knew just what she meant. I couldn't even imagine how much more horrendous it would have been if I'd had children in that situation. I have endless admiration and praise for women who are able to get out of domestic violence situations when there are kids involved. Those women are a real inspiration to me. But, in fact, I suspect that I did fall pregnant to Joe a couple of times. I had contraceptive pills, but I often forgot to take them, given the state I was in. However, if I was ever pregnant, probably the bashings led to early miscarriages—unusually heavy periods that felt not quite right and came at the wrong time.

I wasn't eating much, and when I did it was mostly junk. Sometimes we would go to Joe's sister's flat for Sunday dinner, and sometimes we'd be there long enough to actually eat a decent meal before Joe would start up and we'd have to leave. I was thin, with bags under my eyes, which were often bruised and blackened; I had cuts and stitches and bruises all over me. I wasn't dirty, but even that had a kind of horror attached to it.

Throughout the years when I'd been drinking and drugging, with no real place to call my own, I'd always kept myself clean, using the showers wherever I was working, or going to a friend's place to wash. Now, Joe would bash me so that I bled—often if he'd attacked me on the mattress, I'd be left lying in a pool of my own blood. Then he'd say the blood disgusted him, and he'd pull me up and force me to walk through the house, bleeding, bruised and hunched over with the pain, to the bathroom. There I had to have a cold shower—I was never allowed hot water.

The cold water felt like electrodes on all the cuts and gashes and bruises all over my body. I'd be crying or moaning with pain, but Joe didn't care. He'd just force me to stay in there, with blood running down the drain. I'd get out of the shower, shivering violently, and barely make it into the hallway before he'd start bashing me again, all the way back to the bedroom.

I remember one time before I stepped into the shower I caught sight of a figure from a ghost story, floating on the other side of the bathroom. When I was little, one of the spooky stories kids used to tell to scare one another was the tale of 'Bloody Mary', a ghoul who would materialise in front of you with blood streaming down her face. My heart froze when I saw her face just feet away from me. Then with a different kind of horror I realised it was my own reflection in the bathroom mirror.

Chapter Seven

The week before Easter, in April 2000, we were at Joe's father's place and Joe was attacking me with his fists when he picked up an iron bar, a kind of short crowbar or jemmy that he kept. He hit me hard on the forehead. I reeled from the blow. I felt concussed and my head was bleeding heavily. I tried to run away from him, but he was pulling me back. Someone called an ambulance, I still don't know if it was a neighbour or a member of his family, but next thing I knew the paramedics were there.

They took me to the Prince of Wales Hospital and a doctor stitched and dressed the wound. I was there for a few hours altogether, and then went back to Murrong Place. Sore and just wanting to rest, I went straight through to the middle room and lay down. Joe came in and started yelling at me: What had I told the coppers? What did I say to the doctors? Did I dob him in? I kept my eyes closed and pretended I was asleep.

He knelt down beside the mattress and started touching me. I kept my eyes tight shut and tried to roll away. He started rubbing against me and pulled my pants off, then lay down beside me. He was trying to kiss me. I was disgusted and told him to get off me, to leave me alone. I tried to curl into a ball to get away from him. Then I felt him push something into my vagina. At first I thought it was his penis, but it couldn't be, his body position was wrong for that. Then I realised it was a bottle of hair mousse that had been on the ground next to the mattress. He was pushing it into me.

I was so shocked, I screamed out and jumped up. I freaked out. I was screaming at him that he was sick, what he'd done was disgusting and putrid, and that it was rape. He backed off. Normally when he bashed or raped me, I was stupefied with drink or drugs and far beyond defending myself. But now I was more alert. I'd been all that time at hospital without a drink and when I'd come home I'd lain straight down. What he'd done was so shocking that I reacted without thinking.

I lost it, yelling at him. At first he tried acting like he hadn't done anything, but my outrage must have really surprised him because he left the room and left me alone for the rest of the night. I was too upset by what he'd done to take any pleasure in this very small victory, and it was never repeated.

Less than a month later I needed more stitches when Joe attacked me on the street, just near his father's house. He smashed a beer bottle over my head and then laid into me with his fists and feet. It seemed to go on forever and I was badly hurt. Someone called an ambulance and he backed off while the paramedics treated me, stitching up the cuts on my face and head there and then and checking the other damage, including a big lump on my forehead. The police patrol came and their report notes that Joe ran from the scene as they arrived.

When the ambulance and police had driven off, he started dragging me down the road towards the house, continuing to hit and kick me all the way. Then he shoved me inside, into his bedroom, barred the door and turned the music right up. I knew things were about to get worse, and they did. He forced me to give him oral sex, saying, 'Do it or I'll bash ya worse.' Then he raped me. I said no, but he said, 'I can do what I want to you, you're my woman.'

A few days after that he attacked me in the lounge room, using a woodworking chisel to stab me over and over on the shoulders, arms and back, then sticking a fork into my leg, then hitting me with his bat and raping me again.

RORY BRENNAN: I knew of Joe Timbery because he'd gone to La Perouse Primary, but I didn't know a great deal about him. I didn't know the reputation he had. It was Koorine who told me they were together. She said, 'He's no good. I think he's been locked up and he's just out …' Naturally, I wasn't happy about it but it wasn't until months later that I started getting occasional calls from people in the community ringing to say, 'I saw Lani with a black eye.' I'd ring and have a word with her and she'd deny it all. But it was hard to keep tabs on everyone because I was nursing my mother who was living in one place, I was living in another area, Koorine was somewhere else and Lani was somewhere else again.

For a long time we thought it was just a black eye and a fat lip. I confronted him a number of times, including one day down at Maroubra Junction. Lani had a little bit of a mouse under her eye, a bit of a black eye. I got right in his face and I gave it to him for ten minutes. He wasn't saying anything. In the end I started getting a bit worked up so he bolted and ran off up the road and jumped onto a bus. I went down to the mission a number of times too, looking for them, but they wouldn't answer the door.

Then as time went by I did get a couple more phone calls from people down at the mission saying, 'Oh Rory, the police have just been here. There's an ambulance. Lani's been belted by Joe.' I felt shocked and very angry. No domestic violence is good. I'd had the mother-on-son violence growing up. And with me and Kathryn, I was a very violent drunk but most of my real violence was in the street or in the pub. In the home I'd mouth off a lot, I'd punch a hole in the fibro wall and I would have hit Kathryn on a number of occasions, so it was a nasty scene, but there was never an ambulance called or police called. It was just the usual: the bloke comes home drunk, banging on the door, throws the dinner across the table, swearing and ranting and raving, then hopefully just passes out and goes to sleep. What Lani experienced, that was totally another level. We had no idea how bad it was, otherwise I would have acted a lot harder than I did.

KATHY BRENNAN: It wasn't until a long, long way into that relationship that we found out what was really going on. We went out there to try to see her, but no one would come to the door. We didn't know until much later the extreme violence that was going on, but even so it was terrible to think she was going through any of it. At one point I got her back here to my house, and she was battered and bruised. I couldn't believe the state she was in. It was terrible to see. All domestic violence is unacceptable, but even though I went through it I never got treated that way. The way she was going, I didn't think she would live until she was twenty-one.

There were so many attacks and beatings I won't detail them all, but some of them became very significant later on.

On Sunday, 25 June, we were at Joe's sister's flat for dinner when he started up; her kids were home, but that didn't stop him. It was clear he was going to keep getting more and more worked up, so I ran out of the house, hoping to take the aggression away from the little ones. He pelted out the door after me and tackled me onto the concrete out the front. He got his hands around my throat, choking me, then dragged me to the next building along and shoved me inside the vestibule, where he could bash me out of view of passers-by on the street.

He was punching and kicking me, gouging his fingers into my throat, smashing my head against the walls and the stairs. I was screaming and crying. The noise must have been horrendous, echoing up through the flats. I don't know if it went on for twenty minutes or forty minutes but it felt like an eternity. I thought I was going to die. People in the flats must have called the police and the ambulance. I've never been so glad to see uniforms. Those people saved my life.

Joe took off when he saw the police vehicle approaching, but he didn't get far. They pulled up their paddy wagon in front of where he was running, stopping him. I learned later that they asked him his name. He said, 'Joe Timbery, what's it to you?' Then they asked him about the blood he had over his clothes and hands. He said, 'What the fuck are you talking about?' One of the officers said to him, 'Where did the blood come from?' He said, 'No blood there.'

On it went, with him accusing them of 'picking on' blackfellas and telling them to 'get fucked'. Then they arrested him for assault and put him in the back of the wagon.

The police came up to talk to me, and he could hear us from his cage in the back of the wagon. I had blood coming out of various big cuts on my scalp and face, blood from my mouth, an eye that was already turning black and something was wrong with my jaw, which felt like it was loose and in the wrong place. One of the police officers went in and checked inside the foyer, then photographed all the blood on the walls and the floor.

The ambulance came and the paramedics started looking at my wounds. I was so upset and hurt, I wouldn't have remembered exactly what I said. But because of the arrest and the statement the police made at the time, I have a record of everything. They asked me if I'd been with Joe when the injuries happened, and I said, 'Yes, we had an argument, but I'm not giving you a statement. He's my man.' They then led me into the foyer and asked if it was my blood. I said yes, and the officer said, 'You need to do something about this.' I said, 'I know, but I don't want him in jail, he's on parole.'

The whole time, as the police noted in their statement, Joe was in the back of the van yelling out, 'Don't tell them white cunts nuthin'.'

They took us both back to Maroubra Police Station, him under arrest, and me so they could take photographs of my injuries and try to convince me to make a statement. I continued to refuse, and afterwards the officer concerned made a note of how upset and scared I was. A statement from me wasn't necessary, anyway—the police could, and did, charge Joe based on what they'd seen.

Even though I've tried so hard to explain about how afraid I was, I know that some people who haven't experienced the kind of mental and physical torture that terrorises every part of you might still have trouble understanding why I acted the way I did. Why didn't I accept the help I was being offered here? Why didn't I reach out to the police when they reached out to me? Simply because I thought if I did, Joe would kill someone I loved, most likely my grandmother or my brothers. He'd told me if I ever spoke up he'd make me pay, and I believed him.

It wasn't just me, either. The police spoke to two witnesses that night—the residents of the flats who had called them. Neither of them would give a statement to the police, and when they were subpoenaed to appear in court to give evidence on the charge neither would come, saying to the police they were too afraid of retribution.

The reason my jaw felt wrong was because Joe had broken it. I had to have surgery under general anaesthetic to wire it back together and couldn't eat properly for months afterwards. I remember the shame and humiliation of waking in the hospital and knowing all the nurses and doctors knew what had happened. The police came, urging me to get away from Joe. Through a fog of painkillers I saw Mum and Aunty Carol and I saw the shock on their faces at how badly I'd been hurt. They were crying and begging me to get help and get out. But I knew soon Joe would be there, and he was. There was no way out. He would always be there, hunting me down, threatening the people I loved. I was chained to him until I died.

The charge against Joe over this incident, 'assault occasioning actual bodily harm', ended up being dismissed by Waverley Court. There was a period of years when I thought this had happened because the police had lost evidence—the photos they took of me and of the foyer. But according to the official records that's not what happened. The first hearing date was 18 December 2000. When neither the witnesses nor I appeared at court, a second hearing date was set for three days later and, according to court records, a warrant was issued to enforce my appearance. But I knew nothing about the warrant so I didn't turn up then, either. At that point, the charges were withdrawn.

> CAROL SIMON: I was always at Lapa driving around, picking up clients, taking them somewhere. If I saw Lani and Joe together I wouldn't pick the two of them up, I used to drive past them. If Lani was by herself, I would never not pick her up. If I ever did see her on her own I'd try to get her to go home. I'd pick her up, drive her home in the car, but she wouldn't go in, or she'd have an argument with her mum and take off.
>
> By this point Lani looked glazed all the time—stoned, confused, frightened. One time one of my granddaughters said, 'Nan, Lani's down at the chemist'—this is Lexington Place—and I went down there. She was off her head just sitting there on the ground and Joe was standing in front of her, yelling and screaming. I went over and he swore at me and carried on. And I walked away, left her there. I feel terrible about that. We should have rung the police and got them to come but we were frightened, everyone was frightened of him.
>
> Another time Kath rang and asked me would I take her to the hospital to see Lani. She'd had to have her jaw wired after he'd bashed her. Her eyes were so black and

blue, she couldn't even open them. Her face was twice the size of normal. I'll never forget walking in and seeing her like that. Of course we tried to persuade her to get away from him. She wanted to leave. She'd look at us and she wouldn't say anything, she'd just cry. She felt that she couldn't get away from him, he wasn't going to let her go.

I was back at the Prince of Wales Hospital eight weeks after that attack, with what the doctor reported as 'a massive swelling and bruising surrounding the left eye and also some blood issuing from the eye'. That was the result of a beating that included being hit in the face with a crowbar.

In all, I was in hospital with injuries Joe had caused me eight times between April and October 2000. They were the worst of what I copped, but for every beating that put me in hospital there were dozens more that I just had to deal with myself.

I lied about what had happened when the doctors asked. I would say I'd been beaten by a gang of girls in a park, or hit from behind by a stranger with an iron bar while leaving a pub. One time I even said I'd fallen from a horse. I guess they knew the stories didn't add up, because every time I turned up I was covered in older bruises and cuts and scars, along with the fresh ones. They just did their best, treating my body but unable to break down the barriers fear had built around me.

Things kept on getting worse, and on 29 September Joe hurt me so badly I could have died. It was my friend Petra's birthday. I'd known her since we were at school and she was having a party. She'd invited me, and I fixated on the invitation, dreaming of a night's escape from the torture. When the night came, I was determined to get there, somehow. I got dressed and was finishing getting ready when Joe came into the bedroom and said, 'You won't be goin' nowhere. Take your clothes off, I want a fuck.' I said, 'I don't want to, I'm getting ready to go to Petra's party.' He said, 'Lie down and do what I want or I'll shove this VB bottle up ya.'

So I lay down and let him do what he wanted, trying to zone out. Sometimes I could manage this, letting my mind drift off to a safe little world somewhere, while my body waited for him to finish. As soon as he got off me, I stood up and went to have a shower, then I got dressed again and walked into the living room, on my way out of the house.

Joe was sitting on the couch, which was one of those old ones with a metal frame and bare wooden arms. He was mulling up some yarndi for the bong, using a ceramic plate painted with Aboriginal designs that I'd got back when I worked at the Cultural Centre. He got up and said, 'You're not going nowhere,' and shoved me, sprawling, onto the lounge. I started to struggle up, saying, 'I'm going. You can't stop me.' He picked up the plate and broke it across the wooden arm of the couch. It didn't shatter, just broke cleanly in two. Then he lunged towards me and slashed.

I looked down at my left thigh, blinking, trying to work out what had happened. I couldn't understand it. There was blood everywhere and I could see right into the flesh of my leg, it was cut so deep. I was still staring down, trying to catch up, trying to shake out of the fog that seemed to have closed in around my brain and figure out why I could suddenly see blood, so much blood. Dimly I heard him say, 'See, I told ya you wouldn't be leavin'. You can't walk out of here now.'

The cut was so deep and it was bleeding so heavily, I'd gone into shock. I started forward like a wind-up toy, jerking my way out the door, with blood pouring, gushing from the wound. I took a few steps out into the yard and the people across the road, who were outside their house, saw me and cried out. My leg was hanging open and I started to stagger towards them. They immediately came to hold me up and said I had to go to hospital, now. The shock was protecting me from feeling the pain and all I could think as I started to black out was that their car looked so new and white and I was going to bleed all over it.

They raced me to the Prince of Wales Hospital and I woke up lying in a pool of my blood on the hospital gurney. Then I felt the pain: it was horrific. The doctor told me they couldn't operate until all alcohol was out of my system so they admitted me and stabilised me for the night. The next morning I went into surgery. It was a full-thickness cut, right down into the muscle, stretching across my thigh. It took thirty-four stitches to close it, as well as metal clamps to hold the top skin in place. My leg was protected by a sort of half-cast: solid at the back and bandaged at the front, over the clamps.

After a period in post-operative recovery I was moved to a ward, where I drifted in and out of consciousness. At some point in the evening I realised Joe was there, standing by my bed. He ordered me to get up and sign myself out. I said, 'I can't go yet. I've just had an operation. I have to stay.' He said, 'I'm not leavin' ya here to dog on me. Get up.'

He was getting more and more worked up, so I sat myself up and managed to get dressed somehow. He was right on my heels as I went to the nursing desk and signed myself out against medical advice. They gave me a pair of crutches, some information on how to look after the wound, some painkillers and an appointment card for follow-up checks.

I was shakily trying to make my way along with the crutches. Joe was kicking out at my damaged leg, telling me to hurry up. We went back to Murrong Place where his brother was sitting out the back, smoking cones. Joe went out and had some too, then came into the bedroom, where I was resting. He said, 'You don't need that cast. Get it off.' I tried to say no, but he started bashing my leg with his wooden bat. Blood began showing through the bandages. I thought if I agreed to take the cast off, he might not hurt me as badly. He told me he wanted to fuck. I said, 'No, my leg. What about my leg?' I was crying and already in pain, but he didn't care. In fact, it seemed to spur him on. The more badly I was hurt, the more he seemed to want sex. He said if I didn't do what he wanted, he'd rip open my stitches.

By this time I was nearly hysterical with pain and fear. He raped me vaginally, then forced me onto my stomach and pinned me down and raped me anally. I was crying, sobbing. I was in agony. When he finished, he just got up like everything was normal, like I was nothing and what he'd done was nothing, and walked out of the room. It didn't matter at all to him then, or in the days after, that I had this terrible injury. He just used me and abused me whenever he liked.

At some point in the next week or so, a home nurse came to see me. (I think it must have been arranged when I failed to turn up for my hospital outpatient appointment.) She took one look at me and told me I had to get to the hospital. The clamps had come loose, stitches had torn, I had an infection in the wound and I was running a fever. They admitted me to the Prince of Wales Hospital, put me on an antibiotic drip, cleaned the wound and gave me painkillers. They kept me in for two nights, then I went back to the man who'd caused all this damage to me in the first place.

Not long after this I worked up the courage to try to escape. I was so terrified and desperate, I was sure if I stayed he would succeed in killing me. I fantasised often about him dying and thought about killing him, but I couldn't imagine taking another life, even his. I thought my only chance at freedom was to take off one day when he'd gone out for a little while, and one October day I did. I shoved some of my few possessions into a bag and went first to visit Wha Wha—something I didn't do much any more, as I'd been trying to shield her from my situation. Then I went to my dad's house at Cronulla. I thought I was safe there because while people on the Mish had Dad's mobile number, I didn't think anyone had his home number or address.

But within a few days Joe had tracked me down. He rang the home number. It was awful that he'd found me, but then he said something that chilled me to the bone. He told me that if I didn't get back to him straight away he would go and kill my grandmother. I was freaking out, telling him to stop, but he said he was going to her house right away, and hung up on me. I was too frightened to say anything to Dad. By this stage I well and truly knew what Joe was capable of. This wasn't an empty threat. I believed he could do something as evil as kill a sick old lady just to get back at me.

I raced out of the house and ran to the train station. I had to get the train to Bondi Junction, then a bus to Clovelly, where Wha Wha lived. The whole way I was frantic, desperate to get there before he did. I ran to her door, and went inside dreading what I might see. Thank god I'd made it there before him. I tried to talk to Wha Wha as if I'd simply come for a visit. But the whole time I was keeping a lookout, and sure enough before long he turned up, walking around menacingly out the front, trying to remember which place was hers. I went outside and he said I'd come with him or he'd go inside right then and kill her. Of course I went with him, copping abuse all the way back to the house and knowing I was in for a severe beating for having dared to defy him.

> RORY BRENNAN: She came to my place at Cronulla a couple of times, one way or another. We'd talk black and blue: 'Don't go back to that arsehole.' And she'd listen and say, 'No, no, I'm not.' But he'd be trying to ring her and suddenly I'd go to work and, bang, before you know it she'd be gone, headed back.

On the night of 23 December 2000 we were drinking in a group at the Mish, not far from Joe's father's house. He decided someone had looked at me or I'd looked at someone—the usual excuse he made to himself—and he got up and started dragging me back home, hitting me as we went. When we got inside and into the bedroom he started again with the 'If you want to act like a slut, I'll treat you like a slut' abuse. He ordered me to get my clothes off, pushed me down on the bed and anally raped me, then turned me over and vaginally raped me. I was crying and shaking and furious and afraid, all at once. I said, 'I'll be leaving you soon. I'll leave you when you least expect it.' He pushed me down and told me to shut up, all the while continuing to rape me. He said, 'You'll never get away. I've fucked you up for life.'

The next day when I got up, he was still asleep and I saw my chance to take off. I had nothing with me except a bus fare, not even shoes. I went to Koorine's. She took me in and Mum came around too, and they saw the state I was in. They were shocked and upset and begged me to get away from him before he killed me. That night I stayed at Dad's place and he looked after me. I couldn't really relax for fear of what Joe might be planning, but just being with Dad made me feel safer.

When I woke up, it was Christmas morning. I had breakfast with Dad and Vera, then went over to Mum's place. I had a lovely few hours there with the boys, still young enough to be excited about their presents, and Mum and Tommy. I saw my friend Rachel. Then I got a call on my mobile from Joe's younger sister. She said she wanted to see me, to talk about what her brother had done to me and how I needed to get away from him. I thought, sweet, it will be great to see her without Joe breathing down our necks. She was at her mother's place, just a short drive away and my mum offered to give me a lift.

As soon as I walked in the door, I felt that something was wrong. Then I saw that Joe was there, lying in wait for me. Long afterwards, when I was able to sort through what happened, I realised I couldn't really hold it against his sister. My guess is that he terrorised her into making the call. My heart started pounding when I realised what was going on. It felt like it was going to break right through my chest. He punched me in the mouth and started telling me how stupid I'd been to think I could get away, and how if I didn't come back to him there and then he would go and hunt down my family.

I knew I had no choice. I had to go back with him to Murrong Place. When we got there he started a bonfire out the front. He had already got well into the grog. I started drinking to catch up and numb myself as quickly as possible. I knew he would make me pay for having tried to leave. I didn't have to wait long. He walked into the house and came out again almost straight away, with a hammer in his hand. He lifted his arm up and swung down, hitting me with the hammer over and over.

I was trying to shield myself and scrabble away from him. I desperately tried to get further from the front door. If he was attacking me with a hammer in daylight in the front yard, I couldn't breathe with the thought of what he might do to me if he got me inside the house.

But he was stronger. He dragged me through the door and down the hall, hitting me all the way. I was twisting and turning, trying to break free. He pushed me again and I fell, spraining my ankle. I cried out with the pain. There was a little wooden table nearby. He grabbed that and starting hitting me with it. He shoved me into his room and said, 'Get on the bed.' I fell onto the mattress. He said, 'Jerk me.' I was crying with pain and fear. I said no, swearing at him to leave me alone. He said, 'I'm gunna bash you worse,' and he picked up his wooden bat and then the golf club, swinging at me with them in turn, smashing them into me, all over my body.

He told me to take my clothes off, and started pulling them off me, continuing to hit me at the same time. He forced me down and then reached to the floor and picked up an electrical extension cord that was lying there, one of those thick bright orange ones. He wrapped it around my neck and then shoved his penis into me. He was raping me and pulling the cord tighter and tighter around my throat. I was sure that this was it, I was about to die. There was no way I could survive this. I couldn't breathe. I kept passing out and coming to again. Sometimes when I came back to consciousness he was raping me. Sometimes he was bashing me. Sometimes both.

He raped me over and over that night, choking me with the cord till I passed out, then loosening it just enough so I'd come back for long enough to see and feel what he was doing to me. Then the air would be gone and I'd black out again.

All night it went on. Hour after hour of torture. Sometimes I prayed to die. Inside my head I was screaming out to any god listening to end the pain, just let me go, let me die and be free. At other times I prayed for the sun to come up. I kept trying to turn my head to see if I could make out any hint of light coming through the window. I thought that maybe when the night ended I'd have a chance to get out—out of the bed, out of the room, out of the house. There were times, too, when I cursed whatever god might be listening, letting me go through this unendurable agony. I was sure I would never see my family again. I was going to die right here, tonight, at the hands of this animal. I felt so very alone.

Chapter Eight

But somehow I did survive. Even now, all these years later, I can hardly believe it. I woke in the blood-soaked sheets, bruised and battered from head to toe. Every tiny movement sent more pain stabbing through me. Joe was there, to see his handiwork. He said, 'Get up, we're going to Maroubra Junction.' He had to report to the police station there as a condition of his parole, and it was clear he wasn't going to let me out of his sight for even a minute.

I slowly started to stand, gasping with the pain. I couldn't straighten out properly and every step I took was agony. I tried to clean myself up as best I could. We caught the bus from La Perouse. I must have been quite a sight: barefoot, with strangulation marks around my neck and other bruises and traces of blood showing. No one said anything on the bus, but there's no way he could have walked me into the police station looking like that and he knew it. Straight across the road from the station was a McDonald's. He told me to go into it, and come to the front window nearest the street. He said, 'Stay there where I can see you while I go in to report.'

Joe didn't know, but on Christmas Eve Dad had given me a prepaid mobile phone. I'd put it into my pocket—in the clothes Joe had thrown off me—and in the terror that followed Joe's sister's call, I had completely forgotten about it. Joe had taken away my usual phone, but as we'd approached Maroubra I realised the one Dad gave me was still safely in my pocket. I was petrified that I might have shown something on my face as I discovered this, and Joe would search me. But he hadn't noticed.

The second he walked through the police station doors, I jumped up and ran to the toilets. There I called Dad. I was hysterical, screaming and crying, trying to tell him what had happened. I told him I would be walking up Anzac Parade towards a dealer's house Joe had said we were going to. It was not too far from where we were now, and there was only one route to take. Dad said he was on his way. I hung up, hid the phone and went back out to the tables near the street.

I had to act normal: everything depended on the next fifteen minutes. I couldn't let Joe get any hint that I'd moved while he was reporting. I couldn't let him become suspicious. We had to stick to the plan and walk up to the dealer's house so that Dad had time to drive over from Cronulla and find me. I saw Joe coming back across towards me and I desperately tried to keep my cool.

We started off up the street. I was trying to keep track of the minutes in my head, counting the seconds till I could expect to see Dad. We walked along past all the normal people living their normal lives, happy to have the Boxing Day holiday and so far away from my life they might have been from another planet.

Then suddenly, there he was, Dad, come to save me. Joe saw his car pull in, yelled out a few things as Dad was getting out, then took off, running away for all he was worth towards a bus that had stopped. I am in no doubt at all that my father saved my life that day. Months earlier it had been the police who showed up at a critical moment. Then, the danger was that Joe wouldn't stop the frenzied attack he was making on me. This was different. I was certain that if he got me back to Murrong Place, Joe would attack me again and keep on going until I was dead, if not that night then the next or the one after. It seemed miraculous that he hadn't killed me the night before. I didn't believe I was going to get another chance like that.

Something had snapped inside me. As terrified as I still was of Joe, there was something else there too, something new. I'd tried to leave before and always been dragged back. Now I had passed a point of no return. I could not go back—I just couldn't. I could not ever let Joe get within arm's reach of me again. I didn't know how it was going to be possible to make that happen, but at last I was ready to put all my faith in my dad, my mum and the other people who loved me and who had been so desperately worried for me. Along with the fear that still ran through my inner being, there was a kind of reckless determination, too. My escape had to be now or never.

I was so happy to see my father. My rescuer. He was very upset when he looked at me and started to realise the state I was in. I told him some of what had happened—nothing about the rapes, I couldn't bear to mention those. He was shocked at what I'd been put through, and I'm sure if he'd had Joe there on the spot Dad would have killed him for what he'd done to me. But his main focus was on me. More than anything he wanted to help me to get away for good this time, and to make sure Joe never did this again to anyone. I spoke to Mum on the phone, then Dad took me to Maroubra Police Station.

I was shaking with fear and pain. I knew what Joe was like—he'd run away from Dad, but he'd be sneaking around somewhere nearby, hiding behind a corner, trying to spot me. I imagined I could feel his eyes on me as I walked through the police station door. I knew he would know what I was doing. Even with Dad by my side, it took every bit of willpower to make myself take another step forward, then another.

Dad explained to the officer behind the front desk what I was there for, and a policeman, Senior Constable Shane Smith, took me to an interview room and asked me to tell him what had happened the previous night. As I spoke, he typed it all down. But after five paragraphs I just couldn't go on. He tried to encourage me to continue, but I was so upset and afraid I just couldn't. He took some photographs of my injuries. Then he asked me to sign the statement I'd made, but I couldn't do that either. I explained to him that Joe would kill me if I went any further. He asked me to think about it and come back to finish the statement when I felt strong enough.

But even what they had was enough for the police to press charges—they had reasonable grounds to believe that a crime had taken place and they could act on that. They did, charging Joe with assault occasioning bodily harm, and also with common assault. (On 30 December the charges reached court and the following day the *Sunday Telegraph* covered it in a brief story that ran under the headline 'Attacked with a Hammer'. It mentioned Joe by name, saying that the court was told he had 'attacked his former girlfriend with a hammer and tried to strangle her'.)

RORY BRENNAN: I went to work on the garbage run on the morning of Boxing Day, then when I finished, about nine in the morning, I went to my mother's flat in Clovelly. She'd had a stroke and I was loading up her clothes because she was getting ready to go into a nursing home. I got the phone call from Lani, screaming, desperate for help, saying, 'He's bashed me, he held me hostage …' It was going to take me a few minutes to get there but she said she couldn't just run straight to the coppers because he was in the station reporting, so I told her to stall for time.

I jumped in the car and raced up. I saw him waving his arms around, ranting and raving like an idiot. I came to a screaming halt beside him. He looked pretty shocked. Later on Lani told me he said, 'Don't you say nothing to him.' We had a bit of an altercation and he bolted, taking off across the road with me after him. He jumped onto a bus and there was all sorts of commotion with the people on the bus. I went back over to Lani. She was there crying. I got hold of her and said, 'This is it, I've had a gutful of this. We're going over to the coppers and see if we can bring an end to this rubbish.'

So off we went over there and that was the first time I heard how bad it was, although she still didn't mention the sexual assaults. The copper taking the statement was in shock and I was in more shock. We could see that she had hit rock bottom and she was really desperate for help.

CAROL SIMON: For all that Lani was angry with her mum and dad, when she got into trouble she rang her mum or she rang her dad. She didn't think of ringing me or ringing anyone else. She knew that she could count on them to be there, and they were.

I didn't find out that she'd finally got away from Joe until a couple of days later because they were all so worried about Lani, and worried about repercussions. They were worried about what would happen with the boys, and Koorine and everyone; Joseph Timbery had shown his face at Kath's house and at the boys' school, so they knew he knew where they were. I was so relieved Lani had got away because if she'd stayed with him I have no doubt in my mind that he would have killed her.

After I left the police station, Dad took me back to his car and drove me to Wha Wha's place at Clovelly, where I could stay and be safe. My poor grandmother was in hospital again, but at least that meant I could hole up there for a few days without worrying her. Dad said, 'You need help. You know that, Lani, don't you?' He'd spoken to Mum, who completely agreed, of course. He proposed I go into rehab and get clean and sober. For the first time, I understood that what he said was true. I did need help. I had to change my life or I would die. I was finally ready to do the hard work and get myself back on track.

I was scared of what it might mean and of how difficult it would be—I'd seen enough people in AA over the years to have some idea of what to expect—but I was desperate. As damaged as I was, and as terrified of every possible option, I was also at breaking point. I couldn't handle the beatings and rapes, I couldn't handle the steel-clawed grip alcohol and marijuana had on me, I couldn't handle the voices in my head. If Dad had told me that jumping off the Harbour Bridge would have helped, I'd have done it.

I did talk to Dad about my fears—how worried I was that Joe would carry out his threats to hurt or even kill one of my family in retribution for me leaving and telling the world what he was like—but Dad reassured me. He told me the family was standing together, that they could all look after themselves, but they were all looking out for each other as well. He told me not to think about it, they would all be fine. I just needed to focus on my own healing.

Mum, Tommy and Dad took care of everything. I stayed at Wha Wha's place and didn't go out. I was scared that Joe might try to track me down, but Dad checked in on me regularly, and I just stayed inside with the door locked. Because it was Christmas time, it took a bit of doing to get me into detox, which is the first step in rehab. There was a charge that had to be paid; Tommy stepped up to take care of that. And I was going to have to wait two days for a space to open up.

There was no alcohol—the drinks I had at Murrong Place on Christmas night were the last ones I ever had. But there was a bong and a stash of pot in a bowl under the bed that I'd left there on a previous visit and I basically smoked away as much of my physical pain and mental anguish as I could, putting myself in a dazed state to get through those forty-eight hours.

On 28 December I was admitted to William Booth House down near Central Station in the heart of Sydney. This is a place run by the Salvation Army as part of its Bridge Program to rehabilitate people with alcohol, drug or gambling addictions. The first step is detoxification—literally getting rid of all the alcohol and illegal drugs in your system (though you were allowed to keep smoking cigarettes, and I did).

When you first arrive, they go through the paperwork and show you to your room. You agree to abide by the conditions of the program, including the fact that if you leave you are not allowed to return. Then you have a shower and sit down with a doctor and go through your patterns of drug and alcohol consumption and your general medical history. In the record of my interview, the doctor noted that I had 'bruises all over, especially left ankle, right thigh and knee, left thigh, right scapular [shoulder blade], ribs sore, eyes, cheek+nose, right hand+left ring finger' and that this was a result of the domestic violence I'd been through.

In those early days and weeks I was scattered and mistrustful of everyone other than my family. I was nauseated and constipated and everything ached constantly as my body got completely free of drugs and alcohol for the first time in many years. So I did what many addicts do in the first period of detox: I started scheming to find a way out of there.

I hated the boarding house set-up. I hated the emphasis on reading the Bible and going to chapel. But most of all, I hated having to look inside myself. The Bridge Program has three parts: first is detox, then a long period of personal growth and reflection, then reintegration into the 'real world'. You have to participate in one-on-one counselling and group therapy pretty much from the beginning. I couldn't even meet people's eyes, I felt so ashamed and worthless. With no self-respect left and no confidence, I felt lower than low and I was suspicious of everyone.

There was a lot of emphasis on examining your childhood, on the basis that a lot of the thoughts and feelings that result in people becoming addicts start there. I didn't like that one bit. Inside me was a huge, fiery tangle of resentment and self-doubt. I didn't want to even glance at it, let along delve right into it. Didn't they understand? That's why I drank and smoked yarndi in the first place, so I could avoid reality.

Well, of course they understood—they'd seen it all before. I was blind to that then. All I knew was that I was being prodded to do things I did not want to do. Now, looking back, I can see how much I needed to go through that. If I couldn't understand what led me into addiction, I'd walk straight back out that door and fall right back into it. But at the time all I could think of was that people were talking about me and looking at me and judging me. I only had one response to that: fury. I tried to hold it inside—on one level I really did know how lucky I was to be there, safely out of Joe's grasp—but my emotions were such a swirling mess that I seethed most of the time.

One thing the counsellors kept saying over and over was 'Fake it till you make it.' What they meant by this was that if you kept on going with the program and the AA steps, even if it felt like they weren't working and you ached to go back to your old addictions, at some point you'd realise you had fundamentally changed, and the new clean life was the one you genuinely wanted after all. I knew that's what they were saying (though I didn't think it would ever really work for me), but I chose to interpret it to my own short-term benefit. I decided that if I faked it by pretending to agree with everyone and pretending I could see the point of their rules, I would make it out of there—they'd let me walk away and I could do what I liked.

Instead, after about two and a half weeks of detox, they transferred me to an out-of-town facility for the next stage of the program.

Selah farm is a women's only rehab facility near Berkeley Vale on the New South Wales Central Coast, about an hour and a quarter's drive from central Sydney (its full name is Central Coast Recovery Services Centre (Selah) — not surprisingly we always shortened it). We went by car and it was already getting dark when we left; the trip seemed to take forever. I'd really never spent much time outside the city, so it was strange to be on a farm in what felt to me like the middle of nowhere. It was strange, too, to be around so many other women. But then everything was strange in those early days of sobriety.

At first, for me, it was all about escape from Joe, but gradually I began to see how it was more than just a change of location or a period of time-out. Even then, though, I resisted it for much of the time. The Bridge Program incorporates about seven to eight months living at the farm (or somewhere like it). This period is supposed to be 'an intensive phase of growth through group and personal reflection'. I'd spent so long avoiding any kind of reflection on my life it was hard to start now.

Everything about the place was a shock to the system. We had a roster of chores, which were compulsory. As well as making our beds and keeping our rooms tidy, we each had specific jobs to do. I was put on egg duty, which meant feeding the farm's chickens and cleaning out their coop, collecting the eggs and cleaning them so they were ready to be sold. We were also required to attend AA or NA (Narcotics Anonymous) meetings, which were led by people who would come in specially.

All of that I could cope with, but the emotional demands put on me were something else. We had to take part in individual counselling as well as group sessions. The groups weren't so bad in theory because they were a bit like an AA meeting, where you knew that everyone there had a story to tell about their own messed-up lives. But at an AA meeting you don't have to share if you don't want to; some people go for months just listening, never saying a word. But here, everyone was expected to open up. We were all supposed to tell our own stories, and to make supportive comments when other people opened up.

I found this so hard. I fell straight back into my usual defence, just pretending everything was fine. I had done this back at William Booth House. Some of the other residents there knew that I'd been through domestic violence, either because they saw the marks on me or they overheard that I'd had a call from the police checking on how I was doing and seeing if I was ready to sign the statement. But I kept putting up my front. I didn't really talk at all in those group sessions other than to say, 'I'm okay. Yeah, everything's good.' There were other Aboriginal people there, elders, who spoke kindly to me, saying, 'Lani, you know you've got to start letting things out.'

By the time I got to Selah, part of me wanted to talk while another part was still desperately trying to keep all my inner turmoil hidden. As the fog started to lift, now that I was away from drugs and alcohol, safe, eating well and living right, I started to talk about things from my childhood, little by little. As I did, I gradually came to realise that everything bad that had happened in my life was because of drugs and alcohol.

My grandmother had often said 'A problem shared is a problem halved.' I used to act like I agreed, but I'd never truly understood what she meant. I thought that letting other people in on your dirty secrets only caused more problems. But now I began to see she was right. I started to open up a bit in group therapy. It was easier there because I didn't feel the spotlight was on me the way it was during one-on-ones. Everyone around the circle was trying to change their lives and move up from the depths. I'd speak a little and listen a lot, and sometimes afterwards I'd seek out one of the other women who'd said something in the session that let me know she really understood what I was going through.

But still there was a huge trust issue. I couldn't seem to shake off the feeling of 'If I tell this person about my life, are they going to use it against me?' That was especially so in the one-on-one counselling sessions. The therapists could plainly see I had anger issues, so they didn't push my buttons too hard. They tried to let me set the pace, but at the same time they had to prod me a little, otherwise I would have completely retreated. I can see that now, but back then I hated them for what they asked of me.

I found it so hard to express my feelings; I found it even harder to face up to what those feelings were. If I looked inside myself, and thought back to the choices I had made, I felt so much self-loathing it was hard to bear. I told myself that I didn't care what other people thought of me, yet even the idea that they might be looking at me sideways or talking about me flooded me with anger.

I seemed to have only two emotional settings: red-hot anger and a cold numbness. I hadn't experienced genuine emotions like happiness and contentment for longer than I could remember. In fact, walking out after one group meeting I realised my face hurt. It took me a second to figure out why my cheeks were so sore, then I realised: I'd been laughing, hard. I hadn't even known that what I'd thought was laughter before that had been fake—like a smile that doesn't reach your eyes. I'd forgotten what it was like to really let go and feel something without being self-conscious about it. But my progress was very slow.

At first, the program didn't allow visitors. Once you'd been through the detox and settled in you were allowed to have phone calls, and I'd get calls from Dad and from Mum. In one of the early calls I got, I could tell they were hiding something from me, and they finally admitted that Wha Wha was once again in hospital because she'd had a stroke. The way I responded to this news shows clearly my messy thought process at this time.

First I was angry that they'd known and I hadn't. Then I was angry that I was 'locked up' and couldn't go and see her. Then I thought, 'This is my get-out-of-jail card. I can just use it as an excuse and say I have to go because I need to visit her.' Finally I thought, 'If I leave, I'll probably just slide straight back into my old life and I won't be any use to Wha Wha anyway.' So I stayed.

I started to open up to the counsellors. In one session, I told my counsellor about the night Joe had cut my leg so badly. I hadn't spoken about what really happened that night to anyone and I'd always kept the scar hidden. That day I asked if the counsellor thought I should show my mum the scar, and she said yes.

After a little while I was allowed to have visitors at the farm. Mum and Tommy drove up and brought the boys. It was good to see them, though we were all trying to adjust to the strange circumstances. I took Mum aside at one point and showed her the scar and told her what had happened. She was horrified but comforted me, telling me I was safe now.

Visitors were allowed to bring food and other approved gifts, and my family had picked up some hot roast chicken, which we ate as a picnic lunch under the trees. They were also allowed to bring cigarettes, which was fantastic—like in most closed institutions, smokes were very valuable. Once a week we had a 'buy-up', where we were allowed to spend any money we might have. This was usually a small amount left over from the dole after money had been taken out to pay your way in the program, which was partly covered by Medicare. Your family could also give you a little extra money, which Mum did for me. The hot items were cigarettes, sweets and special toiletries to use instead of the plain soap that was supplied. But if you ran out of smokes early you just had to wait for the next buy-up or try to scavenge them off other people.

One boiling hot Saturday afternoon I went to the AA meeting that was always on at that time. A few of the other residents were already sitting there, and there was someone else, a woman I recognised from years before—Patsy Gray. I'd known her through my family since I was a girl, though not especially well. I went straight over and sat beside her. She explained that Tommy, who was an old friend of hers, had let her know I was at Selah and asked her to come and visit. Patsy worked as a drug and alcohol counsellor in the nearby Hunter region. She was visiting as a friend, not a counsellor, but because of her professional experience she had a really clear idea of the rehab process.

When the meeting was over we went and sat outside in the shade of a tree and talked. She had such an understanding manner and was so sympathetic that I found it a bit easier to open up to her, although afterwards she said her impressions of me were how guarded I was, and how fearful and ashamed. She asked me about the scars on my face and my leg. I told her about Joe and how he used to bash me. Then hesitantly I shared something I'd never said to anyone before: I told her how he used to rape me. She listened with great kindness and concern, but eventually it was time for her to leave. That conversation was completely unplanned on my part, but years afterwards it became critically important in my fight for justice.

At Selah, up to four people shared a room. The poor girls I was put in with must have wondered what they'd done to deserve this, because my nightmares had begun. The more I examined my true feelings and revealed parts of what Joe had done to me, the worse they got. Before long they were coming every night. One of the women I was friendly with who was also going through rehab suggested I get a dreamcatcher.

Dreamcatchers are originally Native American. They're a kind of hoop with a net or web woven in the middle, and natural, calming things like feathers hanging down. The idea is that they will catch the bad dreams and protect you in your sleep, only letting the good dreams through. I really took to the idea. The next time we were allowed to go to the local shops (always under the supervision of one of the Selah workers) I bought two, and from then on whenever I could I added more. I became obsessed with the idea of them—and I didn't hold it against the dreamcatchers when the nightmares kept on coming.

I also became fascinated with the idea of runes, small stones marked with ancient Viking symbols that you can 'cast', then interpret with a guidebook (like you do with tarot cards) to see into your own subconscious and try to tell the future. With all the therapy and time to think, I was starting to see a change within myself. I was looking at my actions and responsibilities and trying to understand how it was that I had travelled down the path that had led me here. I was reaching out for meaning and trying to find a way forward into a different future.

In the area around my bed, my own little space, which I was free to decorate as I liked, I had my dreamcatchers up and I also put up photos of my family and copies of poems that made sense to me. I had the Serenity Prayer, the verse famously used by AA, which begins 'God, grant me the serenity to accept the things I cannot change, the courage to change the things I can, and the wisdom to know the difference.' I had another poem called 'Drug Addict' and inspirational quotes.

I kept a scrapbook where I pasted in phrases I liked from the various pamphlets we were given at AA meetings. To try to calm myself when sleep wouldn't come I'd get textas and pencils and sit colouring them in, making the pages pretty. I also kept a personal journal—everyone did, we were required to. You had to write about your feelings. I guess they made you do this because a lot of the women there were like me and had spent years avoiding their real feelings. The journal was a really good thing for me, it helped a lot. I still didn't trust many people at all, and there were many, many things I didn't feel comfortable opening up about in front of others, even the counsellors. So instead, I'd write it down. I kept the journal close by me, carrying it around in my bag, and any time I felt bad or fearful or was in mental pain, I'd write it down. I used to write and write.

I've long since lost the rehab journal, but if I were to look inside it now I'd probably think, 'Oh my god, how psycho was I?' My mind was scattered in all directions and I had a lot of 'noise' inside my head: suicidal thoughts, homicidal thoughts. I was a fruitcake. I was the youngest of the thirty-six or so women at Selah—I'd turned twenty at William Booth House—but I was by far the angriest. That was a big call, considering everyone in there had their own resentments and their own anger. But for a lot of the time I was there, I walked around behind a front that said, 'Come near me and I'll kill you.'

Anger, intolerance, impulsiveness and selfish thinking are common in the early days of sobriety. Some people call it the dry drunk. You can't break free of all those self-destructive, furious thoughts, they just keep spiralling around and there's no alcohol or drugs to numb you from them. You don't yet have any other way to deal with bad feelings now that you can't hide under your addictions. But even in a place where the staff had seen it all before, I stood out.

I was like a pressure cooker, constantly just moments away from exploding. Anyone who was in my path might cop it—verbal abuse and suggestions of worse. Except on the pages of my journal, I couldn't seem to express any feelings other than anger. Now I can see that I was only angry because of my decisions and the life they'd led me to, and because I was so unhappy with myself, but back then I couldn't see that. I thought it was everyone else's fault. I'd always been like one of the boys, I'd never really hung around with other girls or women, and now here I was surrounded by them twenty-four hours a day. I found it overwhelming. Everywhere I looked I seemed to see bitchiness and arguments.

Just over a month after I'd arrived at Selah farm it all came to a head. We had a group therapy session that started out just like normal. The idea of the sessions was that you could talk about all sorts of things—things that were to do with your addictions, but also things that you were going through now. One of the women in the group said she wanted to talk about me.

She said I was walking around with such a huge chip on my shoulder and so much anger that she felt scared of me all the time. She didn't think that was right, not being able to feel safe in rehab. Then another woman backed her up, and another one, saying, 'Why don't you let your anger out in counselling sessions? Why don't you talk about what's happened to you?' I tried to explain, saying it was true, I was hugely angry almost all the time. But, I said, 'You've got to understand where I've just come from. I've been bashed and raped. Don't expect me to be walking around all rosy as if everything's great.' Some of them tried to be sympathetic, saying, 'Lani has come a long way. She does talk to people.' But more joined in saying they felt like I was a loose cannon, and they were constantly afraid I'd go off without warning.

I got more and more frustrated that they couldn't see it from my point of view, even though I'd really only given them tiny glimpses of what had happened with Joe, which probably made it hard for them to understand why I was the way I was. The counsellors tried to get me to talk about it and to agree to act differently, otherwise I'd have to leave the farm. They couldn't have everyone being upset and afraid because of one person. I just got angrier and angrier; I felt like everyone had turned on me. There were other Aboriginal women there but I still felt that I was being picked on because I was black, even though some of the people defending me were white, including a friend I'd made in there called Ali.

Maybe I would have reacted differently if they'd taken me aside and told me privately, but as it was I felt cornered. I was sure they'd all been talking about me behind my back and plotting against me. Feeling sideswiped and humiliated, I couldn't handle the pressure of everyone talking at me and demanding things of me. Inside I was scared about what getting kicked out would mean for me. I erupted, kicking and throwing furniture. Everyone ran out of the room and the counsellors barricaded them all into a room where I couldn't get to them.

Other workers went upstairs to my room to try to quickly pack up my stuff into garbage bags. I raced up and went berserk, screaming and hitting the walls. They threatened to call the police on me if I wouldn't go. I snarled that I would go, but then turned around and grabbed one poor woman who was nearby and tried to throw her off the balcony. (As it happened she was probably the biggest woman in the place, luckily for me.)

I was in a blind red rage and I don't even remember how many it took to get me off her and down the stairs, but I was out of there. Thrown out after just one month instead of the planned seven, not to mention the two months of carefully supervised re-entry into normal life that were supposed to follow time on the farm. My official record reads: 'Lani was discharged for threatening behaviour. I will not accept Lani back into program under 6 months.'

When I got down to the front door, there was Ali, packed up and leaving too, because she said she didn't agree with what had been done. We walked outside together and when we got to the big gates I turned back and yelled out, 'Well, fuck you all, I'm going to go and get totally off my fucking face. Fuck you.' And I remember one of the ladies who ran the place—Cappy, she was called, because she was a captain in the Salvation Army—said calmly, 'If you want to go and have a drink, the pub is just down the road. Go ahead and have a drink then, Lani.'

She probably saved my life with those words. I think she had me all worked out. She knew that if someone told me to do something, if it felt like an order, I'd do the opposite. So when she said that to me, I immediately thought, 'Right, well fuck you. I'm not going to have a drink. I'll show you.'

Chapter Nine

Ali and I got on the train together at Gosford; the Selah staff had given us money for tickets. She could have been from anywhere—we'd never spoken about where we each came from—so I was amazed when she said she was going back to Cronulla, where she lived with her husband. I was going there too, to Dad's place. After all the turbulence and upset, it was a great comfort to spend a couple of hours travelling with her.

I didn't call Dad along the way. I was so worried about disappointing him. I didn't want to tell him I'd been kicked out of rehab, because I felt like I had failed him again, and I was afraid he'd think, 'Oh, Lani's up to her old tricks, she's going to get back on the grog and drugs.'

So I waited to make the call to him until I'd arrived at the train station, just ten minutes' walk from the house where he and Vera lived. He was certainly surprised I was there, and I'm sure he was disappointed and very concerned about what might happen next, but he opened his arms and welcomed me in. Vera was also very warm and welcoming.

Straight away I filled my days by going to AA and NA meetings. Dad was going to them too, so sometimes I'd go with him, sometimes I'd go alone and sometimes I'd catch up with Ali if it was a meeting in the Shire (as the area around the Sydney suburb of Cronulla is known). It felt to me as though I was living at meetings, clinging to them for dear life. I would generally do one meeting at lunchtime, one at 5 pm and another at 8 pm. I did that for months.

To be honest, I didn't know if I wanted to stay sober and clean. I'd never really been able to understand that squarehead approach to life. But during the seven and a half weeks I'd spent in detox and rehab, I'd felt the fog that surrounded my brain start to lift, at least a little. I caught glimpses of different possibilities ahead for me. I desperately needed the voices inside my head to stop, and I couldn't risk going back to my old ways.

I was now able to recognise that there's no way on earth I would ever have ended up in a relationship with Joe if I'd been sober and clean. And I was afraid that if I busted my sobriety and started using again I'd end up back with someone like him. The terror of that thought gave me strength to keep going, staying sober one day after another.

At first, though, I felt like the meetings were just brainwashing. People who'd been on the path before me told me that feeling wasn't uncommon. I was reminded of the 'fake it till you make it' approach. So I did. Once again that took the form of me acting as if everything was sweet and I was fine while really those voices were going psycho in my head. I didn't say much in the meetings in that early period of going to them. But I hung in there.

The other saying I heard was 'Those who get around stick around.' It meant that people who make the effort to get to meetings, no matter where the meetings might be, are more likely to stay sober. Dad put it another way. He used to say to me, 'If you'd go anywhere for a drink or drugs before, you can go anywhere for an AA meeting now.' I completely avoided La Perouse and Maroubra and all the other places where Joe or his family were likely to be. But other than that, I'd make a real effort to travel for meetings. So I used to go to meetings at the Redfern roundhouse, where I'd gone with Dad when I was little, sitting under the table doing drawings with Koorine. Or I'd go right into the city for a meeting, then come back out close to Dad's place for my last meeting of the day. Doing that brought me some peace: it felt like my head was more at ease.

The more meetings I did, the stronger I got, but it was slow. AA's famous motto is 'One day at a time.' For me in those early days it felt like one second at a time, then later a minute at a time, then an hour. It started getting easier in tiny steps. Even though I could see that what I was doing was helping me, I still felt like I was only just hanging on. Inside my head things were chaotic, but something strange started to happen. People started coming up to me at meetings and commenting on how much I'd changed, how they could tell from the way I looked that I was doing well.

I couldn't really see it myself at the time; I was too focused on how far I still had to go. And I found it almost impossible to believe when anyone said anything nice or kind to me—I was still locked into the mental patterns that Joe had branded me with, thinking I was just damaged goods, nothing more than a worthless piece of shit. But after enough people had made a point of coming up and telling me they could see positive changes, I looked at myself again and I could see that they were right. I did still have a long way to go but at least I was on my way.

One thing I'm so grateful for was that my family protected me from the threats Joe had been making about me ever since the day I'd left him and gone with Dad. I was sheltered while I was in rehab and in those shaky months afterwards. A good while later on, when they figured I could handle it, people told me he'd been walking around La Perouse with a shotgun, saying he was going to hunt me down and kill me, even firing bullets in the air and making sure people saw he had others left over—he said they were for me. At one point a friend of my dad's saw him on the street and laid into him for what he'd done to me. It didn't stop Joe, though. He even went around to Koorine's at one point and walked straight into her place, making threats and demanding to know where I was. She pulled out a kitchen knife and that scared him off. But I knew none of this, thank god, because I wouldn't have been able to leave the house if I'd had even an inkling of it.

It was only when I looked back on it all, during the writing of this book, that I realised how much effort Dad, in particular, put into keeping me safe. He would often arrange for a mate who was going to a meeting to pick me up and take me, or he'd drive me himself even if he'd just finished work and was exhausted. Without me realising, he kept me off trains and buses, where Joe might see me, as much as possible.

While I was still at William Booth House I'd had a call from another police officer, Senior Constable Vanessa Burns, the Domestic Violence Liaison Officer stationed at Maroubra. Shane Smith had followed procedure and contacted her after I'd started to make a statement to him on 26 December. She called to see if I was okay and to check if I was ready to finish the statement. I told her that I was, but I needed some time in detox and rehab first.

She contacted me again, via Dad, after I left Selah farm. This time I said I was ready to meet, but I couldn't come to Maroubra. I was terrified Joe might hear I'd been there, or that I might even run into him. She understood and offered to meet me at Cronulla Police Station instead. We set a date for 13 March.

Dad took me there and supported me, even though he didn't have much faith the police would actually do anything. This time it took hours. I found it very hard and couldn't look up from the floor. I told Officer Burns about the physical attacks Joe had made on me, and when. As I spoke, she typed up my words. She also made a note of my injuries which, while healing, were still clearly visible seven weeks after the final attack. When we were near the end of the eight-page statement, she asked me if there was anything else I wanted to say. I could not open up about the rapes, I felt so ashamed. Instead I said that other things had happened, but I just couldn't tell her about them then. I guess in her job Vanessa Burns had seen a lot of things and understood how hard it was for someone to come forward. She said, 'Were those other things of a sexual nature?' I mumbled 'Yep', but couldn't say any more. I signed the statement and she told me the police would be in touch to let me know what would happen next.

Five years later, Vanessa Burns was asked to describe the process of me making that statement. She did, in detail. A sceptical lawyer asked her how she could remember this one case so clearly after all those years, given how many cases she dealt with. She said it was so unusual to have an Aboriginal woman proceed with a domestic violence case against an Aboriginal man that it stood out very clearly.

Later on I ran into another officer who looked after domestic violence cases and had often tried to get through to me when

I was with Joe, despite the fact that I kept denying anything had happened and kept telling the police to leave me alone. He admitted to me how surprised he'd been when he'd heard I had made a detailed statement and signed it. He said to me, 'We thought you'd never go through with it. You were an alcoholic. We thought you were going to keep going back to him.'

Shane Smith had laid those initial assault charges back in December, and a court date to hear them was set for 2 May. Joe Timbery appeared in court twice before that date, on 9 and 21 February, on unrelated charges of common assault, possession of a firearm in or near a public place, possession of a loaded firearm in a public place, and possession of a shortened firearm (a sawn-off shotgun). But he didn't show for the May hearing on the assault charges over what he'd done to me.

Unfortunately, what neither Senior Constable Vanessa Burns nor I knew at the time was that the next step that should have happened—the issuing of a warrant for Joe's arrest—didn't. Right around the time a warrant should have been issued, the case had been handed over from Shane Smith, who had resigned from the New South Wales Police Force and moved to Queensland, to another officer. The task of issuing the warrant had somehow fallen between the cracks. It was human error, a mistake; we all make mistakes, but it was very frustrating and distressing when I eventually discovered that's what had happened—though that wasn't until much, much later.

Thinking the legal wheels were in motion, I just kept my head down and continued going to my meetings. The Redfern roundhouse one was the natural choice to be my home meeting. In AA terms, this is the meeting where you feel most comfortable and accepted, the one where you find yourself opening up. Going back to the roundhouse was like coming full circle for me—there were people there I'd known since I was a six-year-old making them pictures. Now I was back as a young woman admitting I needed help.

It was at this meeting that I first started opening up, both to the group and to people who spoke to me before and after. Pretty much everywhere else if people asked me how I was going, I'd just say, 'Fine.' Here, I started telling the truth. I could see they really wanted to know, they weren't just being polite. So I'd be honest. People would say, 'How are you?' and I'd say, 'I'm off my head. I could kill something. I'm just not handling it very well at the moment.' They'd listen, really listen, and before I knew it we'd be talking about feelings and what we were both going through.

Even so, I could never imagine being in a relationship again. I thought I hated men, or at least men who were looking for a woman to be with. I was sure no one would want me or have me, but I didn't care because I didn't want to ever let anyone close enough to hurt me again.

But I had to admit it wasn't only the sense of acceptance that drew me to the roundhouse. Dad used to catch up with his old mates there, some of whom (like Tommy) he'd got sober with. One of these was John Duckett who, along with his wife (whose name was Maria, but everyone called her Delly), had made me presentable before Dad and Vera's wedding. I'd been in and out of their house since I was tiny—they were almost surrogate parents to me. I knew their boys, John (junior) and Chris, too, but not as well, because they were often away in boys' homes or jail. John, who was ten years older than me, was away the more often of the two brothers, so of all the family I knew him least.

He'd started getting into trouble in his early teens and then it had escalated as he'd fallen into the world of drugs and alcohol. Like a lot of heroin addicts, he turned to crime to feed his habit, so he was inside more often than he was out. I'd seen him once in recent years but I was so out of it I wouldn't have recalled it if I hadn't been reminded of it later. I had a black eye and a busted lip where Joe had just punched me on the street. We were in Waterloo and I saw a pub nearby and went into it, hoping to get away from him, at least for a short while. John Duckett was by the pool tables. Little did I know, but he'd got himself clean and sober some time before that, so while he was in a pub, he wasn't drinking. I recognised his face and went towards him. He said hello, and asked how I was going. When Joe saw that I knew him, he stepped back outside. Eventually I had to leave, and Joe was waiting for me, but it had been a brief escape.

One time when I went to a meeting at the roundhouse, John was in charge. By then he was thirty and he'd been sober for two years. Dad took me up to say hello. He said to John, 'You remember Lani, don't you? Can you keep an eye out for her? She's just got out of a bad relationship and gone through rehab.' Dad knew that I was still uneasy being around men, and he wanted someone he trusted to look after me when he wasn't there.

I remember thinking John looked nice, and feeling like I could trust him. I noticed what he was wearing too (a white Nike tracksuit), which should have been a clue that I was attracted to him. But I was so sure that I wasn't interested in any man that I really didn't acknowledge what was going on deep inside me. In fact, other people picked up on it first. I always made an effort to look neat when I was going out to meetings, but Dad started teasing me about how I'd make an extra effort for the roundhouse ones. Then on our way out after the meeting, Dad's mate 'Gangster' Dave would be there and the pair of them would crack jokes until I blushed, teasing me about how I really listened when John spoke, and how I watched him whenever he was in the room.

I denied it, of course, but if I let myself stop and think about it, I had to admit something strange was going on. When I thought about seeing John I got feelings I'd never had in my life before, butterflies in my stomach like I'd always heard about. I found him really attractive. He had a roughness in his looks that I found appealing because it was contrasted by his inner gentleness. When I saw him, I found it hard to talk normally. I felt hot and flushed and I couldn't seem to get my words out in the right order.

But this was crazy. For one thing, AA is very clear on the fact that you shouldn't start any new romantic relationship until you are completely comfortable with your sobriety. I was just at the start of my journey to a clean life. The timing was terrible. Then there was the fact that I knew his parents so well that it was weird to think about a Duckett in that way. It was almost like fancying your cousin. It just seemed wrong.

I was determined to steer clear of John. Like me, he didn't only go to the Redfern meeting. Once I realised how I felt about him and decided that it wasn't appropriate, I spent a couple of weeks figuring out his patterns so I'd know what meetings to avoid so as not to bump into him. For a few months this worked.

What I didn't know was that John had also had feelings for me from that first moment we spoke at the roundhouse. He had been in a relationship and had a young son, but the relationship had ended. He wasn't looking either, but the instant attraction was there for him, too. As with me, though, it was the people around him who recognised the spark between us before anything had happened.

I remember once, during the months we were trying to keep some distance between us, a friend and I had gone to John's parents' house for a visit. Various other family members happened to be there too, including John and his uncle. As my friend and I walked out, I said a general goodbye to the group: 'See you later, I'm off. I'm going to another meeting.' I kept walking so didn't hear what followed, but apparently John absentmindedly said, 'Okay, see you, babe.' His uncle turned around to him and said, 'What did you just say to Lani?' and only then did John realise what had come out of his mouth.

We continued trying to keep away, but in the end the attraction was just too strong. We were drawn together. I stopped avoiding meetings where I knew I would see him, and we started talking and getting to know one another. By late July, we were an item. If you'd told me when I went into rehab that six months later I'd be in another relationship, I would have said you were crazy. For a start, I didn't trust anyone, especially men. Second, there was that AA warning about not rushing into new things during your recovery. Third was the fact that I felt like damaged goods. I felt dirty and ruined inside, and I could never have believed someone would want me—not someone worth being with, anyway.

But here was John, looking right into my eyes, listening when I spoke, making me smile, making me feel like someone who might have a chance at happiness. I worried that things were moving too quickly. I was scared of what it might bring—scared that if he saw how much anger I had inside me, he wouldn't want anything to do with me. And scared that I wouldn't know how to be with a good man, how to build a healthy relationship. But despite all that, I couldn't deny how strong my feelings were.

And then there was the fact that he was so different from the kind of men I'd known. Lee was gentle, but he'd been still a boy when I knew him. John was a man who'd lived a hard life, and seen and done plenty of troubling things in his time. People who don't know John only see the frown he has on his face, but I could see he was actually a gentle giant, tender inside.

He was softly spoken, which I really needed at that time. I couldn't handle someone if they were aggressive, verbally or otherwise. I felt like every time I spoke to him he really understood where I was coming from and he never, ever put me down. No matter what I told him about my messed-up feelings or the things I'd been through, he always made me feel better about myself. He was so compassionate—I didn't know blokes could be like that. I felt so comfortable with him.

JOHN DUCKETT: My life before I met Lani was pretty well all over the shop. I come from a family where there was a lot of alcoholism. I like to think I had a pretty good upbringing in a lot of ways, but it was dominated by alcoholism. There was domestic violence too. My father was the perpetrator against my mother and also me and my brother. But we lived by the attitudes 'Loose lips sink ships' and 'What happens in the home stays in the home.' That's just the way it was. I honestly thought that was normal; I never knew any better. Most of my extended family was the same.

I had a very good sporting ability with cricket, but there was a lot of pressure about winning with that from my father. When I found drugs and alcohol myself I thought I'd won the lotto. Before you knew it I was introduced to crime and it became a way of life. From there I was in and out of boys homes and eventually progressed to jails.

When I was about fourteen or fifteen, my father put his hand up and said that he was an alcoholic. It was a big reality shock but when I found out what he was, I knew deep down that I was too. It still took me another fourteen years or so before I gave in and gave myself up to sobriety. It was a long hard road.

In my last year or two in jail I had the opportunity to actually get out and go into rehab, but I declined. They looked at me and said, 'Hey, don't you want to get better?' I said, 'No.' I wanted to stay in jail where I could get my heroin and coke and whatever. I could get all the drugs I wanted in there plus have my own room. That was the way I used to think. When you start thinking like that, you know there's a problem. Normal people don't think like that.

But then I rang my mother. She said, 'Did you hear the news?' I said, 'No, what?' She said, 'Your brother put his hand up. He went to rehab.' He was three years younger than me. I was thinking, 'Geez, I'm left on my own now.' My father was sober, all my uncles. I had an old mate who used to say, 'Instead of trying to give up, give in.' You know, giving up is just too hard so give in instead. So I did. I was twenty-eight when I found sobriety. I'd been sober for close to two years when I saw Lani at the Redfern roundhouse.

Her father had actually helped my father get sober. I remember Lani when she was about six or seven, then I didn't see her again until she was eighteen or so. It was in Waterloo. I remember her walking into a pub there, and that fellow was following her. She didn't look good. She looked very battered. You could see the black eye, busted lip, dry blood. It's pretty sad when you see a kid at that age like that. She walked in and stood near the pool table and I was standing near there and he wouldn't come across. She was talking to me, because she knew who I was. When I eyeballed him, he hooked it. Even knowing what we know now, I can only imagine what she went through.

Then I saw her at AA a couple of years later. In walked this girl. I was thinking, 'Wow, she is gorgeous.' I was so distracted that my father walked up to me and said, 'You all right?' He saw where I was looking and said, 'You remember her?' I said, 'No.' He said, 'That's little Lani.' I said, 'You're kidding.' It's funny how life is meant to be. I'd been going through a pretty hard time with my ex-partner. I just accepted that was my life. I wasn't looking for anyone. I had my son and I thought, 'This is the best it's going to get.' But then I met Lani and I fell in love from the start. But because of the relationship I'd been in, I held my emotions back.

Eventually, though, I just felt that it was meant to be. I went with my heart. In AA it's highly recommended that you don't get in a relationship so early in sobriety, but I thought I had a chance in life to be happy and I took it, with both hands. It was a risk but I was just so in love. I was a gambling man so I just took a gamble with life.

Being with Lani made it a lot easier to stay sober, because we had a commitment not just to each other but to AA.

AA came first for both of us.

Real life isn't like the movies. It's not all neatly tied up and wrapped in a bow. Even though I was in a better place than I had been for years, and even though what was happening with John was so good, I still had a seething pit of anger inside me, ready to flare up and take over when I least expected it. Sometimes I could feel it starting and I would leave the room or walk away from the conversation—do something, anything, to control it. Other times it flashed up and the red mist had taken me over before I even knew what was happening. Unfortunately, Vera was the victim of one of the worst of these incidents.

Vera was a lovely person and she'd been so good to me over the years, despite everything. I knew that but still I lashed out at her: I was a powder keg and one day I exploded. Dad and Vera were at home, and Darryl and Garri were there too. I had a pot of hot wax out in the living room, ready to wax my legs. I was running my big mouth, going on at Vera, calling her every name under the sun. She'd tried talking to me, but that wasn't doing any good, so she came over to me and gently put her hand over my mouth to try to get me to stop.

That tiny little bit of physical contact made me snap. I jumped up, knocking the hot wax all over the rug, and punched her in the face. Not just once, either. I was yelling, going crazy, screaming, 'You shouldn't have touched me! You shouldn't have touched me!' Vera had blood pouring down her face. Dad jumped in and pulled me off her, and I dimly registered the hurt and shock in his face and in the boys' faces at what I'd done.

Dad took care of Vera, who was crying and bleeding and in pain, and then told me that was it, I had to find somewhere else to stay. Of course, I can't blame him for that. They'd been so good to me, and this is how they were rewarded.

RORY BRENNAN: When Lani called after she'd been asked to leave rehab, well, knowing Lani it wasn't a great surprise, but I was happy because she hadn't picked up. Usually when you leave a rehab or detox like that you'll go and pick up a drug or a drink, but she hadn't.

She came to stay with Vera and me. She was hard to live with. I was happy she wasn't drinking and drugging, and she was away from that mongrel and I knew she was safe. But she didn't want to help around the house; she was moody. It was hard for Vera and it was wearing her down. A few times she said, 'I can't put up with much more of this.' In between nursing my mother and everything else, I probably wasn't paying enough attention to what she was talking about.

Then one day it just broke out over a simple thing. Lani was lying on the lounge watching TV and she'd done something with the washing. I can't remember what. Vera came in and had a go at her about it and then Lani came at her with a mouth full of 'Fuck you!' and blah, blah, blah. Vera said, 'Don't speak to me like that, swearing at me,' and put her hand across Lani's mouth. Lani exploded, and started bashing into her. It only took me seconds to get to them, but by the time I did the damage was already done. I told Lani to pack her bags up and get out.

There is no excuse for what I did to Vera, but at least now I understand it better. What I later learned from the experts who have studied survivors of domestic violence is that we suffer from post-traumatic stress disorder (PTSD). (Karen Wilcox talks about this in her interview at the end of this book.) Most people think of PTSD as something that happens after a single terrible event, like the Bali Bombing or the 'inland tsunami' that hit Toowoomba, or something that comes from being in a war. But the symptoms I had after escaping Joe Timbery, which many other domestic violence survivors have too, are textbook PTSD: nightmares, sudden flashbacks, emotional numbing on the inside and a deadening in the way you show emotions to others, insomnia, feeling like you have no future, and uncontrolled outbursts of anger. Those symptoms and behaviours swirl around inside you like a witches' brew. You never know, one minute to the next, let alone one day to the next, how you'll be feeling or what might set you off.

If I was a returning soldier or someone who'd been in the Twin Towers on September 11, I would have been offered counselling and given the tools to get through it. But I didn't know any of this back then. I knew I was damaged by the actions of that evil man, but I didn't know that with the right treatment I could recover and that, with time and help, the PTSD symptoms would fade, though they might never disappear entirely. And of course, none of the people around me knew either. I'm sure my family must have doubted that I'd ever be able to have normal loving relationships with them again.

My immediate problem was finding somewhere to stay. I phoned John and told him what had happened. Straight away he offered to take me in where he was living, with his uncle in

Waterloo. I still didn't really know John, not fully. And there was a lot he didn't know about me. The biggest thing he didn't know was the full extent of the violence I'd suffered. He knew about the assaults, although he didn't know how bad or how frequent they'd been, but he didn't know anything about the rapes.

We'd only just started our journey together. Moving in together was a huge gamble and if it went wrong, the results might be disastrous. But my options were limited, and I wanted to believe. So I said yes. Here I was, not yet eight months out of Joe's grasp and not properly into a new, sober life and I was suddenly not just in another relationship but actually living with John.

Another big change happened shortly after I moved in: I got a job. I needed to work for many reasons. One of them was to burn off some of the energy I had. In this early post-rehab period, my body ran itself in top gear. It was as if I was on a huge natural high, with endless, restless energy. I only slept a couple of hours a night, but I wasn't tired. I wanted to be doing something constructive.

A job came up as an Aboriginal Respite Officer with the Benevolent Society. I applied for it and was straight with them about the fact that I'd recently completed rehab and become sober and clean. I lied about one thing: I said I didn't have a criminal record. I knew that in due course, when I had to do the mandatory police check, I'd be found out. But I really wanted them to see how well I could work, what I was capable of, and judge me on that, not on my record. And that's how it worked out. By the time the check was done, they knew I worked hard for them and did a good job. I explained why I'd lied, and they were very understanding about it.

My job was to work with the Aboriginal carers of people with disabilities. When the carers needed a break, I organised respite care to take over. I covered the eastern suburbs, from Bondi down to Cronulla and beyond. It was the first job I'd had that really involved helping other people in a meaningful way, and the first one where I wasn't just out for myself. It was hard to accept praise. When my bosses, colleagues or our clients would say, 'Thanks, Lani, you're doing a great job!', my first thought would be, 'Why are they saying that? What do they want? What's in it for them?'

I knew this was wrong, and I made myself understand that they were expressing a genuine appreciation, but it felt strange. A lot of the people I was dealing with knew my family through the extended Aboriginal network and that made it a lot easier to feel accepted. Many of them were openly supportive of what I was going through, saying what a good thing it was that I'd cleaned myself up and started making something of my life. A lot of them were also amazed that, of all people, I'd been able to clean myself up. They gave me kindly encouragement to keep up the progress.

I was still using my old familiar mask most of the time, keeping a smile on my dial no matter how I was really feeling inside. I didn't seem to be able to change my own mood, but I could put up a good front with everyone except John. I had no time to dwell on any inner turmoil, though: I kept myself too busy. I was flying around so much, I didn't have time to sit down and think.

I had to be in the office for work occasionally, but I much preferred to be out on the road, going out to our clients. I loved being out and about, but there was always a streak of fear at the possibility of running into Joe. Whenever work took me close to La Perouse, I could feel the fear rising. But the more I did, the more I wanted to do. I worked on weekends when I was asked. On my lunch breaks I'd be running off to AA meetings. My boss was flexible about letting me take time for meetings; he knew I'd make up the hours and was supportive of the changes I'd made in my life.

I kept myself so busy I hardly saw John, and that suited me. I was smitten with him, but I was afraid of being close. It was hard for me just to be with him in the way people are in the early days together. I didn't like it when he said things like, 'You're so beautiful.' I didn't trust it, and I didn't believe him. When he'd say things like that part of me would be thinking, 'What does he want? Why is he saying that? Is he just trying to get a bit?'

I'd never had a man say that to me before, not when they were sober. People will say all kinds of stupid things when they're drunk; none of that means anything. It took me a long time just to accept that a man could talk about his feelings and express what was inside him, even when it made him vulnerable. I'd never known a man who did that before John. It really threw me.

Sex was really hard, too. I didn't like him looking at me naked. I made him turn away while I got myself into bed and covered up with the blanket, and the lights had to be out. I kept telling myself he wasn't Joe, but in those early days together I was always on full alert, waiting for him to do something to hurt me or force me. But nothing bad happened. There was no roughness—just the opposite. He took things soft and slow, and sometimes we'd start fooling around and just leave it at that, not go all the way. I was amazed. Gradually I started letting myself believe that this bloke really was different. He really was a good man.

The other thing that was different about John was that he listened to me. I felt like I could open up and really tell him what was going on inside. I'd been well trained during my time in rehab to talk about myself: 'I feel this ...' 'When you do that it makes me feel this way ...' Talking about things helps you work your way through them and stops you just reacting in an out of control way. It was a challenge for me—that much was obvious from the way I left rehab. But I tried, and being with John showed me how it was possible to talk honestly about even the bad stuff, and how it helped.

I could say to him, 'I feel dirty,' and even though he didn't yet know about the rapes, he was understanding and sympathetic and kind. He never made fun of me or threw it back in my face later. He was just there for me.

Chapter Ten

Before long, John and I decided we needed to move out of Waterloo and get our own place, where John's son could come and live with us. We found a little flat at Dolls Point, on the peninsula that separates the Georges River from Botany Bay. It was close to the water, which I loved, but all the way round on the other side of the huge bay from La Perouse, so I felt relatively safe.

We didn't have much. We shared a single mattress, which was on the floor because we couldn't yet afford a bed frame. We had some plates and cutlery, a kettle, a frying pan, a saucepan and a tiny black-and-white TV with a coathanger for its aerial. But it was a start.

My boss at the Benevolent Society knew I wanted to increase my income and was very pleased with the work I was doing as respite officer, so he arranged for the society to offer me a second job. It was helping out at a nursing home, doing the overnight shift, giving out medication, helping the old people with their dinners and showers, getting them settled for the night and then staying on the premises in case anyone needed assistance during the night. I leapt at the chance.

I was still on that post-rehab high, not sleeping much, otherwise it would have been impossible because I was working around the clock. I'd work in my respite officer job from nine till five, rush home, grab dinner and a quick shower, and run off to start at the nursing home at 6 pm. I'd be there for twelve hours, then have three hours till my day job started again. I'd grab a two-hour sleep in that morning crossover, and I could generally sleep for at least a few hours on the night shift when everyone was settled and quiet.

It was kind of crazy and I don't recommend it for everyone, but it worked for me at the time. I did get a bit ratty sometimes, but mostly I loved it. It kept my mind occupied and it kept me busy doing something active and positive. I felt energised knowing that I was working again, making a contribution, and just generally being back in the real world, doing normal things.

John was a stay-at-home dad to his son, also called John, who was just five. I hardly saw them during the week, just when I was dashing in and out between jobs. But that was a good thing too, because sometimes when I was with John I'd find myself trying to push his buttons. It was all part of my fear and mistrust: I couldn't believe that he was as straightforward as he seemed. I thought there was a hidden side to him, the way Joe Timbery had kept his evil side hidden at first. So I'd say things to John just to see if he was going to snap and turn on me. The fact that he never did didn't stop me—I guess, somehow, I just thought I had to push harder.

Looking back, I can't believe what he put up with. Often I'd be on edge because something completely unrelated to him had sent me off earlier in the day—a person glimpsed in the street, or a sound or a snatch of a song, some tiny innocent thing that would trigger a flashback. It might only last for a few seconds and to the rest of the world I might seem fine, but inside I'd be jangling, anxious and upset for hours. When I saw John hours later, I'd lay into him with verbal abuse, carrying on and calling him all sorts of names. Nothing ever pushed him to lose control.

Towards the end of November, I started feeling different, physically. I didn't feel sick exactly, but something was going on. It couldn't be that I was pregnant—I'd seen doctors a couple of times since I'd escaped Joe, including in detox and rehab, and when I'd described the severity and frequency of the beatings I'd suffered, they'd told me I almost certainly wouldn't be able to have children. I was only twenty, and this was a horrible thing to hear and hard to cope with. But I wasn't surprised; I'd been kicked and punched in the stomach countless times.

The feeling didn't go away, it just got stronger. I became convinced that I was pregnant after all. I got an over-the-counter urine test and it came up negative. I didn't believe it. I got more tests and they came back negative too. I went to the doctor and did a urine test there and it came back negative. But I just couldn't let it go. Somehow I was sure, no matter what the test results said. I asked to be given a blood test. Unlike the urine tests, you didn't get the results on the spot. I counted the days and finally the news came back: yes, I really was pregnant!

I was thrilled. Straight away I started thinking of the little one growing inside me as my miracle baby. John was with a mate down in Nowra, two hours or so south of Sydney, when the news came. I phoned him up. He was so excited. He cut short his visit and jumped on a train to come straight home.

My thoughts were swirling. I was filled with joy that this impossible thing had happened—I could have a baby after all. But John and I had only been together four months. My life was just getting started. I was still finding my feet. I had work that made me feel good. Now everything was thrown into the air again.

Even so, I never thought about not going ahead with the pregnancy. It was such an unexpected blessing and I figured I was already helping to raise little John, so it wasn't such a big step to add another child to the mix. I guess I should have thought about what would happen if John and I broke up but that didn't even cross my mind. We were in this together and somehow it was all going to work out okay.

CAROL SIMON: When Lani came out of rehab, Kathy called me. I was working with South Sydney Youth Services, which helped people aged up to twenty-five, and Kathy asked me to get Lani in there. At that point she was still vulnerable; the anger was still there, and the hurt. She was quite teary. But she tried to settle herself. She started to talk to her mum, and to Tommy who had helped her get to rehab.

Then she got together with John. I was concerned about it, because she was so vulnerable and picking up with someone else so quickly. I was just hoping it was a good relationship. Then she found out she was pregnant. I went over there and she even had the name picked out, Tymekqwa—no one had ever heard of it. She was so excited about it all.

My family were excited for me too. Even though they'd been concerned that I might be moving too fast, they were pleased that John and I had hooked up. They knew him, they knew the depths he'd sunk to and how far he had raised himself back up. They knew he was a strong man who had rebuilt his life and they were confident he would be a force for good in my life. They were over the moon that we were settling down to raise a family together—I was having the life that had seemed lost to me forever when I was with Joe Timbery.

In fact, there was only one person who raised the idea of me having an abortion, and that was John's father. Things had been strange between me and John's parents ever since John and I had started our relationship. Before that I'd felt so close to them and they'd been affectionate and protective towards me. But instead of being pleased for their son when we got together, they became very distant towards me. They now seemed to see me as a home-wrecker, which was ridiculous. John's relationship with his son's mother had been troubled for a long time. He'd tried to fix things, but it was beyond saving, so they'd broken up. It had nothing to do with me.

John senior suggested to his son that we didn't need to go ahead with the pregnancy, he didn't need to be tied down to me, it would be easy to get rid of the baby. My John said we were having a child together and that was that. Things between his parents and me just deteriorated from there.

Pregnancy proved to be a breeze. I think I only went to one antenatal class, but I felt great. I had to give up the nursing home job after a while, but I was able to keep working as a respite officer. The daytimes were fine, but nights were another story: I started having nightmares again, reliving what had happened with Joe.

I didn't know I was dreaming, so it was like reliving the horror again and again. But when I woke up I didn't remember anything about what I'd dreamed. I only knew that I felt upset and agitated when I first woke, and I couldn't work out why.

It was John who saw what was going on, and who copped it. Apparently, the first night it happened I was kicking out and punching, saying, 'Get off me, you dog, stop! This is rape!' I was fast asleep, in a frightening dream of being back with Joe Timbery. Thrashing about in the bed, I whacked John hard several times, but I didn't know anything about it until the next day.

As we were getting ready in the morning John said to me, 'I heard your dreams last night. Sounded like you were pretty upset. Is there something you want to talk about?' I didn't know what he meant. When he explained a bit more, I felt a bit freaked out. What had I said without knowing it? What had John picked up on? I denied that anything was wrong and just shut the conversation down.

But the nightmares kept coming. I don't know if it was related to the fact that I was pregnant or not. A lot of women do say they have particularly vivid dreams when they're pregnant. For me, that was just one factor among many. It was twelve months since I'd escaped the violence and got free of alcohol and drugs. It was six months since John and I had become involved, and it was clear he wasn't going anywhere. I'd been through so many huge life changes in such a short time, maybe everything would have started coming to the surface whether I was pregnant or not.

While the nightmares continued, there were some golden dreams too, and these were definitely pregnancy-related. In one, I dreamed the baby I was carrying was a little girl. I dreamed I saw her face after she was born, and I dreamed her name—I saw it written down: 'Tymekqwa'. When I had an ultrasound in due course and they offered to tell me the baby's sex or leave it a surprise, I said, 'Tell me.' I was already certain, but they confirmed it: yes, she was a girl.

The nightmares didn't stop, and John kept letting me know in his calm, supportive way that he was there for me, ready to listen. Sometimes now I'd scream out in my sleep and wake myself up. I'd be confused and occasionally a little panicky, wondering what I'd said, but I'd look over at John and he'd seem to be asleep—tucked away as far as possible from my thrashing arms and legs. He didn't get in my face about it, so I didn't feel pushed or threatened, and eventually I was ready to start talking to him.

JOHN DUCKETT: The nightmares just kept coming. Most nights I would get hit or punched as she was trying to protect herself in her sleep. I started to sleep curled in as near as I could to the wall. I never thought about giving up on her, but I knew I had to get her to talk. I tried not to force the issue because it was very emotional. But finally I started working on her hard because I thought, 'This is not right.'

It took a while for her to disclose what she'd been through. I knew she was a knockabout. People were scared of her, they were intimidated by her anger. I think it was just frustration and the hurt she'd been through. You have to come from that sort of background to really understand. I didn't know then what she'd been through but once you're drinking and drugging like that, you know what happens. Everyone's got their war stories. But she didn't open up for a long time. Once a few cracks opened up she let it all out. And it was massive.

I just thought, 'How could a person go through this?' Straight away I started talking to Lani about going to the police. I said, 'You need to charge him.' She said, 'That's a dog's act.' I said, 'I'm telling you, from my point of view that's not a dog's act. Any man who would do that to a woman, they're not worth a crap.' I knew he needed to be held accountable for his actions.

It was hard. I felt so ashamed and dirty, and angry too. Other men might have run from what they were hearing or run from the turmoil I was revealing within myself. John was staunch. He said what had been done to me was wrong, simple as that. Joe Timbery should be made to answer. I had to go to the police and make another statement. I thought it was better not to stir up any more trouble. I couldn't imagine sitting down with a police officer talking about those things.

But as the weeks passed and I thought more about how wrong the things that had happened to me were, I decided John was right. Joe Timbery should not be allowed to get away with doing this to me or any other woman. In early May 2002 I contacted Vanessa Burns, the Domestic Violence Liaison Officer I'd made the statement to fourteen months earlier. When she heard what I had to say, she arranged for me to go to Maroubra Police Station and make another statement.

CAROL SIMON: The idea came up of her signing a new statement and getting charges pressed. I remember when I heard about it I was scared. Kath rang me and I went over to see her and Tom. Kath said, 'What do you think?' I said, 'I'm frightened for Lani because of the repercussions.' I didn't want her to go ahead with it. I was just thinking of the violence that could have happened—he wasn't in custody. I thought, 'You're doing well, forget about it.' I tried to talk her out of doing it. I didn't realise it would be a part of her healing.

RORY BRENNAN: I wasn't really talking to Lani at this point, but when I heard she'd started talking about going to the police I was against it. I've never had many good experiences with police. I thought, 'You've moved on. You've got a new man. You're off the drink; you're off the drugs. You made your own life. Is it worthwhile bringing it all to the surface again?' But at that time I still didn't know how bad it was.

KATHY BRENNAN: When she got together with John, I thought it was fine. I knew the family. I like John. He's very straight up, down to earth. He speaks his mind, he says how it is. I knew John would do the right thing by her, and he would look after her. They were stable but they were really struggling. Who doesn't struggle? So the boys and Tommy and I would go out there on weekends and take food and stuff. One night my boys and John's son were asleep and Lani was too and there was this noise. I said to John, 'What's that screaming?' He said, 'Kathryn, she does this every night.' I said, 'What are you talking about?' He said, 'It's Lani, come and have a look.' She was in the bedroom, curled up on the floor asleep, screaming. I thought, 'Oh my god.'

When she said she was going to go back to the police, I thought for a better peace of mind, yes, that's a good thing, but it could be a bad thing in terms of retribution. I was worried for her safety, and John's, and the boys'. And worried for her having to relive everything that she went through, even though we still didn't know the extent of it.

Despite all the misgivings, I decided to go ahead. On the appointed morning in mid-May 2002, when I was six and a half months pregnant, John drove me to my police appointment. He pulled up to drop me off, but I wasn't sure I could even get out of the car. I said to him, 'This is hard.' In his straight-talking way, John said, 'This is just the start. It's going to get a lot harder than this.' I looked at him and I saw that he had faith that I could handle it, and that he'd be there for me every step of the way.

Even so, I felt like turning around and walking out of the station when a male officer came to where I was waiting and said his name was Senior Constable Graham Sims and he'd be taking my statement. He was nice enough, but the thought of describing those things to a man was excruciating. Still, I'd come this far, I had to go on.

So we sat down and I gave him an extensive, thirteen-page statement. I had to describe the specifics of the rapes: whether they were vaginal or anal or forced oral sex, what Joe Timbery had said to me while he was doing it, every little detail. There were times when I broke down and had to stop. But I could see that Graham Sims believed me and I really needed that. It was late afternoon when we finished, and I felt shaky and drained, but

I also felt the determination at my core. John came and picked me up, and I went straight to an AA meeting to regather my strength.

I got on with my life while Senior Constable Sims set about gathering evidence. He got a statement from a doctor at the Prince of Wales Hospital that listed all the times I'd been admitted from April to December 2000, what the injury was each time and what treatment I'd had. He went to Murrong Place and spoke with Joe's father, who refused him entry into the house. It was at around this point that Graham Sims realised the warrant that should have been issued the previous year hadn't been, so he issued one. On 20 September he tracked down Joe Timbery in the police cells at Sydney's Central Court. He was there after being picked up on charges of assault, having a knife in public and giving a false name to police. He refused to participate in an interview.

It didn't matter, he was arrested anyway, and the court ordered a brief of evidence concerning the assault charges be served upon him. Graham Sims then took the next step and spoke to the officer who had taken over the domestic violence role at Maroubra from Vanessa Burns. Graham Sims offered to make sure the brief was served, but the other policeman told him he'd take care of it. He didn't.

The police did some brilliant work on my case; without them I could never have sought justice. But there were two really distressing and frustratingly avoidable slip-ups along the way: the failure to serve a warrant on Joe Timbery was the first, and this was the second. The result was that because no brief of evidence had been served, the matter was withdrawn when it came up at the court date that had been rescheduled after Joe's non-appearance back in May. Joe must have thought he was going to get away with it all scot-free. (He would also have been cocky about the other charges he was in court for—around this time he was found guilty of having a knife in a public place and despite his criminal record was given a $150 fine, and a few months later got just 100 hours of community service for having a sawn-off shotgun.) I knew nothing of any of this at the time.

When we'd found out I was pregnant, John had applied for public housing. He'd requested something in the Sutherland Shire, the area of Sydney that takes in Cronulla and the long stretches of beaches around the suburb. I was too afraid to be anywhere near La Perouse, but I'm a beach girl, always happiest when I'm near water, so the Shire seemed to fit the bill perfectly. At the start of July, when I was eight months along, we got word from the Department of Housing that a place had come through. It was, they told us, in Menai. I thought I knew most of those beachside suburbs, but I'd never heard of Menai.

It turns out that the Sutherland Shire stretches a fair way inland. Menai is kind of near water, but it's the Woronora River, not the sea. Cronulla Beach is sixteen kilometres away—about twenty-five minutes' drive, and that's not accounting for traffic. Still, it was a house, it was big enough for John, me, John's son and the baby who would soon be here, and the rent would be cheaper. So I took maternity leave from my job and off to Menai we went.

I didn't have much time to worry about the change because we were just a couple of weeks off my due date by the time we moved. I was booked in to give birth at King George V, which was then the maternity section of Royal Prince Alfred Hospital in Newtown, right near the city. To make sure I was able to get there, we asked John's uncle to come and stay with us in the lead-up to the birth.

The days passed and nothing happened. John's uncle was a drinker, and he was impatient to leave and go back home because he wasn't allowed to drink in our house. I couldn't risk him going, so I decided to try the two things I'd heard were likely to bring on birth: drinking castor oil and having sex. John went down to the chemist and got a bottle of the oil and I drank a heap of it; I didn't know you were only supposed to have a couple of tablespoons. To this day I can still taste it in the back of my throat. It was the most revolting thing I'd ever drunk and I was almost heaving, but I kept it down. Then I took John off to bed for the second part of the method.

We both fell asleep, then in the early hours of the morning I woke up in pain. Because I hadn't been to more than the one antenatal class or read any books about birth, I really didn't know what to expect. These days I guess I'd have spent half the pregnancy on the internet finding out every little thing, but it was different then. I didn't really know what was going on, but when the pain kept coming, worse and worse, I thought maybe this was what contractions were. I needed some advice. I wanted to talk to Mum, but I didn't have any credit on my mobile phone, so I couldn't use it to make a call.

I left John and his uncle sleeping, got dressed and set out to walk to the nearest public phone. It was about half a kilometre away—there were two big hills along the way, but even so it would have been just a couple of minutes' walk for someone who wasn't nine months pregnant and didn't have to stop, doubled over in pain, every few minutes. It seemed to take me forever to haul myself there.

Panting and groaning, I called Mum. She asked me what I was feeling, told me they were definitely contractions and asked me how far apart they were. I told her, 'About five minutes.' She said, 'What are you waiting on? Get to hospital!' I said, 'Oh, I'm waiting for my waters to break.' She said, 'It doesn't have to bloody break! You're in labour. Just go now. I'll meet you there.'

I lumbered home, put the kettle on and woke the men up. I gave them a quick cup of coffee to get them up and moving. We got in the car and drove in—thank goodness there was hardly any traffic because it was not yet daylight.

The way I'd pictured myself giving birth was all natural—a calm and peaceful water birth at the birthing centre with no drugs. Unfortunately, as often happens, nature had other plans. The baby had turned inside me into a breech position—feet-first instead of headfirst. I'd experienced a lot of pain in my life, but this was something else again. The agony just went on and on through the whole day and the following night as I stuck to my 'no drugs' plan. I couldn't seek relief from warm water because I couldn't bear to sit or lie down or kneel, even in a bath. I had to stand the whole time and walk around.

Hours and hours passed and the midwives said to Mum, 'You may as well go home and get some rest, she probably won't have the baby until the morning.' They made John a comfortable bed on the ground and he was lying there, snoring away. But only about half an hour after Mum left, when I'd been labouring away for thirty-two hours in all, the monitor showed the baby's heart rate was dropping. There was no choice: I needed an emergency caesarean, and I needed it now.

I really didn't know anything about caesareans, how they worked or what to expect. The anaesthetist gave me an epidural to block all feeling below the upper chest, while the nurses tried to wake John. I was so stressed out I was screaming at him to get up. If I'd have been able to reach him, I'd have probably added a persuasive kick or two to get him on his feet sooner. He got up and phoned Mum, who was really upset that she'd been sent home and might not make it back in time for the birth.

They wheeled me straight into the operating theatre, with John there to support me. In the theatre, the woman is lying on a trolley, obviously, while the doctors get to work. The man stands up by your head and his job is to be there and support you through what can be a frightening experience, especially if it's your first time and you haven't been expecting it.

There is a low cloth screen on your chest so you can't see what's happening down there, but of course the man can from his standing position. A lot of men keep their attention on their partner's face—maybe even turning away from the operation. But for some reason John couldn't stop looking at what was going on and giving me a running commentary! He started explaining what they were doing—cutting through the skin, then the fat layers, then the muscle, then into the uterus to get the baby out. I said, 'Stop telling me,' but he was fascinated. He said, 'It's unbelievable. Your belly where they're cutting through it is this thick,' holding his fingers apart. 'It's sort of like *E.T.* when they get down to the baby.' I felt faint, and exhausted, and freaked out enough already. I yelled at him to shut up.

Finally, the baby was out, and after all that drama and worry, she was fine. In fact, she was perfect. She looked just as she had in my dream—my little Tymekqwa. We gave her the middle name Koorine, after my sister.

RORY BRENNAN: Vera had only stayed a few weeks more after Lani bashed her and that was it. There were other problems—we were in financial difficulty and my mother'd had the stroke. But that was the icing on the cake. Vera had never experienced anything like that. With my family, sad to say, nothing in life shocks you. You're used to people getting belted and then forgetting about it. You'll go into a pub and you'll get the hell bashed out of you or you'll bash the hell out of someone else, then the next day you're back drinking together and it's all forgotten. But for people that have had a normal upbringing, it's shocking. They've never experienced stuff like that and they just won't tolerate it.

I stayed in touch with Lani a bit when she was living at Dolls Point, but once it really sank in that Vera wasn't coming back, I thought, 'That's it.' I was really pissed off because that changed my life completely. I was pretty keen on Vera, and she was a really nice girl, but that was the end of us. I was dirty with Lani. I would see her at my sons' football, but I would stand on the opposite side of the field and once it was over I'd be gone.

It was only when she had Tymekqwa that I got to a point where I thought, 'I can't go on forever like this. It's my daughter.' I started thinking that I'd grown up violent and maybe part of the violence was because I came from a violent home. And then when I looked at Lani's life, I thought, 'Well, gee, what she went through with him, and the way she's been with her drinking and drugging, her violence is a pretty normal reaction, I suppose.' So I went to visit her in hospital with the baby and we got over what had happened.

I took to motherhood right from the start. I didn't have the kind of shock to the system that new mothers often do, it just all seemed to flow very naturally. I enjoyed breastfeeding and just hanging out with my little baby girl.

It was just as well I liked it, because Tymekqwa was just over three months old when I found out I was expecting again. (I'm living proof that nursing one baby doesn't stop you falling pregnant with another!) My babies would be born almost exactly a year apart, like Koorine and I had been.

JOHN DUCKETT: I'd been there when my son, John, was born, but when Tymekqwa was born I was sober and that was a big difference. I was amazed. It still amazes me thinking about it today. From the moment she was born she was gorgeous. She was aglow. You just have to look at her today. She's still gorgeous.

Lani was an easy, natural mother from the start. But even though she was happy with the baby, Lani was still in turmoil in those early days and she would push me to see if I'd snap. It really didn't worry me. Once I found out what had happened to her with the domestic violence, I got to know the triggers. The first five years we were together, I don't think there was ever a day that we had any peace.

Motherhood and pregnancy were fantastic, but I was not enjoying living out at Menai at all. It was so far away from my family and friends.

I became friendly with my neighbours on one side and there was one other family up the road who used to stop and chat, but to the beach at Maroubra, we had a nasty confrontation. John was in having a swim when I caught sight of his parents further down the sand. I swallowed my pride and feelings of hurt at the way I felt they'd been acting and went over to them to say hello. I got Tymekqwa out of her pram and held her out, to give her grandparents a cuddle. She started crying, and they all but threw her back at me, making out like I'd deliberately got her to cry somehow.

That was it: I was furious and hurt. I said, 'She doesn't know you. Why do you think she's going to be sweet with you?' I said a few other choice things too, but there was no getting through to them, so I turned around and struggled off with the pram through the sand. Delly, who had multiple health problems, was in a wheelchair by this stage, having had her leg amputated because of diabetes. But that didn't stop her trying to chase after me along the beach in her chair, abusing me all the way. We must have been quite a sight. From then on the hostility was open and unrelenting.

We also had a visit from the Department of Community Services, accusing us of neglecting and abusing young John. Welfare officers came around to talk to us and went through our cupboards, checking if we had food. It was humiliating, but of course they found the accusations were all baseless and cleared us completely. As well, they visited young John separately, at the primary school, to ask if I'd been hitting him. Again, they found he was being well looked after, but unfortunately, it put ideas into the young boy's head. I can't really blame the child, but he turned it into a tactic for having his own way, all the time. Every time I told him to tidy away his things or do some little chore to help out around the house, he'd say, 'I'm not going to and if you do anything about it, I'll go to the police and say you bashed me.'

He'd also act spitefully to the girls, telling them all the things his Nan and Pop had given him, and where they were going to take him on his next visit with them. John's parents showered young John with birthday presents, but didn't even send a card when my babies were born. At Christmas we took young John to their place and the girls and I had to wait in the car while John took him in—we weren't even allowed into the house.

It got harder and harder to cope with. A few times I left and went to Mum's for a night or two, but I always came back. The thing that made it all so much worse was that I felt like I had to deal with it myself. John wasn't working but he was often out at AA meetings, so he wasn't there a lot of the time when young John was acting up and he seemed blind to the level of nastiness coming from his family. I thought talking to him about what was going on with his son would only make things worse, so I tried to find a way through on my own.

Iesha wasn't even six months old when I found out I was pregnant again—we'd been using contraception, but the test came back positive. (So much for never being able to have kids!) As understanding as the Benevolent Society had been about extending my maternity leave, it was clear I wouldn't be going back to work any time soon and I resigned.

Eventually, I just reached breaking point. I put in an application with the Department of Housing for a place for me and the kids back in the eastern suburbs, even though I knew Joe Timbery was still on the loose there. I didn't tell John about it. I wasn't intending to leave him, but I knew I couldn't stay at Menai the way things were.

The pressure built and built until one day it was all too much. I packed up the whole kit and caboodle, all my stuff and the girls', and I said to John, 'I'm out of here. I'm leaving for good.' John asked me to talk about it, to really tell him what I was feeling. I did, and he listened. He said he was there for me. He could see what his family were doing was wrong, and he told me he'd have nothing more to do with them. I knew how hard this was for John, because he loved his parents and had always put his mother, especially, on a pedestal. It was what I needed to hear. I stayed, but we agreed that when a place in the east became available, we'd take it.

Chapter Eleven

John laid down the rules with his son. He was kind but firm: if young John couldn't respect me, we would have to make another living arrangement, but if he could, everything would be fine. We all made an effort.

Finally there was good news on the move: I'd been allocated a house in Daceyville, my old stomping ground, and it would be available soon. It was also part of the area of Sydney where Joseph Timbery hung out, and my fear of him remained intense. Even so, we said yes immediately. I simply couldn't continue to live at Menai. Back in the east I would be near my family and friends, and even if such closely spaced pregnancies meant I couldn't go back to work, there would be plenty of good things to fill my days.

I'd found that even though some of the people I loved continued to use drugs and drink in a dangerous way, I could be around them without feeling I was going to go back to the bad old days myself. I was never even really tempted, because I used to project myself a little way into the future. I'd think, 'Yes, it would be easy to sit down with this person and have a smoke or a drink now, but what's going to happen in an hour's time and then in two hours' time?' I knew that as an addict I wouldn't stop at one or two or even three; the first sip or the first smoke would be enough to send me crashing back down to the depths. And knowing that, being able to think it through in that way, meant that even when the opportunity presented itself, I wasn't interested. The compulsion just left me.

Even so, I didn't take anything for granted. I knew I'd always need to abstain, my whole life long. One slip would be enough to lose everything I'd worked so hard to build up. I said to John many times, 'If I ever pick up anything—any kind of drugs or a drink—you just take the kids and go, no questions asked. Just go straight away.' Because I knew how out of control I could get under the influence. I wouldn't be fit to be around anyone.

John was staunch in his sobriety, too. But unfortunately, there were a couple of things he was keeping from me. He'd lasted a couple of months maintaining a distance from his family, but gradually he'd resumed contact with them on the sly. I can see it from his point of view now: he really loved them, but he didn't want to hurt me, either. After a while I realised what was going on, and I wasn't thrilled about it, that's for sure. But as long as they kept out of my face, I could live with it.

But there was something else going on with John, and it was much more of a problem. He'd started gambling. I didn't even spot it for a problem at first. Like a lot of people, I like a punt, and if ever we had a night out away from the kids we might go to a club for dinner and then have a bit of a go on the pokies afterwards. It was just a bit of fun for me, a little excitement. I thought it was the same for John too, but it wasn't. It was something more serious for him, though it took me a while to realise the extent of it. For him it was betting on horse-racing, not so much the pokies, and it was bad.

I didn't know at the time that his problem was not at all unusual among reformed alcoholics and drug addicts—they can turn to gambling even after they've been sober for years, as John had. I also didn't know how sly gamblers can be. John would just take off for hours with no explanation then walk back in again like nothing was wrong. I'd end up going off my head at him and he'd just shut down, he wouldn't say a word. This went on for months. Money would disappear: I'd know exactly how much money we had to get through the week, but when it came time to buy a few groceries, some or all of the money would be missing. So many times I said, 'If this doesn't stop, I'm out of here.' He'd promise to stop then gradually I'd notice the secrets and lies had crept back in. I was beside myself with worry and pain at having this man who'd stood by me through so much breaking my trust.

It was during this period we moved from Menai, with me a few weeks away from giving birth, just as I'd been when we moved in there. Luckily I had plenty of energy and felt good, and I was just so happy to be moving, so it all went smoothly.

When you've had two caesareans there's no choice about it: giving birth naturally is too great a risk in case the internal surgery scars tear. So I was booked in to the Prince of Wales, just up the road from our new home. It was all organised well in advance, but when I woke up on the morning I was due to go in, John was nowhere to be found. He knew I was going in that day and that he had to drive me. So where was he? I got breakfast for the girls and double-checked my hospital bag, but he didn't appear. That's when I knew he hadn't just gone up the street to get the paper or some milk. He'd snuck off, gambling the little money we had.

I knew the local club, Souths Juniors, was his favourite. At six o'clock in the morning on 3 September 2004, the day our baby was going to be born, I had to ring the club and have John paged. They put the page over the loudspeakers, but no one answered. I rang back and ended up speaking to one of the bouncers who said, 'Is your bloke a tall, dark guy?' I said yes, and he said, 'Oh, he just went bolting out of here.' John turned up at home minutes later and copped an almighty serve from me.

With the birth of our third little girl, Lateia, we had three children under three years old. John came up with the name Latei. I wanted to make it a bit more unusual so I added what was meant to be a silent 'a' at the end. And we gave her the middle name Maria, after John's mother. (Now everyone calls her Tia and reckons I named her Tia Maria after the liqueur. As if!)

Forty-eight hours after I'd given birth to her I signed myself out of hospital—they usually keep you in for a week after a caesar, but I felt fine and I wanted to be at home, in my own space. It wasn't a happy homecoming because I walked in with my two-day-old baby to find John's family sprawled about the place, smoking cigarettes inside my house—something that wasn't on, because of the children—and making a mess everywhere. You'd hope that if you came home just after giving birth and found people in your place, they'd be there to help. I let them know how I felt, but the last straw came when little Tymekqwa, still just a toddler, locked herself in the toilet and none of them even noticed or offered to help me get her out. John had gone out saying he needed to get more supplies, and I ended up having to get the door off myself, stitches and all.

***

After a while John's son decided he wanted to try living with his mother for a while. John kept up their relationship, but the girls and I really didn't see much of him from then on. It also meant I didn't have to have any contact with John senior or Delly at all, which suited me just fine. The girls and I had nothing to do with them for a few years after that. Part of me wished it didn't have to be like that—after all, family is family—but they were so negative when they were in our lives that we were better off without them.

I am happy to say, though, that at the very end, Delly and I were able to make peace. Her various medical conditions got worse and worse until, a few years after that confrontation in my house, she was dying. She was in hospital, and she knew it was the end. She sent me a message that she wanted to see me and the kids. I didn't know what she might want, but I couldn't refuse a dying woman her wish, so we went. She told me she wanted to apologise for what she'd put me through. She told me it all came down to jealousy. She'd been jealous that John had started a new life where he didn't depend on her, and didn't depend on the rest of his family. I was so independent, used to coping on my own, and she said she'd been hurt by that. She'd expected me to ask them for help, and when I didn't she'd taken offence. But, she said, she could see that it was all so unnecessary and it had cost her all the time she might have been spending with her granddaughters.

I knew what it must have taken for her to say that, and so when she asked me to forgive her, of course I said yes. She asked to see the girls and they all came into the room. She seemed to have been waiting for that, and soon afterwards she passed away.

Sadly, things didn't end up so well with John's dad, and my girls still have nothing to do with their paternal grandfather or uncle. But who knows what might happen in the future? I remain hopeful.

In the months after Lateia's birth, John's gambling got even worse. It almost did what nothing else had been able to and drove us apart. He was missing in action—not there when I needed him (and as you can imagine, with three children so young, I needed him there a lot). Money kept disappearing and he'd have some dodgy explanation or no explanation at all. He'd stay out till all hours and take off early. From being my rock, he'd become someone I couldn't rely on for even the simplest things.

I had threatened to leave him so many times over the gambling, but I didn't really mean it. For a start, how could I, with the girls? Plus I really did love John and believe in him. And then there was the fact that I was still fairly naive about the extent of the problem.

I knew the effect it was having on me, and the inconvenience it was causing us as a family, but I didn't really understand the severity of the situation because I knew far less about gambling than I do now. I thought he was just getting carried away, and I could understand why he liked it. I didn't see that it was another form of addiction. I now realise that gamblers are more shifty than drug addicts and alcoholics because with gambling you can't see it—they can keep what they're doing hidden until things have become really, really bad.

Fortunately, John was able to stop himself before he sank to that level. I guess he recognised the danger of losing me and the girls if he kept going the way he was, and he knew he'd beaten drugs and alcohol so he had the strength to beat this, too. There were some bumps in the road—when his nan died he relapsed. Her wake was held in a club, and I walked in there and went off my head when I saw him sitting at the pokies.

It wasn't too long before he stopped for good, but there was one occasion after that when having a bet meant he was in the right place at the right time—maybe not according to the legal system, but according to the law of everyday justice.

In the background of our lives the whole time was the spectre of Joseph Timbery. I'd overcome my mistrust of the police and my fear of retribution at his hands in order to make my detailed statements about what had happened. Vanessa Burns and Graham Sims had been sympathetic to me and professional in their approach. But more than two years had passed since I'd made my second statement detailing the assaults and rapes that had taken place, so why had nothing happened?

I was always on edge when I was at home with the babies and John was out; I jumped at every unexplained sound, I couldn't sleep. My anxiety was through the roof. Constantly in the back of my mind was the thought that Joe might find out where I was and come and get me—and make sure I could never testify against him. It got so bad I wanted to pick up again—to take drugs and wipe myself out so I could get some sleep and stop worrying, at least for a few hours.

> CAROL SIMON: During this period when Joe Timbery still hadn't been picked up, everyone was walking around in fear. His mother and I stopped talking. I was worried for Lani's family and I lived by myself at the time too. Everyone was just walking around on eggshells trying to work out what was happening. It wasn't good.

Both John and I had contacted the police numerous times to try to find out what was going on. We were told things were in motion, it was all being taken care of, but still nothing happened. Joseph Timbery was doing as he liked, free as a bird. I lived in fear of seeing him on the streets. I would catch a glimpse of someone I thought was him and instantly I'd be shaking and fighting back tears, trying to act like nothing was wrong so I didn't scare the girls. Then the man I'd thought was Joe would turn or get closer, and I'd see it wasn't him, but I'd be shaky and upset for hours afterwards.

I did see some of his family members and every time I had to fight the panicky urge to run. We never spoke—we'd cross the road to avoid each other—but I knew they knew I'd been to the police; everyone in the La Perouse community did, by now. I knew most of them didn't support his actions in any way, but I also knew they were so scared of Joe they would probably stand up for him in court if it ever made it that far.

The police didn't seem to be able to find Joe, but he was right there, walking the streets as if he owned them, and while I never ran into him, members of my family saw him. One afternoon during this period when we were growing increasingly frustrated with the lack of action, Koorine happened to be on the street in Kingsford, just minutes away from my house in Daceyville. She'd seen John shortly beforehand going into the nearby pub—even though he didn't drink, the pub had a TAB betting facility, so he sometimes went there to lay a bet. Then she noticed Joseph Timbery at the bus stop right outside the pub. She ducked inside and told John.

John came outside intending to confront him, but I think as soon as he saw Timbery his fury at the suffering this evil man had caused me just swamped him, and without even thinking he laid into him with his fists. He gave him a hell of a beating that day. Given John's own criminal record, that was a really risky thing for him to do because it could have landed him back in front of a judge. But he didn't stop to think, he just acted. Even though it all took place on the street, in full view of passing traffic, and the police did come in response to a passer-by phoning them, nothing happened afterwards. Timbery wasn't in a position to report it, given that he should have been arrested long before then.

JOHN DUCKETT: Time passed and we heard nothing about the case. I started ringing the police regularly. I'd say, 'What's happening? Why haven't you picked him up?' They'd say, 'We haven't seen him.' But the whole community knew where he was. Sometimes I'd drive past him and I'd tell them that.

As soon I saw him outside the pub that day, I saw red. I just jumped on him, flogged him pretty bad. I actually thought I could kill him, but I stopped myself. He didn't put up a fight—he'd only pick on someone weaker than himself.

I just turned around and walked back into the pub. The bouncers knew me. They knew I didn't drink, that I'd just come in and have one or two punts a week. They said, 'Just go in and clean up.' The police came because someone driving by had called them. They said, 'We've had a report. We're looking for …' The bouncer said, 'We don't know what you're talking about. No one came in here.'

More time passed and I was still ringing the police all the time, Graham Sims or whoever I could talk to. But still nothing was happening. We were getting nowhere.

I kept asking myself, if this happened to a white woman would we be here? Is there something going on where they think, 'It's black on black; let them kill each other'? I still think if this had happened to a white woman and a black man was the perpetrator, every man and dog would have been looking for that bloke.

I'll admit I rejoiced in the fact that Timbery had been paid back by John a tiny fraction of the suffering he'd caused me, although it wasn't the same as facing justice in a court. But then I got even more scared. Where he'd been was so close to our new house. Had he found out where I lived? Is that why he was there? Or was I just being paranoid? I had no way of knowing.

I'd got to the point where I was ready to give up. I felt like I'd been stupid to put my faith in the system and try to seek justice. People I trusted, including Dad and Aunty Carol, had tried to talk me out of going ahead with the case. They'd said I should just move on. I heard it, too, from a lot of people in the community: they had no faith in the criminal justice system and thought I was making myself a target for retribution. They thought I should drop the whole thing—nothing good would come of it, and perhaps by withdrawing my statement I'd be safer. I wondered if they were right.

I found myself spiralling back into those dark thoughts of feeling dirty and ashamed, like damaged goods. My inner turmoil led me to frequently lashing out verbally at John and other people close to me. I was tense almost all the time.

John stayed strong, though. He made his calls to Maroubra police more frequent, until he got to the point where he was ringing at least once a week, often more than that. He kept telling them that Timbery wasn't hiding out—he was living in La Perouse and easy to find. They just kept putting us off, without any real explanation of why he hadn't been picked up.

So John ramped it up. He contacted the local paper and the office of the Police Commissioner and the state Ombudsman. Finally, in May 2005, four years after I'd first signed a police statement, Joseph Timbery was taken into custody on charges related to what he'd done to me. Even then it only happened after his own father rang the police to say his son had assaulted him and to tell them where they could find him that day—at a drinking hole in the city.

It turned out that even though the charges had been laid for his attacks on me, no warrant for his arrest on those charges had ever been issued. No bloody warrant. That was why he had been picked up on other offences, fingerprinted, held in cells, taken to court, found guilty, and then let go time and time again during those years.

Even after he was picked up, I didn't hear it from the police first. I was at home when I got a call from someone I knew who knew someone who'd seen him arrested. I listened, but I didn't really believe it. I'd heard before that he'd 'definitely' been picked up and those stories had turned out to be false. I called Maroubra police and asked for Vanessa Burns, but she wasn't there. So I asked the desk cop who answered, and when I explained who I was he confirmed it: yes, Joseph Timbery had been picked up on the charges concerning me. I hung up feeling angry and let down. Why hadn't the police rung to tell me? Then Graham Sims called back and explained it had all just happened. The grapevine had delivered the news within minutes of the event, before he could call and be the one to let me know.

As I said earlier, there have been fantastic cops who worked on my case over the years—and another real gem was about to come my way once the trial started—but there were some really dumb, avoidable mistakes along the way too, and the fact that it took the police so long to pick up Joseph Timbery was one of them. I am completely sure that if I had been a white woman it would have been a totally different story. Not because it was a conspiracy or anything like that. But because if I was white, Joseph Timbery's actions would have been seen as outrageous by every single person who heard about them, and the police would have made the pursuit of justice a top priority.

But I was a black woman, and a former addict to boot, so details of my case were able to slip between the cracks. It wasn't a case that was given resources and attention and vigilance in the way it would have been if I'd been a different person with a different history and different skin.

Not long after we got the news about the arrest we got some even more important news: I was expecting another baby. I'd managed to conceive one child while taking the mini-pill and another while using a contraceptive implant that is placed under the skin of your arm and is supposed to be effective immediately, and good for three years. Sometimes it felt as if John and I only had to pass each other in the hall and I was pregnant again!

Even though we hadn't set out to have so many children, we considered the news a blessing. I feel like I was made for motherhood. I breastfed for five years straight, and was pregnant for much of that time and I just loved it. I know some people find kids really try their patience—they totally love their children but they also find themselves driven mad by them occasionally.

Despite the fact that anger had burned so hot in me for so many years, I found I simply didn't get angry with kids.

Being around children makes me feel like a kid myself. It lets me be joyous and silly, and I guess that's why I sometimes feel more comfortable being around kids than adults, the more the merrier. As my own family grew, the girls would often have their little friends over and I'd frequently end up with a gang of fifteen or more kids of different ages running around my house. It would probably have driven other people mad, but I absolutely loved it. Being a mother really has brought out the best in me.

Joseph Timbery was kept in custody while the police and the Office of the Director of Public Prosecutions went about preparing the case against him. A fantastic police officer named Scott Johnson was assigned to the case. They explained to me that the reason they weren't charging him with attempted murder, even though I could easily have died many times over on that last horrific night alone, was because to prove that charge you have to prove intent. If the defence can say convincingly 'He never intended to kill her', the accused will be acquitted of the charge. That was too great a risk.

While the legal team was preparing the case, John and I got on with raising our family and living a good life together. The nightmares continued, but we just had to live with those.

Even when things are working as they should, the justice system grinds along very slowly. Finally we heard that a court date had been set: the case would be heard in the New South Wales District Court, starting on 6 February 2006. It would be a jury trial, so while there would be a judge to oversee things, it was twelve randomly picked ordinary people who would decide Joseph Timbery's fate.

I was twenty-five years old and had five years of sobriety under my belt, and five years of rebuilding my life since escaping the horror of that relationship. Now I was going to have to be stronger than ever. I would need to stand up and tell the whole world what Joe Timbery had done to me. And I'd need to be in the same room with him for the first time since 26 December 2000. I felt sick at the thought, but there was no way I was backing out now. I could do this. I had to do this.

Shortly before the start date of the trial, one of the lawyers on my team and an Aboriginal Witness Assistance Officer came to Mum's house to see me. I didn't know how any of this stuff worked, but I was about to get a crash course. The way it goes is that police have the job of looking into whether a law has been broken. Simple breaches of the law, like driving too fast, get dealt with on the spot: the police issue you with a speeding ticket. It only goes to court if you want to challenge it. But more serious crimes go to court automatically.

If the police think a law has been broken and they know who is responsible and think that person should face the charges in court, they refer the case to the Director of Public Prosecutions (the DPP). If the DPP agrees that the evidence is strong enough to stand up to a court case, they take it over and run the case. They do this as representatives of the public.

So while I was the person making the allegations (I was 'the complainant'), the case against Joseph Timbery was actually being made on behalf of society in general. That's why the head lawyer, or barrister, on my side was called the Crown prosecutor. (Technically the head of state in Australia is the British queen, which is where the 'Crown' comes from.)

I could never have afforded a barrister—they charge thousands of dollars a day. But I didn't have to because the DPP supplies one for the cases it prosecutes. The lawyer within the DPP who gives the barrister the information they need to run the case is the instructing solicitor. They do all the legwork and the barrister gets up and does all the talking, basically. (The defence side is also publicly funded for people who have been granted legal aid, so there is a defence barrister who goes head-to-head with the Crown prosecutor.)

The lawyer who came out to see me was called Josephine Cashman; she was the DPP's instructing solicitor. I liked Josie from the start, and not just because she was indigenous and had some sense of where I was coming from. Kind, sensible and well organised, Josie was a real lifeline for me. As I said, I had no idea what to expect but Josie explained things and told me what was likely to happen. The support officer, Samantha Smith, was lovely too. Josie and Sam asked me what I was going to do with the children while the trial was on. I hadn't figured it out. All the people I would normally have asked to mind them for me were people I wanted there at court to support me—my mum, my dad, Koorine, Aunty Carol.

Thank heavens a brilliant lady called Aunty Shirley phoned the Gujaga Child Care Centre at La Perouse for me. It has a huge waiting list, that place, but when the people there heard my circumstances they made arrangements to take the girls in as soon as I needed and keep them for as long as the trial ran. I'll always be grateful to Gujaga for that. My little ones had never been in childcare at all, and it was hard to send them off all of a sudden, no easing into it—Tymekqwa wasn't four yet, Iesha was only two and a half and little Lateia was only seventeen months old—but I knew they were in wonderful hands.

I also met the Crown prosecutor who'd been assigned to the case—as a lot of them are, he was a freelancer the DPP hired as needed. I had a very different reaction to him than I did to Josie. Of the thousands and thousands of barristers in Australia (there are nearly 3000 in New South Wales alone), only about twelve are indigenous. I didn't get one of them. I got a man who was very good at the job of standing up to the defence side in court and making a judge and jury understand the facts of a case. But like the majority of barristers, he was rich, white and male, and had probably led a very privileged, sheltered life. We may as well have come from different planets.

When he spoke to me in private outside the courtroom it seemed to be mostly lectures ('Don't wear anything showing cleavage, don't wear too short a skirt') or harsh challenges to my evidence. I can still remember my shock and disbelief when he said to me in a hostile way, 'How could you get anally raped without lubricant?' Jesus, did I really have to spell it out to him that Joseph Timbery wasn't asking my permission, that he didn't care how much pain or damage he caused me? I don't know what I would have done if Josie hadn't been there.

JOSEPHINE CASHMAN: I knew it was a big thing Lani was doing in coming forward. Not many people come forward about matters like this in any community, not just the Aboriginal community.

The week before the trial was going to start I went out with the Witness Assistance Officer, Samantha, to see Lani at her mother's house. I found Lani to be very articulate, but she had no idea what she was letting herself in for. She asked me what might happen and I said, 'I'm not going to lie to you. We've got no control over the outcome.' I said to her, 'Read all your statements,' because that's what I tell everybody. Any little diversion from them in court, even though they were made so many years ago, any little slip of the tongue will be leapt on by the defence.

What Lani had been through was horrific. I'm working now as a senior solicitor in Arnhem Land and there's nothing that comes close. Sometimes you might get a frenzied attack when someone's drunk, but Joseph Timbery was cruel. It was also the emotional abuse and the fact that she stayed with him and she was so isolated. She was being raped and she was so vulnerable. I don't think anything to that extent would happen in the Northern Territory because usually you'd find that the woman's family would come in and deal with him if it was that bad. I think Lani's case is unique—I've never come across anything like it.

As the trial date approached, I knew I had to prepare my family. None of them knew the full horror of what had happened. John knew the most, but even he didn't know all the details. I knew I couldn't let them find out about it for the first time when they were sitting in court. So I gathered them and asked them all to read the statement I'd made to Graham Sims in 2003. I said to them, 'I want you to walk into that courtroom knowing what you're going to hear without me having to say it to you.'

I had two copies, so they took turns. Everyone was silent, reading through the pages, then each reacted in their own way. John and my dad were so angry. They were determined to see Joseph Timbery pay. I'd never said anything to anyone, but in the back of my mind I'd thought about what would happen if he got off, what I'd do. I thought about somehow trying to attack him myself, right there on the steps of the court. Of course, I couldn't really do it; I had my children and my family to think of, apart from anything else. But it meant that when I caught John and Dad plotting together about taking him out if he was acquitted, I knew just where they were coming from. They were talking about it as a practical problem—who would do it and how. Dad was saying things like, 'I should do it. I'm older and I don't have as long to go, but you have to be here for the kids.' I knew it was their way of dealing with the rage they felt about what he'd done to me.

Meanwhile, Mum was devastated. It brought up a lot of the skeletons of what had happened in her own marriage to Dad when he was still drinking. She'd locked those bad memories away and kept them hidden all these years, but the shock of finding out what I'd gone through released them. It was the beginning of her feeling she could be more open with me about the domestic violence she had experienced. It had the same effect on Dad too, as time went by. He started to be able to talk more about the abuse he'd suffered as a boy from his mother when she was drunk.

We don't generally sit and talk about feelings; it's not our way. Instead of hugging or crying, they all just started bustling about, making me coffee, seeing to the kids. Even though they didn't show it the way other people might have, I knew they were all deeply affected and I also knew that whatever happened, I had so much support and love. This tight inner group would always stand by me, no matter how bad things got.

Chapter Twelve

Finally, 6 February came around. I hardly slept in the days leading up to it, despite being eight months pregnant and constantly busy with my girls. Josie had shown me what the courtroom looked like beforehand, and pointed out where I would enter and sit. I had looked over my statements to refresh myself on the dates of specific events. There was nothing more I could do but speak the truth and trust in the jury.

Because I was a witness—the prime witness—in the case, I wasn't allowed to be with anyone else when the court was in session or talk to anyone about the case until it ended, even my family. Things didn't get underway until the afternoon of the first day. One of the court officers led me to a small room. There was hot water, tea and coffee, a TV and that was it. I had to just sit there on my own for hours, trying not to go crazy, wondering what was happening in the courtroom and when I would get called up.

I knew that on that first day they would be choosing the jury, and it would take a while. From reading the transcripts after the case was over, I know that after that happened there was a fair bit of legal back and forth between the lawyers and the judge, including discussing how long the case might last—the defence barrister thought five days, the Crown prosecutor thought ten at most. Then came the reading of the charges.

Joseph Timbery was led up from the holding cells into the dock. As the accused, he was in court during pretty much every part of the trial, all the witness testimonies and the opening and closing arguments. The only time he had to leave was during the technical legal sections between the lawyers and the judge, when everyone but these 'officers of the court' had to go out of the room.

The charges were read out. That simple bit of court procedure took quite some time because there were twenty-three charges (including one that was known as an 'alternative') for attacks that had occurred between April and December 2000.

In their full form, the charges were stated like this. 'Charge 1: That on 16 April 2000 at La Perouse in the state of New South Wales [Joseph Timbery] did maliciously wound Lani Brennan. Charge 2: Further that he on 16 April 2000 at La Perouse in the state of New South Wales did have sexual intercourse with Lani Brennan without her consent and knowing that Lani Brennan was not consenting to sexual intercourse.'

Charge 3 was that on 12 May 2000 Joe Timbery had again had sexual intercourse without consent, this time 'in circumstances of aggravation, namely that immediately before the sexual intercourse he did maliciously inflict actual bodily harm'. Charge 4 related to the same date; it was for 'assault occasioning actual bodily harm'. This was the 'alternative', which only came into play if Timbery was found not guilty of Charge 3—if that happened then the jury could consider Charge 4. Charge 5 was also for the same date and it was another charge of sexual intercourse without consent (each different type of rape—vaginal, anal, oral—drew a separate charge).

Charge 6 was worded as a date range, rather than a specific date—'between 1 May 2000 and 30 May 2000'—and was for sexual intercourse without consent, in circumstances of aggravation (meaning that, again, Joseph Timbery had inflicted malicious bodily harm before the rape).

Charge 7 concerned 18 May and was also for sexual intercourse without consent in aggravated circumstances. Charge 8 was for another occurrence of the same offence on that same date. Charge 9 was maliciously inflicting grievous bodily harm on 25 June 2000 (the bashing in the foyer of the flats near Joe's sister's flat). Charge 10 was from 21 August and was also for sexual intercourse without consent in aggravated circumstances. Charge 11, from the same date, was another occurrence of the same event; Charge 12 was a third instance from the same date and Charge 13 was for sexual intercourse without consent on the same date.

Charge 14 concerned 29 September (the night of Petra's party) and was for sexual intercourse without consent 'in circumstances of aggravation, namely that immediately before the sexual intercourse he did threaten to inflict actual bodily harm on Lani Brennan by means of an offensive instrument, namely a beer bottle'. Charge 15 was for malicious wounding on the same date (cutting my leg with the plate). Charge 16 was for assault the following day, 30 September (when he bashed me and forced me to take the cast off), and Charges 17 and 18 were for sexual intercourse without consent in aggravated circumstances that same day.

Charges 19 and 20 were that between 30 September and 15 October 2000 he'd had sexual intercourse without consent, and sexual intercourse without consent in aggravated circumstances. Charges 21 and 22 were for two instances of sexual intercourse without consent in aggravated circumstances on 23 December. And Charge 23 was for sexual intercourse without consent in aggravated circumstances on Christmas Day.

In short, there were eighteen unlawful sexual assault charges, of which fourteen were aggravated, with an alternative charge of assault occasioning actual bodily harm to one of these; two malicious woundings; one malicious intent to inflict grievous bodily harm; and one common assault. They covered eleven different episodes of abuse.

Even though I had suffered many more attacks than the twenty-three charges covered, each charge had to be pegged to some kind of evidence such as hospital admissions, because the law says that charges have to be proven beyond reasonable doubt. Otherwise it was just my word against Joe Timbery's, and no matter how much I had truth on my side, the jury still had to be convinced that he was guilty beyond reasonable doubt based solely on what they heard in the courtroom.

It was up to the Crown to prove the case to them, given that our legal system works on the assumption of innocence until proven guilty. What the jury wasn't allowed to know was that by the time Joseph Timbery had been picked up in May 2005 he had a charge sheet of previous offences that was nineteen pages long and included assault, malicious damage, interfering with a witness in a court case, several armed robberies, inflicting grievous bodily harm, demanding property with menaces, having a loaded firearm in a public place and several escapes from custody. They also couldn't be told he'd been convicted of a domestic violence assault on a previous partner.

One by one the long list of twenty-three charges was read out, and to each one Joseph Timbery responded, 'Not guilty.'

The Crown prosecutor explained to the jury what the charges meant and gave them an indication of the witnesses he would call. Then they were formally empanelled and the judge had to spend some time filling them in on their responsibilities and explaining how things worked—how they were required to choose a foreperson, how they couldn't talk to anyone outside the jury about the case, how they were forbidden from trying to do their own research on the case, and most importantly, how it would be them and not him who would decide whether Joe Timbery was guilty or not guilty. When he gave them an idea of how long the trial would run he went with two weeks, which he considered a generous estimate.

I was still sitting it out in the witness room during all this, worrying about my children and how they were coping without me, trying unsuccessfully to get comfortable with the baby wriggling around. I had no idea that, in the absence of the jury, the defence barrister told the judge that he and the Crown were working on an agreement to alter the charges, in exchange for Joe Timbery altering his plea to guilty.

At first this might sound like a really good thing. But what it meant was they wanted to drop a whole lot of the charges and instead have Joseph Timbery face lesser charges, and it was on those he would plead guilty. It's formally called charge negotiation but it's better known as plea bargaining. The DPP does it sometimes because it avoids a lengthy trial and it means there will definitely be a conviction.

Josie and the Crown prosecutor came in to tell me about it. They were going to reduce the charges so that Timbery would plead guilty and most likely end up with a sentence of just six months in jail. He had evidently agreed to do this. I went off my head. I just lost it. I'd waited so long, and fought so hard for this, and now after all this time we'd finally made it to court and they threw this in my face?

Josie had explained to me before things began that you never know going into a trial what will happen. You have to prepare yourself for the worst outcome while still hoping for the best. I understood that, and I understood what they were trying to do with this new strategy, but I said to them, 'You've dragged me all this way, through all this shit, just to give him six months? No way. Not now.' I explained that this trial was about the (hopefully guilty) verdict that would be handed down, of course it was, but it was also about me speaking up and telling the world what had happened. It was about me showing Joseph Timbery I wasn't going to be intimidated into silence. If the plea bargain went ahead, I wouldn't get to say my piece. He would plead guilty and the next step would be for the judge to sentence him. I told the prosecution team I wouldn't accept their recommendation to make this deal, and I wanted to talk to the head of the DPP.

The lawyers passed what I'd said on to the DPP decision-makers, but my feelings were overruled: the DPP instructed the Crown team to go ahead and make the plea bargain deal. I was bitter about it, but I also knew it wasn't the end. I warned them: 'You don't know him. It's just mind games, that's all it is with him. He won't take the plea. You'll see.' I could tell they didn't believe me.

The next day the trial should have got properly underway, but, sure enough, instead the defence barrister had to get up and tell the judge that Joseph Timbery had changed his mind about the plea bargain—he was going to plead not guilty after all. The consequences of that were huge. First, the defence barrister resigned from the case. Lawyers have to abide by a code of ethics and once a client has admitted their guilt, as Timbery effectively had done by agreeing to plead guilty to lesser charges, their hands are pretty much tied. Knowing their client's guilt, when they are cross-examining witnesses they can't say, 'Well, this didn't really happen at all, did it?' because they know it did happen. They can't do the job that is expected of them.

Second, the jury was stood down because they couldn't be kept hanging around doing nothing while the Public Defenders Office was trying to find a barrister to take over the case. It was Thursday 9 February and we'd spent four days on legal wrangling, wasting thousands of dollars of taxpayers' money and tying up a courtroom and judge, all because, it seemed to me, this man who'd already done so much damage had decided to play stupid games.

The following Monday the case resumed. All the preliminaries had to happen for a second time—the jury being chosen, the original charges being read and the pleas entered. Again, I had to wait away from everyone while all this happened but at least now I had Sam Smith, the Aboriginal Witness Assistance Officer, with me. She'd been in court with someone else the previous week, but now she was here to support me throughout the trial.

A new defence barrister had been found. In my view he played the race card right from the start. In the absence of the jury he addressed the judge, questioning whether this was even a case that should be heard in court, saying, 'This is clearly a trial that involves the Aboriginal race and their conduct to one another ... What persons in the general community might accept as reasonable and acceptable conduct ... might not necessarily be the accepted conduct of persons who fall within the earth people of this land. The accepted and proper tribunal may be, for these people, tribal councils and elders of the community.'

In other words, rape and aggravated violence were something a court should deal with if they happened to white people, but when it came to indigenous people ('the earth people'!), they could just bugger off and sort it out among themselves. Thankfully the judge rejected this racist nonsense and the trial finally got underway. Well, almost. There was one piece of drama before I was brought into the courtroom and sworn in.

In the same way that my mum and dad and John and Koorine and Aunty Carol were there in the courtroom to support me, various members of the Timbery family and a friend of theirs called Crystal were also there watching. Before the main part of the proceedings could begin, they handed the defence barrister a note that they said recorded comments made by my family, including a threat to them. The defence barrister handed the note up to the judge and said it might be evidence in an application for an AVO by them against my family members. (Again, I knew nothing about this at the time.)

Let's put aside the fact that if anyone felt threatened in this situation it was me and my loved ones. When the barrister did this, he would have known perfectly well that AVOs are not something a District Court judge has any involvement in. The application needs to be made through the Local Court and is then judged on its merits. If he knew all this, what was his tactic in raising the matter with the trial judge? Well, I'll leave that to you to decide.

What I wonder was if the Timberys had revealed to him that the week before the trial had been due to start they had actually already applied for an AVO against me. On behalf of the DPP—an organisation that is very careful in what it says about people—Josie Cashman wrote to the presiding magistrate at Waverley Local Court where the application had been made, noting that the applicants (Joe's married sister, with his father and other siblings also listed on the form) were immediate family members of the accused in an upcoming trial at which I was a Crown witness. She wrote, 'This Office has concerns that a motivating factor for this AVO application may be to intimidate the Crown witnesses before the trial,' and asked that a decision be held over until the trial finished. The magistrate did as she requested, and listed the matter for September.

The registrar of Waverley Court wrote to the officer in charge at Maroubra Police Station, giving them the hearing date and asking that they inform the relevant parties—the Timberys listed on the application and me. Three paragraphs of the five-paragraph letter were devoted to explaining about the trial, our connections to it, and the fact that my address was not to be disclosed. Pretty clear, you'd have thought.

As far as we were able to determine afterwards, the papers the police served to the Timberys didn't include my address. But when the police sent a form back to the court to confirm they had served the papers, they *did* include my address. Despite the letter that had been sent out from their office in the first place, the court registrar hadn't put an entry in the court's database noting that my address should not be entered. The clerk who got the paperwork from the police did what he or she usually did with such forms, and entered all the details. Including my address.

So every piece of correspondence that went out to the Timberys later on about the AVO application, and there were a few, had my address on it. This would have serious repercussions.

The judge gave his instructions to the new jury and the barristers made their opening addresses. The Crown prosecutor outlined the incidents behind each one of the charges, giving brief details of what had happened on each of the relevant dates. He gave the jury an overview of what I had gone through at the hands of Joseph Timbery, telling them that six times in the eight months covered by the indictment I was in hospital with serious injuries; on a number of these occasions I'd had to be brought in by ambulance; and on two of them I'd needed surgery.

He also said to them, 'You may ask yourselves questions throughout this trial as to how the complainant could have put up with this for so long.' He needed to say that, because they would indeed ask themselves and each other that question: it was only natural for anyone who hasn't experienced the powerlessness and terror of domestic violence. Only when they had heard from me about what life was like in those dark days would they really be able to understand.

Then the defence counsel got up and gave his opening address. I understand that defence lawyers have their job to do, and their job is to try to get their clients off. I realise that one way they can try to do this is by making out that the person who says a crime was committed against them is lying. Josie had explained to me in the lead-up to the trial that the other side would try to say that the assaults and rapes had never happened.

I'd prepared myself for that, but even so I still find many of the things the defence barrister said to the jury and to me disgusting, starting with his opening in which he said that what had happened was 'a rather torrid love affair'. He told them there was 'not one scintilla' of evidence of rape and that in fact 'these people ... were in a sexual affair, they were de factos, they were living together', as if somehow that made it all okay.

He would have known that rape within marriage (including de facto relationships) had been a crime in New South Wales since 1981. In other words, for a quarter of a century before my trial the law had recognised that just because you willingly start a relationship with someone and willingly have sex with them that does not mean that you become their possession or that later on they can force you into sex. It recognised that rape was rape, no matter who was doing it. Yet all these years later, male lawyers still stand up in court and say things like that. Worse was to come from the defence.

Finally, at 2.55 pm on 13 February, I was led to the courtroom to begin my testimony. As I stepped in and saw Joseph Timbery in the dock, I started to cry and shake. I was instantly terrified. It didn't matter that he was a prisoner, and the rational part of my brain knew he couldn't really jump the dock and reach me because there were security officers in the court who would stop him doing anything. I still felt as though he had the power to kill me then and there. I didn't look at him after that first glance around the room, but I could feel his eyes burning into me. Instantly, all the old fear washed over me until I was struggling to catch my breath. I couldn't make myself stop crying.

I glanced over at my family sitting up the back of the courtroom in the seats provided for observers. I took strength from their presence and from what I was here to do, and gradually got myself under control so that I could take the stand and swear to tell only the truth. I was facing the lawyers' tables with the jury to the left and in front of me. I took a glance at them while I was trying to get my bearings, then looked around the rest of the court. I could see the various Timbery family members there too, with Joe's older sister in particular trying to get herself noticed. It was hard to catch my breath—it often is when you're that pregnant, but my heart was also racing with fear and stress. I felt so emotional, but I had to somehow get control. I had to focus; I had a job to do.

I knew that the way I gave my evidence was vital; it would make or break the case. It was now five years since the last of the attacks had happened and the police had gathered none of the weapons Joseph Timbery had used or any other physical evidence except for photographs they had taken—and we found out before the start of the trial even some of those were missing. Fortunately they turned up in time to be submitted as evidence.

In the words of Scott Johnson, the officer who ended up running the police side of the case and who stood by me every step of the way, I was the crime scene, the victim and the witness, all rolled into one. It wouldn't matter how many dreadful things Joseph Timbery had done to me if I couldn't make the jury see the truth of the matter. It all came down to me and I had to be stronger than I'd ever been before in my life.

I was determined not to feel intimidated by the process. Anyone who hasn't experienced a trial would be amazed at how technical and long-winded it is, with all the legal jargon flying around. It's often hard to make any sense at all out of what the lawyers and judges are saying to each other. Crime shows like *Law & Order*, my favourite, get the confrontation part of it right, but that's about it. Sometimes it's hard to understand the lawyers even when they're talking right to you. When that happened, and it happened often, I'd say straight out, 'I don't understand what you're saying.' I'd turn to the judge for help and he'd direct them to be clearer, saying, 'Break it down into normal English.'

The Crown prosecutor led me through my evidence, meaning he asked me questions and I answered them, starting with how long I'd known the Timbery family and when the relationship with Joseph Timbery started. All the basics. Then he asked me about the assaults and rapes, going through the events in chronological order. I had to say out loud, in front of all those people, things like, 'He was trying to place a VO5 mousse bottle into my vagina,' and the Crown prosecutor had to ask me things like, 'Did you give him permission to put that bottle inside your vagina?'

It was so hard to sit there with everyone looking at me, talking about these experiences. I tried my hardest to stay calm, but the tears came again. I was so embarrassed and in emotional turmoil. I was crying so much I couldn't answer the next question. For the first time, but not the last, the judge kindly adjourned so that I could take a minute to recover.

We started again, going through each of the incidents in detail: what Joe had said and done, what I'd said and done, how big the wood-carving chisel and the wooden bat were and what they looked like—every little thing had to be spelled out so there could be no uncertainty in the jury's minds. It was an exhausting afternoon, but at least we were underway.

The next day I was sworn in again and continued giving my evidence for hour after hour, with a few short breaks whenever I became too distressed. There was yet more detail and dozens of exchanges like this one. Crown prosecutor: 'When he said "Suck my cock," where was he?' Me: 'He was standing in front of me, over the top of me.' And this one. Crown prosecutor: 'Did you give him permission to turn you over onto your stomach and have anal sex?' Me: 'No.' God, my dad was sitting there listening to all this. But worse was the fact that Joseph Timbery smirked at every mention of sexual things, and his family were laughing and smirking along, jiggling around in their seats, trying to get me to look at them.

At different stages both John and my dad had to leave the courtroom because they were getting so agitated at what they were hearing they almost wanted to take justice into their own hands. They went outside and cooled off for a while, then were able to come back in. I could tell Mum was really distressed too. I just focused my attention on the jury. I listened to the prosecutor's questions, then half-turned when I answered and spoke directly to those twelve men and women. They were the ones who held my life in their hands; at least that was the way I saw it.

At those times when it got too hard to say out loud what had been done to me while looking at someone, I found a spot on the wall and just focused on it until I was able to turn back to the jury. Over and over I told myself, 'The truth will set you free.'

At lunchtime I was allowed to be with my family as long as we didn't discuss the case; my barrister still hadn't decided if he was going to call them as witnesses, which I found frustrating. So most days Josie, Sam Smith, Scott Johnson, my family and I went out to a cheap Chinese place around the corner and got a five-dollar lunch. I would call the childcare centre to check on the girls, and try to relieve the aches that came from sitting in court with such a big pregnant belly. We spoke about everything but the case. I felt shattered and drained but the others would crack jokes and act silly, trying to ease the tension for me. By the end of the trial the owner was practically starting to get our meals ready as we walked in the door, he'd served us so often.

It was an all too brief break. Some days it felt like we'd barely sat down before I had to pick myself back up again and steel myself and go back to the court for more.

From time to time the jury and I also had to leave the courtroom so that some legal argy-bargy could be worked out between the two barristers and the judge over technical points of law. We all had to troop out, them off to the jury room and me to the witness room, then troop back again when we were called. It took all that second day to get through the rest of my evidence-in-chief. That was a Valentine's Day I was glad to see the end of.

I did try going to an AA meeting once during the trial. There had been stories about the case in the newspapers, and everyone knew what was going on and who I was. The minute I walked into the room I was aware of people starting to whisper and look at me, saying, 'That's that girl who was in the paper.' So much for the 'Anonymous' part. I felt totally exposed, and knew I couldn't go back until it was all over.

At the end of a court day it was really only my kids that kept me going. If it had been the bad old days I'd have reacted to so much stress by reaching straight for a bong. I could still feel the lure of that old habit. Not alcohol—that urge really had left me. But I didn't want to hang around anywhere when court was adjourned for the day; I wanted to get inside and close my own door against all the temptations.

I might have felt the old call, but there was no way I was going to give in. Being a mother meant I just had to take care of all the things children need when I got back home each afternoon. I was fine being around the kids, but any other company was really hard to take, even John and Mum and Dad. As much as I appreciated them being there for me, I didn't want to be around anyone and I'd often just go away from them, into another room to be on my own.

The nights, once the kids had gone to bed, were the worst. I just couldn't sleep so I walked around the house drinking coffee for hours and hours in the middle of the night. I'd try to watch TV but I couldn't relax. John was sleeping peacefully, the kids were off in dreamland, it was just me and my mind that wouldn't close down. I'd think, 'I can't take any more, I can't go through with this.' Then I'd tell myself I couldn't crumble now, I'd come so far. Round and round it went. Those nights felt endless.

Wednesday 15 February I was on the stand again, but this time it was the defence's turn to ask me about what had happened—the cross-examination. Before he started asking questions, the defence barrister said to me, 'I apologise at the outset if I am going to upset you.' Then he launched in. His first line of questioning was about my alcohol and drug use over the years. The Crown team had told me to expect that. For an hour and a half—twenty pages it takes up in the court transcripts—he asked me over and over again about how much I had consumed, and about the assaults I had been treated for and the fact that I had not reported the sexual assaults at the time. On and on he went, pushing me on my substance abuse and the fact that I hadn't officially reported the sexual assaults in detail before my statement to Graham Sims. The shame and fear that keeps many rape victims from revealing what happened to them is very well known, but you wouldn't have thought so, going by his questions.

CAROL SIMON: Lani really had no idea what she was in for with that trial, none of us did. We were all there for her, every day. On that first day in the courtroom we were sitting at one end and the Timberys were sitting at the other. The way they were pulling faces and giggling and poking each other, it was quite horrible. Lani was in tears and we were in tears.

I've supported people at court, though not with those serious charges. But I'll never, ever, ever forget how his barrister was to her. He was horrible. The stuff that he said to her, it was horrific. He accused her of being the instigator of the violence, and said, 'He didn't rape you, you wanted him to do that to you.' It was horrible. No woman should have to go through that. It was quite horrible.

It just goes to show how strong she is, that she could sit there. To me, the interrogation was like she was being attacked and assaulted and abused all over again, this time by the legal system. Anyone else would have broken down and been sobbing. She was crying, and she used to come out and swear as she does. But she was strong. She'd say, 'They're not going to get me.'

What she had to tell about was explicit, really, really explicit. The night after that first day when a lot of stuff had come up, I couldn't sleep. I remember saying to Kath, 'It should be a closed court.' And Rory was in there, sitting and listening to what happened to his daughter. He said, 'I'm her father, I'm supposed to have protected her.' Kathy said, 'I'm her mother, I'm supposed to have looked after her.' They felt angry towards him, guilty towards Lani. It was traumatic for them. Kath would have to get up and walk out. Rory would have to get up and walk out because they were feeling the anger and the strain of everything and feeling Lani's suffering.

RORY BRENNAN: In the lead-up to the trial Lani was upset and agitated, wondering, 'Should I go on with it?' Most of the family thought it would be a waste of time, he'd just walk away. But in the end she was adamant she was going to do it. She's a very strong person. If anybody could do it, it would be Lani.

Sitting in that courtroom was pretty intense. I would have liked to grab Joe Timbery by the throat and kill him on the spot. When the bloke representing him started cross-examining Lani, I lasted half an hour. He was giving it to her like Joe was the victim and she was the bad one. And the way they ridiculed her, you know, she was an alcoholic, she was a drug addict. I was really getting worked up so I left. But Lani kept going. She was strong as anything.

JOSEPHINE CASHMAN: During the trial, Lani was completely stressed. She must have called on every part of her strength, and John was supporting her. During the cross-examination what they did was humiliate her because of her being in rehab. She just had to keep her cool. If you're too upset you can't concentrate on the question.

We're not allowed to coach witnesses. We're not allowed to say, 'If they say this to you, answer this way.' That would be completely unethical. We just told her, 'Think about the question before you answer and stick to the topic. Tell the truth.' She's done so much AA work and that's what I think really helped her. In AA you have to get up and tell your story all the time. If she hadn't done that, she probably wouldn't have been as good as she was at getting up and telling her story in court.

Being in a trial is like running a marathon. You just have to hold on for dear life. And whatever happens, you have to cope with it. I had to tell Lani there is always the possibility someone can be found not guilty. You have to keep hope, but you have to be realistic with the victim. 'Beyond a reasonable doubt' is a very high standard, and it is so because if you're going to lock someone away for years and years the community wants to make sure that's the right decision.

The defence barrister continued with his aggressive approach. On it went this way until the late morning break and only after we came back did the Crown prosecutor ask the judge to close the court. This means that everyone except the court officers, the witness, the Witness Assistance Officer and the accused had to leave. It was Sam Smith who pointed out to my barrister that this should have been done right from the start. The law had been changed a while before so that when a witness was giving evidence about sexual assault, all the court spectators had to leave. As soon as he was asked, the judge did it, saying he hadn't been aware of the change to the law—but meanwhile I'd already spent two and a half days on the stand with the Timbery family among the spectators, listening to my evidence.

Chapter Thirteen

The fourth day of the trial continued with the defence barrister cross-examining me on my evidence, but not before he had objected to the fact that a trainee Witness Assistance Officer was accompanying Sam Smith in court—he claimed this might lead to an unfair trial because the jury would see me with two support people and contrast that with Joe, the accused, being accompanied by a prison guard. Again, the judge was having none of it.

The defence barrister grilled me about every incident, asking me something, then asking me again in a different way and again in another way. He seemed to be hoping to catch me out, throwing dates at me and mixing up things from one statement with another. He suggested that I was lying the whole time, saying that perhaps I'd made the marks around my own throat in the photographs taken by the police on 26 December 2000. Interrogating me about the scar on my shoulder from when Joe had attacked me with the chisel, he said that it 'is a pimple, isn't it?'

I just stuck to the truth and held my focus on the jury. I could tell the majority of them were sympathetic to me. There were a couple of the men I couldn't read so well, but the way the women looked me in the eye, I could tell they knew I wasn't lying. Some of them cried, listening to my testimony.

The cross-examination went all through the rest of that Thursday afternoon, and then the court was adjourned until Monday. There was no easing into things when we started again: the cross-examination resumed more fiercely than ever. Asking me about the cut on my leg, the one that Joe Timbery had made with the edge of a broken plate, the one that went down to the muscle and needed thirty-four stitches to close the wound, the defence barrister said, 'I put it to you that that cut on your leg was brought [about] by you using some instrument, a plate or whatever, because you were in need of drugs and you would get them at the hospital.' I replied, 'I would not hurt myself like that.' He said, 'You were beside yourself with the need to have more drugs, and you would get them at the hospital at the time I suggest you cut your leg.' I said, 'I would not cut myself like that.' He said, 'Well, it is a matter of whether or not you did.' I said, 'I didn't.' He said, 'You say that you would not?' I said, 'I didn't. I was telling the truth that Joseph did.' He said, 'I put it to you that you did.'

It went on and on like this. Imagine having a conversation like that in real life, outside the courtroom. Imagine how it would make you feel. But I just had to stay calm and on track, and keep on telling what had really happened.

KATHY BRENNAN: When I found out what had really gone on, what she'd been through, it was terrible. I said, 'How could anyone do this, and why? Why didn't you come and see us, why didn't you …' It was awful when she was on the stand getting cross-examined; it was quite brutal. The defence was tearing her up, making out like it was her fault that things happened to her. She was a mess, upset and crying. But as time went on she got stronger.

That barrister was quite arrogant, twisting everything and trying to manipulate her, trying to mix her up. I think the jury picked up on that.

Just before lunch, the jury and I were sent out of the room and the defence barrister told the judge he wanted to call members of the Timbery family to give evidence. This was a big deal because they had been sitting in the court listening to all my evidence on the first two and a half days. There's a very good and obvious reason why witnesses are not allowed in court as spectators, which is that if someone in that situation was intending to lie they'd know exactly what lie they needed to tell in order to contradict an accusation or support a defence argument.

In the afternoon the cross-examination resumed. The defence barrister put it to me that Joseph Timbery never hit me with a hammer, a chisel or any other weapon, that I wanted to have sex with him and he never forced me to have sex against my will, and that the whole case was a vendetta against Joe Timbery that I had come up with because he had broken up with me. At one point, trying to deal with it all, I started weeping. The judge asked me if I wanted to stop, but I wanted to keep going—the more we got through each day the sooner all this would end.

The barrister said, 'You are tearful at the moment, aren't you?' 'Yes,' I said. 'You are tearful at the moment when I raised about the breakup between you both,' he went on. 'That's not true,' I answered. 'It is very hard, this trial. Very hard to say what has happened.' 'If you are trying to get even with him because you feel that he tossed you out, if this is your way of getting even, it would be very hard, would it not?' the barrister persisted. I replied, 'He has done the wrong things to me and he should be judged on that.'

On and on it went, all the rest of Monday and again when we resumed on Tuesday morning. Having told me that I'd lied about there being any violence at all, the defence barrister now said to me, 'Your relationship with Joseph Timbery, I suggest in respect of violence, was one that turned you on. What do you say about that?' I said simply, 'No, that is not true.' 'Turned you on sexually?' 'No.' It was sickening, but it just had to be endured.

The jury and I were sent outside while another conversation took place between the lawyers and the judge about the issue of using Timbery family members as defence witnesses. The defence barrister was talking about their mistrust of the police and the fact that one of Joe's brothers had been arrested outside the court on an outstanding matter when he had come to watch the case. Talking to the judge about the likelihood or otherwise of any of the Timberys actually appearing if they were asked to, he chose to put it this way: '… we have got indigenous people. They just don't think like us, Your Honour, with respect.' With respect? Yeah, right.

Finally, late in the morning, the cross-examination was over. The Crown prosecutor then got to re-examine me, meaning he could ask me to give answers on areas where the defence had sought to cast doubt—clarifying my sobriety, the precise order of events on Christmas Day 2000 and that kind of thing.

The next step in the trial was to call witnesses, and because I'd finished giving evidence the court was allowed to be reopened to spectators.

The first witness was Dr Ian Chung, the doctor I'd seen when I was admitted to detox. The Crown prosecutor led him through my drug and alcohol history and the injuries that were evident when he examined me. Then the defence barrister cross-examined the doctor, saying to him at one point, 'Based on the history of cannabis use that you obtained, what would you say to the suggestion that Ms Brennan self-harmed herself in order so that she could be admitted to hospital and undergo surgery in order to obtain the analgesia and anaesthetics that she is recorded as having obtained on the twenty-ninth of June?'

Dr Chung replied, 'It would be extraordinarily unlikely that anyone would seek to have admission to hospital to obtain a drug whilst in the hospital that in any way could have a similar action to their drug of addiction. I would believe extremely strongly that this is known to all drug addicts.' At another point, the defence barrister asked about the scars visible in the police photos, specifically the chisel scar that he'd previously tried to claim was a pimple. Asked to describe what he saw in the photo, Dr Chung said it looked like either a scar or an intradermal cyst. The barrister tried to push the pimple idea again. Dr Chung explained that this kind of cyst could be formed when the body heals a wound and that, yes, it could be the kind of wound caused by a chisel.

Then the defence barrister moved on to whether my injuries could have been caused by me falling over drunk. He had no luck there, either. He asked if a person consuming nearly twelve beers each day was 'likely to fall over from time to time'. Dr Chung replied, 'No, under that circumstance their tolerance would be quite high and they would be quite capable of walking quite soberly and not having anything happen to them.'

The next day there was another doctor witness, this time giving evidence about the treatment I'd received at the Prince of Wales Hospital. That went right through until just before 4 pm, when I was recalled to the stand for more cross-examination on things that had arisen from the medical history. On the next day, Thursday, officially the eighth day of the trial but in fact the seventeenth day since we had first come to court, the judge acknowledged that proceedings were going to run all through the following week and probably into the one after. Meanwhile, I was closer and closer to my due date.

I was brought to the stand yet again for more cross-examination about the assaults and the fact that in my fear I had told lies to the police about how I'd been injured. Then the first of the police witnesses appeared; these were the officers who had come on 25 June 2000, when Joseph Timbery was bashing me in the vestibule of the flats near his sister's place. Then came Shane Smith, the officer who had taken my unsigned statement on 26 December. Next it was Vanessa Burns (who had since married and changed her surname), the domestic violence officer who had taken a more extensive statement three months later, after I was back from rehab, and who had arranged for me to go in and make my final statement and who I'd stayed in contact with, trying to find out what was happening about the charges.

That evening when we got home, the deadlock had been taken off my door. The house was open. Mum, who had a key, had picked up the girls and beaten me home. As I walked up to the door I realised something didn't look right. As I got closer I could see the lock had been taken out and when I swung the front door open I could see it lying on the hall floor. I called out to Mum who came down as though nothing was wrong. I pointed to the lock and asked her what was going on. She said it had been like that when she arrived and she thought it was something I'd arranged.

Fear surged through me. Someone had been here, had broken in to my home. The back door lock was wrecked too. We quickly moved through the house, checking every room. Nothing was taken, nothing was moved, but a very clear message had been sent: we know where you are and you are not safe. I was deeply shaken, but I wasn't about to walk away from my pursuit of justice. Dad and Aunty Carol and Koorine arrived, as they generally did at the end of a court day. Everyone was rattled. I called the police first, then the Department of Housing emergency number. They arranged to send a locksmith and everyone stayed until he had been and gone, leaving new deadlocks on both doors. They each asked me if I wanted to stay with one of them, but John and I said we'd be fine there now the locks had been repaired. I don't think I closed my eyes that night, though. I shook for hours.

The next day's first witness was Patsy Gray, who had come to see me at Selah. Her evidence was crucial because during that visit I had told her that I had been raped. Other than saying to Vanessa Burns that something else had happened but I couldn't talk about it, and answering yes when she asked if it was sexual, Patsy was the only person I had spoken to about the rapes before I was ready to make my third statement. The defence was making a huge deal of the fact that I hadn't brought up the rapes at the time when I first saw the police—in other words, suggesting that I had made them up long afterwards. Patsy could confirm to the jury that I had opened up to her in early 2001, and she told them how distressed and fearful I'd been in talking about what had happened.

Then Graham Sims, the police officer who had taken my statement in May 2002, appeared. He said the reason he hadn't searched for the weapons I'd mentioned in my description of the attacks was that when he went to the house in Murrong Place he had not been allowed in, and he hadn't applied for a search warrant because 'considering the limitations of the Search Warrants Act, I believed that any application to a magistrate or a chamber magistrate would be unsuccessful and I based that on the grounds that I've been taking out search warrants for fourteen years in the police and I'm well versed in taking search warrants out for all types of matters including sexual assaults and historical sexual assaults …'

The conclusion of his testimony marked the end of the Crown's case. The court adjourned for the weekend, but we were still a long way from the finish line.

On Monday, when we resumed, it was time for the defence to present its case. Joseph Timbery's barrister told the jury they would be hearing from Joe's sister, my former friend and schoolmate, and that she would say that far from a relationship characterised by brutality, her brother and I were 'quite lovey-dovey, they were friends, they were companions'. He also told them 'the Timberys are a proud group of young people, in persons and family because they are of a tribe at La Perouse and they are of the tribe that welcomed Captain Cook in 1788'. (He meant 1770.) Then he called the accused to the stand. Like everyone who would give evidence, Joseph Timbery was required to swear to tell the truth. For whatever that was worth.

He said none of the assaults or rapes had happened. He said we 'went to movies and stuff together. You know, did a lot of things just like normal relationships do'. And, 'It's obvious we loved each other.' In his version, I started the arguments and I was the jealous, controlling one. 'I wasn't allowed to do anything,' he said. Under oath.

He claimed I gave him black eyes and cut my own leg. At his barrister's questioning he described in detail the foreplay and the willing sex that he claimed was all that went on. He said, 'I don't threaten women for sex. I'm not like that, I don't. I don't abuse women, I look after them, if anything.' His barrister asked, 'Were you brought up with that sort of respect or not?' Joe said, 'Yes, I was.' On it went like that, all the rest of that day. The next day started with more of the same. Joe said the sofa on which I testified he had broken the plate to cut my leg was entirely padded, with soft arms. Not everyone in his camp had been briefed on this, it turned out.

They called me back onto the stand that day to address some things Timbery family members had claimed in statements given to the defence. Normally they would leave this until after the accused's evidence was all finished, but because I was so close to giving birth, no one wanted to take the risk. As the Crown prosecutor put it, 'I think everyone is agreed that we don't want another trial, Your Honour.'

Joseph's mother had suddenly turned up a statutory declaration which she said he had given to her some years before. It was supposedly written and signed by me, and said that the bashing that had happened near his sister's flat wasn't Joseph Timbery's doing. I looked at it for the first time in court and gave evidence that it wasn't my signature and I hadn't written it. Joe also came up with a ridiculous story about me having picked up a typewriter at the police station where we'd been taken immediately after the bashing and thrown it on the ground.

His sister claimed that I hadn't been invited to Petra's party the night my leg was slashed but I'd tried to force my way into going, that at no stage that night did she see blood anywhere in the house at Murrong Place, and that I was the aggressive one in the relationship. Again, under oath, I simply told what had really happened that night and throughout the relationship.

There was tension between the judge and the defence barrister throughout the trial, and this day it came to a head while the barrister was cross-examining me on the claims made by the Timberys. In the absence of the jury, the judge said, 'I want to put something on record. [The defence barrister] in the presence of the jury has suggested that I am biased. I wish to place on record that this is entirely untrue. [The defence barrister] will be quite aware that it was I who raised a number of matters which he had forgotten about for cross-examination yesterday and the day before. The comment was totally unwarranted.'

Soon after, a problem arose with the Crown prosecutor too. The defence had shown me recent photographs of Murrong Place and asked me various things about the rooms. The Crown then showed me the photographs again and asked me about plaster patches on the wall. I said that previously those had been holes punched and kicked in the walls by Joseph Timbery. The judge told the Crown prosecutor this was against the rules of what was allowed because it testified to his 'violent disposition'. It might be true that Joe had a history of violence, but you weren't allowed to say it because it didn't directly relate to these charges. The judge said, 'I think all I can do is tell the jury to put it all out of their mind and wait for the Court of Criminal Appeal to order a new trial.' The defence barrister asked the judge at this point to discharge the jury. He didn't do that, but he did tell the jury to disregard everything they'd heard about Joseph Timbery's actions in the discussion of the photographs.

Then Timbery came back on the stand and spent the rest of the afternoon telling more fairy stories about how I'd hurt myself and he'd done nothing wrong, other than having 'backhanded' me once and given me a black eye. The case resumed briefly on Thursday morning and then again on Friday morning, when the judge told the jury they had to disregard one of the accused's statements: 'I don't threaten women for sex. I'm not like that.' Leaving this in as evidence opened up a black hole for the defence—it allowed the Crown to talk about Joseph Timbery's character, so things like him punching the walls would be okay to reveal, and so would various of his previous criminal activities. No wonder the defence was withdrawing it.

Then it was the Crown's turn to cross-examine Timbery. In answer to the Crown saying, 'I put it to you that you used to hit Lani on a number of occasions and in particular on those occasions that are the subject of the indictment?', he replied, 'Well if for starters a girl was getting hit by a baseball bat by her boyfriend, why would she stick around anyway ...'

I didn't hear any of this. I had something even more important to attend to that day: the birth by caesarean of my fourth daughter, Kiani. The judge had given me permission to not attend court until I was up to going back, but I was determined not to cause any hiccups by my absence. Kiani's birth happened as scheduled and without drama. We gave her the middle names Kathy Carol, after my mum and Aunty Carol, who were so staunch by my side during the trial. As before, I didn't stay in hospital for the recommended seven days. I had somewhere I needed to be. I discharged myself on the Monday morning, only three days after

Kiani's birth, and went straight back to court. It was just as well, because they needed me back on the stand to counter some more lies about what had happened.

The looks on the faces of the judge and jury when I walked back in was classic. The judge knew why I'd been away on Friday, of course, and had informed the jury. I'd been told I could have applied for a three-month break in the trial, under the circumstances, but I wasn't going to let anything derail it now. Still, until the moment I arrived I don't think anyone really believed I'd be back so soon. Some of them had their eyes nearly popping out of their heads.

I was glad I was there, but it wasn't easy, emotionally or physically. Those first days after birth should be a really special time of connection and bonding between mother and baby. I took breaks to breastfeed and kept Kiani with me whenever I wasn't actually on the stand, but it wasn't the same as being able to relax and focus only on her. When I was on the stand, Mum or Samantha Smith or Aunty Carol would hold my beautiful little newborn, rocking her gently and, if she started to cry, quietly getting up and taking her out of the courtroom until she settled again.

I refused the painkillers they give you as standard procedure after you've had a caesarean—it is major abdominal surgery, after all. Having to sit there for eight hours with stitches and dressings and nothing to relieve the pain was really hard, but the last thing I wanted was for the defence to turn around and say, 'Here's this former addict who's supposed to have cleaned up, but she's popping pills now on the stand—how can we trust what she says?' So I just copped it, sober and clean.

On Tuesday, the defence witnesses took the stand—first Joe's married sister, then his de facto sister-in-law, who had lived at

Murrong Place with her children, then his brother. His sister said her brother had never bashed me, that we hadn't been at her place before the 25 June 2000 attack, and that on 25 June I hadn't been wearing the clothes in which I was photographed by the police. Joe's sister-in-law took the stand with two black eyes. She got very muddled, trying to keep her story straight on what dates she was living at Murrong Place. No, she didn't hear any violence—she would have gone to help if she had, she said. Without realising the importance of what she was saying, she testified that the lounge suite at the house did indeed have wooden arms. His brother ran the same line as the others—he hadn't seen or heard anything amiss.

They were the last witnesses; it was time for the concluding addresses from both sides. The Crown prosecutor went first. He reminded the jury of the seriousness of the charges, of the nonsensical argument that I had cut my own leg and how that had been denied by me and rejected by Dr Chung, and so on through the rest of the defence's explanations for what might have happened to me if it wasn't done by Joe Timbery. He said, 'At the end of the day, I submit that you will accept her evidence. She's had the blowtorch applied to her and she has come through unshaken, indeed extremely strong. She was a very good witness, a very credible witness, and a very steadfast witness.'

The defence barrister then gave his address, in which he said I'd been a drunk and a drug user, so how could my memories be reliable; that 'we wonder what may be the motive for all these outrageous suggestions that she is making against this man'; and urged the jury to 'think about what does allow Lani Brennan to tick, is it a payback on this man?'

Finally, on Thursday 9 March the jury retired to consider their verdict. There was no way of knowing how long it would take. Josie Cashman told me that a trial running longer than anticipated is generally taken to be a bad sign in terms of securing a conviction, yet we had felt the sympathy from the jury. It was impossible to know which way the decision might go. There are no words to describe the tension of those days as we waited and waited.

On the following Monday, 13 March, the jury sent the judge a note which said they had reached a unanimous verdict on six counts but not the others, and could he advise them what to do. The laws in New South Wales have since changed to allow a majority verdict, but at the time a jury's decision had to be unanimous. Both prosecution and defence agreed with the judge that the jury needed more time—it was far too soon to dismiss them. The judge had the jury brought back into the courtroom and said something to them that seemed pretty reasonable at the time, but turned out to be a time bomb, just waiting to explode.

He said, 'Ultimately, if you cannot agree, I will take the verdicts on the six counts that you have agreed and discharge you as to the rest and there would have to be a retrial of the other seventeen counts ... In light of that, members of the jury, I urge you, I suppose I can say I plead with you, please go out and keep trying ... Do not be concerned about the amount of time it takes. Trials of this nature often take a number of days for a jury to reach a verdict, but my direction to you is please continue your deliberations. And you ask what the next step is, ultimately to discharge you and have another trial on these matters, a matter which in a trial of four weeks would be just terrible. So I ask you to retire again and keep going.'

The following afternoon came the call we'd been waiting so anxiously for—the jury had reached a verdict. It was more than five weeks since the court proceedings had begun. For the first time, I sat in the body of the court instead of on the stand. Joseph Timbery was staring at me. I was trying not to panic, thinking, 'Has this all been worth it? After everything I've been through he might still just walk. And if he does, he's going to kill me.' The police had spoken to me about going into witness protection if he did get off, but I didn't feel confident that would be enough. We'd already seen what had happened with the supposed non-publication of my address on the AVO the Timbery family members had applied for, and besides, my whole extended family couldn't go into witness protection. I knew what Joe was capable of and how malicious he was. I could hardly breathe.

Finally the foreman stood up and one by one the judge's associate led him through the charges, asking for each, 'What is your verdict; is the accused guilty or not guilty?' One by one he answered: 'Guilty … Guilty … Not guilty …' My ears were ringing, it was hard to take in what he was saying. Scott Johnson was making notes on his copy of the indictment and it was only when he quickly explained it to me after the last verdict was spoken that I understood what had happened.

On Charges 1 and 2, the malicious wounding and rape on 16 April 2000: guilty. On Charge 3, aggravated rape on 12 May that year: not guilty. On Charge 4, the alternative charge of assault on that same occasion: guilty. On Charge 5, rape on that same date: not guilty. On Charge 6, aggravated rape between 1 May and 30 May: guilty. On Charges 7 and 8, aggravated rapes on 18 May: guilty. On Charge 9, the 25 June bashing: guilty. On Charges 10, 11 and 12, aggravated rapes on 21 August: guilty. On Charge 13, a separate rape on that same date: not guilty. On

Charge 14, rape on 29 September, the night of Petra's party: not guilty. On Charge 15, malicious wounding with the plate that night: guilty. Charges 16 to 22: not guilty. Charge 23, aggravated rape on Christmas Day: guilty.

CAROL SIMON: When we walked in to hear the verdict I thought, 'Oh no, nothing's going to happen, he's going to get off.' He was quite cocky when he came in, a bit gung-ho, moving around, looking at everyone with a bit of a smile on his face. When they were reading the verdict out, I didn't understand it. We were all saying, 'What's going on? What's going on?' It wasn't until they said the final sentence that we all looked at each other. I don't think we realised until right then at the end that he was found guilty. We walked out still stunned, and then all of a sudden everyone was crying and cuddling and shaking. It was unbelievable.

JOSEPHINE CASHMAN: I was happy with the verdict. It didn't matter that there were some not-guilty findings. It had taken place so long ago and, as I say, beyond reasonable doubt is a high standard. There were so many counts. If they didn't believe her they wouldn't have found him guilty of anything. Any charge where there was medical corroboration or medical evidence got a 'guilty'.

RORY BRENNAN: My mother had dementia and other medical problems, she was near dead during the trial, but I remember her asking, 'Did that mongrel get found guilty?' I was able to tell her yes, and she was happy.

Timbery been found guilty on ten very serious charges. I was laughing and crying at the same time, and people were hugging me. We still had to wait for the sentence, and that would take some months, but the guilty finding meant I had closure at last.

Or so I thought.

Chapter Fourteen

With Joseph Timbery safely behind bars awaiting sentence, life should finally have been peaceful. But instead of settling down after the verdict, the level of tension increased. There were threatening, supposedly anonymous, phone calls to my home and disturbing encounters with members of the Timbery family when we ran into them locally. My address had been leaked, my family was still being threatened. When would it all end?

As much as I'd enjoyed my Daceyville house, I no longer felt safe there. Then came the final straw: the house was broken into twice in two days. Nothing was taken, the intent was just to terrorise us. It worked.

In April 2006, the month after the jury had spoken, the police stepped in. Both Scott Johnson and Inspector Eddie Bosch of Maroubra police sent letters to the Department of Housing supporting an urgent request for my emergency relocation. Scott's letter explained the trial and verdict in brief, then said: 'During the trial the Timbery family made allegations towards the Brennan family which were found to be untrue and I witnessed these untruths. The Timbery family in an effort to upset Lani Brennan during the trial took out personal violence orders on her and her family.' He concluded: 'I believe that the Timbery family may try and seek revenge upon Lani Brennan for the long jail sentence that Joseph Timbery will receive.'

In his letter, Inspector Bosch wrote: 'Ms Brennan has been harassed by the family of the above mentioned offender when she has frequented such places as the local shops, the local beach and the court. This family is known to the police. Recently phone calls of a harassing and threatening nature have been received by Ms Brennan at her Daceyville address.'

The department swung into action, but even that was not without its drama. One day the removalist truck they had sent pulled up—I hadn't even known it was coming. They said, 'We're here to move you.' 'When?' 'Now.' We had to pack up everything right then and there. Because the new place was a flat, not a house, we also had to leave our pets behind, which upset us all, especially the kids. Mum said she'd take my dog, Nala. I quickly phoned around to find someone who could look after our two cats. In the end I found a neighbour who agreed to take one, but we had to leave the other in an animal shelter until we could reclaim her.

The truck made two trips. First one load, which they moved into the three-bedroom flat that was intended to be the new home for the six of us, then a second load, this time with us following in the car. They wouldn't give me the address before we set out—it was their security protocol—so I just could not believe where we pulled up. I called the case officer and said, 'Geez, do you know where you just put me?' It was behind Joe's married sister's place, so close we were almost sharing a back fence. Most of the second truckload wouldn't even fit in the flat anyway, so I left the furniture that was already in there, hurriedly arranged for the rest to go into storage, and went with John and the girls to stay with Mum until something else could be sorted out.

From Mum's we went on to a safe house in the eastern suburbs, and I was supplied with an emergency call buzzer to wear around my neck: if anything happened I had only to press it and help would be on the way.

On 30 July, my beloved grandmother died. Wha Wha had been in a nursing home for a while now; she had dementia, and a medical check-up after she'd had a fall there revealed she also had cancer. We'd known for a few months that she was dying, so the whole family had tried to spend as much time with her as possible, making her comfortable and keeping her company. Dad was really amazing, going in to see her pretty much every day and staying for hours, trying to help her eat and just being there for her. Their relationship was an incredible example of change and forgiveness.

For obvious reasons I saw very few people during the period when I was living in the safe house, but someone I was in close contact with was Genevieve Grieves. Genevieve was an oral historian and TV producer who was moving into filmmaking and working with Blackfella Films, a documentary-making company with a good reputation. She also happened to be the sister of Josephine Cashman, the DPP solicitor who had been such a valuable support during the trial. Josie had mentioned my story to Genevieve, thinking it might interest her as a possible subject. It did. (Having put us in contact, Josie then had nothing further to do with the project for ethical reasons.)

Genevieve told me my story was one worth telling, though the outcome of the trial would determine whether it was really going to be possible to make it work. She'd never made a documentary before, but from our first meeting I trusted and agreed to work with her. Once the guilty verdict was delivered, she knew the project was a goer. The first step was for her to do some filming with me, getting just enough footage to attract funding for a full-scale documentary. She interviewed me talking about my life on camera, then went away to edit the footage into a form that would get potential investors interested.

We were still waiting for the sentence, but there was nothing we could do to hurry the process, so John and I just got on with living our lives and raising our family. In due course, the pre-sentencing hearing was set for the second week of August. I appeared and presented my victim impact statement in person. In part it said: 'I have permanent scars all over my body from these assaults, including scars on my back, shoulders, a wired jaw, legs, cheekbones and several scars on my face which are all visible. Because of the scars I cover my body. I'm ashamed to wear some clothes as people tend to ask about the scars. These scars are a constant reminder of the assaults and they are a permanent reminder of all these bad memories ...

'Before the trial my family never knew of the extent of what had happened to me. My father especially felt guilt and shame that he wasn't able to protect me as he didn't understand what had happened to me ...

'My current relationship has been affected by what Joseph Timbery has done to me. I met my current partner, John, after I left rehab and I was always waiting for him to hit me, because I thought that this is what would happen ... It still feels like my current relationship is too good to be true. I have a loving relationship with four beautiful children, and our family's life is in a clean, loving, drug- and alcohol-free environment. I never thought a relationship could be like this.

'I was heavily pregnant during the trial and I was having problems with the baby. Her heart rate was going very fast and they thought that I was going to go into labour ... The stress of being cross-examined and being recalled so many times throughout the trial [meant] I felt that I was the one on trial, not Joseph ...

'As an Aboriginal woman I had to stand up and say no ... I feel justice has been served and I believe justice needs to be seen and done in Aboriginal communities. I will never be silenced.'

At the time I didn't know about the defence's pre-sentence legal manoeuvrings in detail, and I'm glad about that. It would have been very hard to handle some of what went on. For instance, immediately after I finished giving this victim impact statement and left the stand, the defence barrister raised the issue of my children with the judge and said the fact that I had gone on to form a new relationship and find happiness showed that the rapes hadn't really affected me as badly as all that because there was no 'frigidity'. The judge pointed out that they had just heard about the emotional difficulties I had in developing trust with John, but the barrister kept on and on. Even now, the lack of compassion appals me. What would he have said if he'd known that by this time I was newly pregnant again?

A little later in the proceedings the defence barrister suggested that Timbery's sentence should be less severe because 'there was a personality clash between both of them' and also, 'when one considers the aggravating circumstances and factors attributable to the victim's behaviour'. The judge responded, 'I just don't know what she did to contribute to this, I suppose apart from staying there.' The defence barrister then said his client was 'unusual, he's different, he's a tribal warrior' and '[w]e put forward that he has had partly himself to blame—the system as well, perhaps—but he's had significant disability through the lack of proper education, through the availability of drugs in the community'.

To top it all off, he submitted that the sentences for the various offences should be served concurrently (at the same time) rather than cumulatively (one after the other) because, in part, 'of the closeness of the relationship between the two young Aboriginal people'. In other words he was saying that being bashed and raped in the context of domestic violence isn't as serious as it would be if you were attacked in the street by a stranger.

> JOSEPHINE CASHMAN: Before the sentencing the defence served us a psych report on Timbery saying he was at low risk of reoffending. If someone is judged low risk, they'd get an earlier non-parole period. But I'd gone through his criminal history and we pulled out a psych statement relating to another woman; it wasn't a sexual assault but it was a similar modus operandi—the way he spoke to her, etcetera. So I subpoenaed the psych expert who did the defence report. We cross-examined her and handed up the facts on the other assault and asked, 'Do you still say he's at low risk of reoffending?'
>
> Most sex offenders have to have a psych assessment to determine their risk of reoffending. But if the expert who does the assessment is briefed by the defence, they might not have a copy of the criminal history. Timbery told her

he'd never done this kind of thing to anyone else before. But then when we showed her his previous criminal history, she conceded that he was at medium to high risk of reoffending. He also had no contrition going for him. He put Lani through a hell of a trial and he wouldn't face up to his issues. The only thing in his favour was that he was still young. But he was twenty-eight, not a baby.

On Thursday 10 August the sentence was to be handed down. Just before that happened, the judge honoured my request to lift the non-publication order on my name. Maybe by speaking out I could help other women living with violence.

Mum, Dad, Aunty Carol, Koorine, Darryl, Garri, Samantha Smith and Scott Johnson met John and me at the court. The Timbery family was there to see it, too. This time the whole thing went quickly—it only took a matter of minutes, but it seemed to me to be unfolding in slow motion. The judge announced his decisions. Again, it was hard to grasp what was going on because each count on which Joseph Timbery had been found guilty was read out, then the total term to be served was stated (the maximum), then the length of the non-parole period (the minimum) and the date it expired. There were twelve of these to get through.

Scott was again writing it all down as it was announced, adding it up, and at the last count he whispered to me, 'Thirty-three years. He got thirty-three years!' Samantha confirmed it—a total term of thirty-three years with a minimum of twenty-four years in jail—and Josie Cashman said she thought it was the longest sentence ever handed down in Australia for these sorts of crimes. I felt like I was tumbling around inside a washing machine, in a swirl of relief and happiness but still not quite believing what I was hearing. The courtroom erupted. Joe's married sister just lost it. She jumped up and started screaming out. Timbery himself started yelling out too, and tried to jump up from his seat in the dock, but the prison officers must have been ready for him—they grabbed him straight away and surrounded him. Meanwhile my supporters were cheering and embracing one another.

We walked outside, hugging and smiling and a little teary. We were over the moon. I thanked everyone for everything they'd done to get to this point. It had been a long, hard road, but it had all been worth it. Then it was time to say our goodbyes and go home to a houseful of little girls who knew nothing of the Joseph Timberys of this world, and never would, I hoped.

When Genevieve had done the preliminary filming with me she'd asked me about all sorts of things, including how hard it had been to get through the court case and my relief that it was over. I answered her in detail, saying right at the end, 'The last thing I'd want to do is have to go back to trial.' She then edited the footage into a short package that gave a taste of what a full documentary would cover and sent that out to various funding bodies. She also sent me a copy on disk. The day I received it I also got an unexpected phone call: it was Josie Cashman, but she wasn't just calling to catch up. She had some news: Joe Timbery had appealed against his conviction. The closure I thought I'd achieved slipped through my hands, just like that.

Part of me couldn't believe what she was telling me, but another part, the part that always expected the worst, wasn't surprised. During the trial Josie had expressed concern at some of the judge's directions to the jury, and the opening they might provide to the defence to appeal. But months had passed, and I'd put all that to the back of my mind. Now the worst had happened. Well, maybe not the worst—we didn't know if the appeal would succeed, but Josie said based on what she'd heard, there was a good chance of it. If the appeal was upheld, a mistrial would be declared. The convictions would be erased. There might be a new trial.

I flipped between anger and despair. I'd worked so hard at staying positive and staunch. I'd even come to regard as a blessing in disguise the fact that it took so long for Joseph Timbery to get picked up, because that had given me time to heal myself to the point where I could stand up and tell the world what had happened. But finding out that I might have gone through the ordeal of the trial for nothing was just too much.

Josie assured me that if there was a mistrial, the DPP would re-prosecute. I felt I couldn't go through it. I wanted to curl into a ball and disappear. Josie didn't try to push me, but she arranged for me to sit down with her and Scott Johnson to talk things through. I told them, 'I can't do it. I just can't go through it again.' They were sympathetic but they also tried to encourage me, saying, 'It's going to be quicker this time.' I still felt I couldn't face it. They told me that if I wished, they could use recordings of my testimony so I wouldn't have to take the stand. I gave it a lot of thought but eventually I called them and told them no, if there was to be a second trial, I would be there, on the stand. There would be a new jury who knew nothing of what had come before. Recorded testimony might be enough to let them understand what I'd been through, but then again, it might not. If it came to that, I had to somehow find the strength to front up to it all over again.

The appeal itself was based on technical legal grounds, difficult to understand unless you have a law degree. There were ten grounds to the appeal, but only five of them were really important. These were: that the judge erred in summing up the case as one in which the fact that sexual intercourse had occurred in the relationship was not an issue and also by directing the defence counsel to correct that part of his address which suggested sexual intercourse was an issue; that the judge erred in the way he described 'corroboration' to the jury; that the way the judge told the jury they were to deal with charges without corroborating evidence suggested this only applied to sexual assault charges; and that the judge's comments when the jury came back to him saying they could agree on only six counts (he urged them to go back and keep trying in order to avoid another trial) put inappropriate pressure on them and led to a miscarriage of justice. Because it's such a big decision to overturn a conviction, and the Court of Appeals process is very detailed and very slow. No one knew how long it might take. We just had to wait.

My pregnancy progressed well and on 25 May 2007, our fifth daughter, Kirrawahn, was born. We gave her the middle name Maureen, after my beloved grandmother. John and I didn't set out to have so many children, I just kept falling pregnant despite all the different forms of contraception we tried, including the pill and implanted long-term hormone release. But we welcomed and loved each one of our babies and never forgot how lucky we were to have them. Other people react differently. I try not to pay attention to the way some people look at us sideways in the street, their eyes full of judgement about the kind of person who would have so many children. I work hard at not letting it get to me, but I'll have to admit there are days when it's really hard to take.

Genevieve had succeeded in getting funding for the documentary, and she started putting the various pieces into place, seeking approval to get court transcripts and doing other background research. I found out that filmmaking has one thing in common with the legal system: the slowness with which everything happens.

The wheels of justice ground on and there was a legal hearing for the appeal in September 2007. Then finally, on 18 December that year, the judgement came down: those five crucial grounds of the appeal were upheld. A mistrial was declared. Joseph Timbery's convictions from the trial were quashed. The Court of Appeal judges who made the ruling did include this note at the end of their 35-page judgement: '… there has to be a new trial. This is much to be regretted as it will be an ordeal for LB.' The events cast a shadow over Christmas, but John and I tried to keep it to ourselves, so as not to taint the celebration for the girls.

> CAROL SIMON: When the mistrial was declared, that was like a kick in the face. You felt like you'd been let down again by the system. Lani thought, 'Why did I bother?' She started to doubt her own strength. She was talking about witness protection and we were all talking about it—does it just affect her or is it all of us? We all started to think, 'Where are we going to go, what are we going to do, how are we going to live around here if he should win the next time?'
>
> She was starting to come apart. That's when John was her biggest strength. He said, 'No, we're not going to let this get to us. We've been through worse than this. We're going to survive this.' I slept at their place several times,

but he was the one always there, with the nightmares and the crying and everything. Their strength came from each other.

The DPP prepared for a new trial. You can't retry someone on charges of which they've been acquitted, so there were only the twelve charges this time: two of malicious wounding, one of assault occasioning actual bodily harm, one of maliciously inflicting grievous bodily harm, one of sexual intercourse without consent, and seven counts of aggravated sexual assault.

I was nervous and stressed in the lead-up to the second trial, but it was nowhere near as bad as the first time. The trial started on 16 April 2008. There was a new judge and I had a new barrister, female this time, a new solicitor because Josie wasn't available, and a new witness support officer, but everything else was familiar. Scott Johnson was there for me again and I knew what to expect day by day. I was still emotional and it was draining to tell my story again, but I knew I had the strength to get through it.

The whole thing ran much more quickly, and that helped. I felt from the start that the jury could see the truth and understand what I'd been through. Joseph Timbery didn't even take the stand this time. That's his right under the law, but I think the jury drew their own conclusions about his decision—and that's their right. Some of his family testified as witnesses again, but they kept getting caught out contradicting each other's stories. With the first trial it had seemed as if it would never end; this one seemed to fly by. There were only five sitting days and then it was over; the jury retired to consider their decision. That went very quickly too. They were only out a day, and on 24 April we reassembled at the court to hear the verdict.

As had happened at the first trial, they read the charges then announced the verdict. This time it was 'guilty' after 'guilty'. Of the twelve charges, the only one on which Joe was found not guilty was the assault occasioning actual bodily harm. He was convicted of all the rest. I was so relieved and pleased—now the world knew what kind of man Joseph Timbery really was. The sentencing would take some time, but justice had been served.

Normal life resumed and Genevieve went on with her work making the documentary. No one was very comfortable with the idea of appearing on camera. Dad was particularly reluctant because he knew Genevieve wanted him to talk about his own direct experience with domestic violence from the early days of his marriage when he was drinking heavily. As she put it later in the publicity material for the film, she was interested in 'the impact of intergenerational violence within a family and community'. Dad's life all these decades later was so different. He'd worked hard to change and many of the people who knew him now didn't know what he had been like back then. Taking part in the documentary would mean dragging all those skeletons out into public view.

In the end though, he agreed. I'm so glad he did, too. A lot of people have commented to me on how well he comes across. He is a real hero of the story, saving me when I called out to him in my time of greatest need and standing staunchly by me ever since.

Before we started I had no idea how much work goes into those things: they film for hours and hours and might only use a couple of minutes of it. I find it hard to sit still at the best of times, so it was a real challenge for me. It's funny, though, you do forget about everything else and just tell your story. I did, anyway, because Gen made it easy for me to feel like I was just talking to her. (All the people who took part in the doco—Mum, Dad,

John, Aunty Carol, Scott Johnson and Samantha Smith—were filmed separately, so none of us knew what the others had said.)

I was filmed sitting on my own on a spotlit chair in the middle of a room. Beyond that it was all dark, which helped me forget about the camera and sound operators. Gen was off-camera asking me questions (and every now and then coming up and putting powder on my face to blot away the sweat). She made it really easy, saying to me that I could stop any time it became too hard, and only give as much detail as I was comfortable with.

Even though the events I was talking about were the same as the ones I'd been describing in court, the experience was very different. In court, it's all about facts. How I felt didn't come into it. Here, in her gentle and compassionate way, Genevieve was asking me not just what happened but what effect it had on me. The fact that she was so understanding made it easier to open up. I still got emotional at times, as I had done when I was giving evidence in court, but I was okay with that—it would help people understand what I'd been through, and that's what I'd hoped for when I agreed to take part.

The new sentencing date was set for 19 September. In the lead-up I forced the issue of having the suppression order on my name lifted (the new case meant a new order). I'd tried to speak about it with my barrister before the verdict came down, but she was very opposed to it. I never could get a real handle on why, although she kept repeating that keeping my identity secret was for my own good.

But I was determined. I felt even more strongly than I had at the time of the first trial that no one would ever silence me again. It was my story and if I could help even one other woman by letting the world know that you could survive this kind of abuse and eventually put the abuser behind bars, it would be worth it. The way I saw it, everyone who knew me knew what had happened. To look upon my story as something that needed to be kept secret would have made me feel like I was still hiding away from the world, like I was still under Joseph Timbery's control. Dad was staunch in his support of me. It was a bit of a tussle, but eventually the barrister agreed to make the application and the court approved it.

The support team who had been with me all the way through this long, long struggle reassembled at court and we listened as the judge read out the sentence. Again, we were trying to keep track, and make sense of the various maximum and non-parole periods. The sentences had staggered starting dates, taking into account the time Timbery had already served in jail, and the earliest was May 2005, when he'd been picked up on these charges. The judge, who had seen his criminal record, didn't hold back, saying, 'I am not going to mince words here. It is my confident prediction that once released from custody, the offender will harm someone else in a serious way.'

When I realised that the maximum this time around was twenty-four years, I felt shocked and disappointed. It was nine years less than the maximum Joe had been given in the first trial.

Everyone around me was pleased, but I took a while to adjust to the lesser sentence. It was something Josie Cashman said to me when I spoke to her afterwards that helped me. She told me to focus on the non-parole period—the minimum he would serve— not the potential maximum sentence. This was eighteen years (compared to twenty-four years the first time). I would have been happier if it had been longer, but it was still a lengthy punishment.

I felt great sympathy for other victims such as Angela Barker (whose story is told by Karen Wilcox at the end of this book) whose attackers seemed to have been let off so lightly.

> CAROL SIMON: After the second trial Lani was more settled. She wasn't as vulnerable. She was stronger in herself and she didn't have the same fear. He was locked up and when his family tried to intimidate us we had the police behind us and we thought, 'We can deal with it.' And we have.
>
> It's very important that women speak up the way Lani did, even though it's so hard. Indigenous women who are suffering domestic violence are often scared of the police, and even scared of the perpetrator being locked up. Welfare and the police are the two government departments that Aboriginal communities are scared of, because of their history. But domestic violence shouldn't be accepted in the community. You just have to be there for those women, let them know you're there for them to help or just to talk to. It is hard. I was brought up with whatever happens in the home stays in the home. But we need no more turning a blind eye.

Because the suppression order had been lifted I was able to speak to the media after the sentencing. The headline our local paper, the *Southern Courier*, put on the interview I gave them said it all: JUSTICE AFTER 'EIGHT YEARS OF HELL'.

Chapter Fifteen

The next year and a half passed relatively quietly. Well, as quietly as they could when you have five children under eight. There was some bad medical news for me. I'd been having trouble with my hands for a while, especially when I did something like use a computer mouse. I'd get terrible pain and my fingers would swell up alarmingly. Eventually it got so bad I went to see my doctor.

Finding out what was going on took quite a while; when I finally got a diagnosis I understood why. It turned out to be something called mixed connective tissue disease (MCTD), an autoimmune disorder like lupus. It's sometimes called an overlap disease because the symptoms are the same as a number of other conditions, which makes it hard to identify. It's also very rare. After a blood test had confirmed that I had MCTD, one medico told me it's so unusual that the average doctor would be lucky to see one case in their working life.

It's a chronic condition that affects the joints, which swell and ache and become permanently damaged (overlapping symptoms with rheumatoid arthritis) and eventually it can damage internal organs including the kidneys and heart. Too much sun exposure can make it worse. The one bit of good news is that it's not genetic, so I don't have to worry about having passed it on to my girls. Doctors don't yet know what causes it. Apparently there is no connection with my alcohol and drug use except, the doctors told me, that numbing myself that way might have masked the symptoms, so I might have had it years ago and just not known.

There is no cure. There are ways of managing it, mostly by taking corticosteroids (drugs like prednisone), but they bring with them their own dangers. I'm in pain pretty much all the time, and the more active I am, the greater the pain. Sometimes by the time night falls I'm in agony. But I just have to keep going. The doctors have recommended that I take painkillers whenever I need them, but that would mean popping them like lollies. I don't want to do that, because for a start, they bomb me out so I walk through the day like a zombie, and second, I don't want to become dependent on substances again.

When I've explained that I don't want to take too many painkillers, a couple of my doctors have quietly said to me, 'Well, people who don't like taking pills sometimes find that smoking marijuana helps. That's why in some places it's medically prescribed for people with cancer.' Hell, I'd love nothing more than to smoke some pot and be able to physically relax and mentally chill. I lost my desire to drink alcohol after I sobered up, but the urge to smoke pot is something different again. But I'm an addict. I can't pick up again, no matter who says it's okay to do that, because I know it's not okay for me. I've worked so hard to be clean and sober and be the mother my children deserve. I'm not going to risk all that.

* * *

Genevieve had been working away finishing up the documentary, which she titled *Lani's Story*, and finally it was ready to go. When I was sitting there being interviewed for it, I knew other people would see it but somehow I imagined it would be a small, local thing, maybe screened in a community centre or the Yarra Bay Sailing Club at La Perouse. I couldn't imagine being on TV and I never in my wildest dreams would have imagined anything like the premiere, which was held on Friday, 7 May 2010, at the Sydney Opera House as part of the Message Sticks Indigenous Film Festival. It was unbelievable.

In the lead-up to it, a friend of mine called Claudia said, 'Alex Perry wants to give you a dress to wear. You can go down to his shop in the city and pick out anything you want.' I thought, 'What the hell!' I knew he was a famous, expensive designer whose clothes were always on the women in the social pages of the Sunday paper. It turned out that Claudia did riding lessons at Centennial Park with the woman who ran his boutique for him. Claudia was chatting to her one day and said, 'Oh my mate's in a doco and it's going to be screened at the Opera House and she's got nothing to wear.' The lady talked to Alex Perry about it and he said, 'Tell Lani to go in and choose a dress.'

I'd thought all his clothes were for those stick-thin model types, but when I walked in they were expecting me and they knew my size and had some beautiful things for me to look at. I chose a stunning black number and got all dressed up with high heels and the whole look and went down to the screening. When we got there, the place was packed. I hadn't known what to expect, but there were hundreds and hundreds of people—it was so full that they'd set up screens in the foyer so the people who couldn't get a seat inside could sit there and watch.

I was trying to take it all in, but it was all a bit of a blur. Someone led me in front of a TV crew for an interview on the way in, then we went and took our seats. Dad wouldn't come down the front with us—he sat right up at the back. Mum and John and Aunty Carol and I were all looking at each other in amazement before it began. Sitting there with that huge crowd was the first time any of us had seen the whole thing, and because we'd all been interviewed separately, it was the first time we each heard what the others had said.

It was so weird seeing myself up on the big screen. I felt in a way like it wasn't really me. But I also felt really choked up because it brought back vivid memories of all the bad things I was talking about. It was also an airing of old secrets for the others. Mum had never spoken publicly about what had happened in her marriage to Dad, but she did in the doco. It opened the door for John's healing too, because he'd always had to be the rock and hold everything together, and he's got his own demons about his mother and father. It let light in for a lot of people and helped them find some closure.

When it finished I felt so exposed, I just kept my eyes down at my lap, then Gen said, 'Look up, Lani.' I said, 'What?' She said, 'Every single person in this whole place is standing.' I looked around and they were: they were cheering and it was a standing ovation. I was spinning out. Then the organisers asked me to go up onto the stage for a Q&A with the audience. Well, I'm not very good in high heels so I ripped them off and walked up there barefoot. Everyone was laughing. I said, 'I wasn't going to fall headfirst on the stage in front of all you people!'

I answered everyone's questions and cracked jokes. I was enjoying it, but at the same time I couldn't believe it was happening—all those people there just to hear my story. On the way out afterwards, Ernie Dingo, whose movie *Bran Nue Dae* was screening as part of the festival, came up to me, very emotional, and said, 'You should have the first DVD ever of *Bran Nue Dae*,' and he signed it and gave it to me. Other people were coming up and congratulating me all the way out.

When I'd agreed to take part in the documentary, I'd said to Gen that if it saved one life I'd do it. At times I'd wondered if it was all worth it—for instance when they decided to film at Mum's house, and they shifted furniture out and rearranged everything, including Mum, who had to stay at my house. It was hectic and it seemed to take forever, but the reaction to this screening showed me it really had all been worth it.

I'd trusted Gen and her team, and that was a big leap of faith. I didn't have control over what they would do with my words, I just had to hope they'd make it honest and show people that despite all the bad stuff, I was living proof you could turn your life around and find happiness. They'd done exactly that.

Two and a half weeks later the doco aired on SBS. Apparently it got a huge amount of coverage leading up to it in the 'What to Watch' and 'Show of the Week' sections of newspapers all around the country. Even though the Opera House crowd had responded so well, I still didn't know what to expect. They were a friendly film festival group; the people who'd be watching on TV might react differently. I didn't know how people in the Aboriginal community would take me telling the world about what had happened, and I didn't want anyone to think I was stereotyping Kooris and saying it only involves them.

But again, the response was amazing. Koorine and my friend Anna came over to my place and watched the doco go to air, and then about fifteen minutes after it finished they said, 'You should log onto Facebook,' so I did and I was blown away. There were hundreds of messages from people who'd watched it. Some were brief, just saying they'd found it powerful and congratulating me, but others were more personal, from women who had survived abusive relationships or were still in them, or from the friends and families of women in this situation.

I decided I had to write back to each one. Because I was so slow on the computer, one of my friends told me I should just write one answer and copy and paste it into each message, but I didn't want to do that. These people had taken the trouble to contact me and I wanted to let them know I appreciated it. I was still getting messages eighteen months and more after the doco aired, from people who had seen it on DVD. Not just from women, either. Men messaged me, stepping up and admitting what they'd done and telling me that now they understood how wrong it was. It's opened the door to talking about domestic violence in an incredible way.

It's also taken me on the road, as people who've heard my story through the doco have asked me to come and speak and take part in workshops. I've been to Victoria, Queensland and around New South Wales on these trips. I've spoken in jails. I've spoken to police domestic violence officers—I told them what that Maroubra police officer had said to me after the charges had been laid: 'You were an alcoholic, we thought you just wouldn't go through with it.' I told them that I can understand they'd get sick and tired being called out to the same places over and over. 'But,' I said to them, 'that one time you could be saving someone's life. It might even be the day the woman decides to follow through.'

I've spoken to indigenous prisoners in Silverwater. I tried not to show it, but walking into jail to talk to those men, I was freaking out. I thought to myself, 'Someone in this room is going to know Joe.' After I did my talk a lot of them came up to me and they were disclosing things they'd done, saying, 'You've opened my eyes. I never knew that that's how she felt.' They'd started looking at things differently. That's huge. For me, it's much easier to talk to survivors, but talking to the perpetrators can be a really amazing way to bring change. Some men can change. Some are just animals, just evil. But some really can change.

It's humbling to feel I've had a part in helping to take domestic violence out of the shadows. The way I see it is that it's just that I had the chance to speak up, in the way that a lot of other women might have done in the same circumstances. I often leave those workshops totally drained because the experience is so intense. But afterwards the energy flows back, because I can see how the simple act of sharing stories changes lives.

JOSEPHINE CASHMAN: It was hard for Lani to decide to seek justice but it's very important that women do. There is a big mistrust of the police from indigenous people, and I say this as an indigenous woman. There is mistrust of the police because a lot of kids have been put in homes and things like that. But I don't want everybody to be painted with the same brush. Up here in the Northern Territory, in West Arnhem Land, indigenous communities have a really good relationship with the police. I think in urban environments it's really hard. More Aboriginal lawyers need to be employed in the justice system. Because I came from that background and had been around Aboriginal people all my life, I could understand the conditions that Lani had experienced and I could talk to her in a way that no one else could. Both for defence and in the DPP they need some more Aboriginal lawyers.

When we brought indigenous sexual assault training in at the DPP, some of those lawyers had revelations. They'd prejudged Aboriginal people. It's a different culture and sometimes aggression or other mannerisms are misunderstood on both sides. Some Aboriginal victims might think, 'Oh, the police don't care about me.' As a Koori person, I had a real mistrust of the police before I worked for the DPP but I got to see that there are really good police out there who do care about people. More Aboriginal police officers and more Aboriginal lawyers will bridge that gap, and also non-Aboriginal people who are trained up, because it takes both.

As for claims that domestic violence is part of Aboriginal culture, I don't believe that at all, not one skerrick. It's untrue. Up here in this environment where the culture is really strong, there are huge consequences for people who bash women. In Katherine and Alice Springs there are problems, but it's usually people who've lost their culture, who drink and then there's violence. It's not the ones who have their land and their culture. I think it's more a reflection of people who are suffering intergenerational trauma.

Fewer Aboriginal people drink than the wider population: seventy-five per cent of non-indigenous

Australians drink alcohol, but only sixty-five per cent of indigenous people do. If you go to Macquarie Fields in Sydney or any other housing commission area you'll find violence that's related to poverty or desperation or depression. Domestic violence is a problem across the board. It's not an Aboriginal problem and it's definitely not accepted within Aboriginal culture.

The impact of the documentary and the awareness work that has come out of it have been so far beyond what even I had hoped for. In a way, I think the documentary and people's responses to it have helped me find peace even more than the justice system did.

It even took me overseas. One day Genevieve phoned me and said, 'How would you like to come to Canada?' Blackfella Films had received a call from the organisers of the imagineNATIVE Film and Media Arts Festival that was to be held towards the end of October 2010 in Toronto. They wanted to include *Lani's Story* and they were going to pay for her and me to go over with it. I couldn't believe it. I said to Gen, 'I don't even have a passport!' She told me not to worry, she'd help me to organise it.

As the preparations were underway we heard the good news that the doco had been honoured in the United Nations Association of Australia Media Peace Awards, winning the Best Television Documentary category and also a special award for 'increasing awareness and understanding of women's rights and issues'. It would also go on to win the 2010 Human Rights Award for Television.

I'd been feeling good about going to Canada, but the day I started packing, I suddenly got nervous. Genevieve was going on ahead, so I'd be travelling on my own. I have a close friend called

Guyleen and as a joke I said to her partner, Brad, 'You should pay for Guyleen so she can come with me.' And he did! She couldn't get on to the same flight as me, but her plane got in just five hours after mine.

Our film was screened as part of a triple bill, along with two other documentaries: *December 6*, about a mass shooting in Montreal in 1989, and *Open Season*, about sex-abuse survivors on Native American reservations. The films were all so intense that the audience in the theatre was very emotional afterwards. Lots of them made a point of coming up and telling me how moved they had been by my story and I found that very touching and unexpected, so far from home.

When our big day was over, it was time to have some sightseeing fun. It was great to have Guyleen there because, like me, she was always up for a good time. Gen is such a squarehead! She'd be forever telling us to quieten down in the motel room and go to sleep, but Guyleen was in for some fun. I hadn't even realised Niagara Falls was nearby until she told me it was just a two-hour bus ride away. We went there for the day and I've never seen anything so beautiful. The only other time I'd been overseas was when I was seventeen and drunk in New Zealand. This was totally different and I was so glad I had a good friend to share it with.

Two weeks before the trip I'd had my IUD removed because it was causing me difficulties. The night before I flew out John had given me an intimate send-off, and within a few days of coming home I knew something was going on that wasn't just jet lag. Yes, I was pregnant again. Our other babies hadn't exactly been planned, but we had just taken our growing family in our stride. But this was totally out of the blue. We'd thought we were done after five children. Our youngest, Kirrawahn, was three and a half; we'd finished with nappies. The time when they would all be at school was within sight, yet here we were right back at the start again.

We did talk seriously about what we should do. My doctors were plain: another pregnancy with MCTD was not recommended. But in the end, there was only one choice—have the baby. I respect other women's choices on abortion, but it wasn't something I could do. We were going to become a family of eight and that was that.

This pregnancy was very different to all my others. About a week after a home pregnancy test had come back positive, I began to feel not quite right. It wasn't anything I could put my finger on, things just felt wrong. A couple of weeks after that I started bleeding and rushed myself to hospital. It was after hours, so the specialist ultrasound staff weren't there. Instead, the doctors in the emergency department wheeled in their little machine. After examining me with it for a while they said they were sorry, but there was too much bleeding. They couldn't stop it and I'd lost the baby. I was to stay overnight and have a full ultrasound in the morning.

It was a terrible feeling to have come to terms with the fact that we were expecting, and then to miscarry. But the next morning when a specialist technician did the ultrasound they told me they had been mistaken: the baby was still alive after all. The bleeding settled down and I was released, then two weeks later I haemorrhaged again, went back to hospital and the same thing happened—using the ultrasound equipment in the emergency department, they told me I'd lost the baby, but the next morning on re-examination they told me the baby was still there. The bleeds kept coming, every fortnight.

In February 2011, when I was about three and a half months pregnant, John went away to Alice Springs for a week to commentate for NITV on the National Indigenous Cricket Carnival, the annual Imparja Cup. (Previously he was a star player for the New South Wales team, and now he gets to sit back and watch it from the commentary box.) I started haemorrhaging so badly there was a trail of blood up the hallway. I had intense contractions, too. The girls called John, who couldn't do anything but worry desperately. Then they called my mum and friends to come and help. Somewhere in there an ambulance was called and it whisked me off to emergency where, unbelievably, for a third time I was incorrectly told I'd miscarried. This time, fortunately, I was transferred to the Royal Hospital for Women in Randwick where they told me I was still pregnant, but both the baby and I were at risk of dying.

They told me I needed to be admitted right away and that I'd be staying there for the whole remaining term of the pregnancy. I couldn't even go home to get clothes or toiletries. I was in a panic. What would happen to my girls at home? John couldn't stay home with them the whole time—he had to work. I phoned my friend Symone, and without me even asking she said, 'Don't worry about anything. I'll stay at your house for the whole time you're in there. I'll look after your kids.' I'm still amazed by what that lady did for me. She uprooted her whole life, including her two sons, preschooler Dheklin and teenager Jerome. Jerome even had to switch high schools. But they did it.

I was on bed rest; I couldn't get out of bed, let alone leave the room. It was really hard to handle being cooped up. I missed my kids so much and longed to see them every day, but even though Koorine and a lot of my friends helped out, things were too busy at home for them to make it that often. Symone didn't drive and John was working flat out.

For the first month I had lots of visitors but then they started fading away. I could understand that—it's such a long time, you can't expect other people to just put their lives on hold. Even so, I started really struggling. By the time I'd been in there for three months, I was losing the plot. I was depressed and anxious. I felt worried about my kids all the time. I started getting angry with the whole world and even resenting being pregnant.

Every couple of weeks I would have another big bleed. The doctors realised that clots were building up inside the uterus and releasing, but they didn't have a way to stop it. As the months went by and it seemed less and less likely that I was going to make it to full term, they gave the baby in-utero steroids to try to develop her lungs, and other medication to give her the best chance of survival. I was also on various medications, some to try to delay birth, some to help me through the painful contractions that accompanied the bleeding.

Despite that, it got to the point where I begged to be allowed just a short break away from the hospital. Finally the doctors agreed. My girls were playing Saturday netball and I had 'gate leave': I could go out for one hour only, then it was back to bed rest. It was 7 May and I was twenty-seven and a half weeks pregnant.

I should have been happy when I woke at 5 am that day, but something felt really wrong. I hadn't felt right since the pregnancy began, but this was a new level of wrong. There was a device in the room that strapped around my belly to monitor the baby's heartbeat. I grabbed it and tried to take a reading, but the results were all over the place. I told the nurse who came that I was taking myself downstairs to the delivery suite. Down there they put me on a bed to examine me. I felt like everything was shutting down. I had my phone in my hand and I managed to ask them to ring John. They tried to call him and my mum, but before anyone could reach the hospital, which was only a few minutes' drive from where we lived, I'd been rushed into theatre and had an emergency caesarean.

The baby was so tiny, weighing just one kilogram. She went straight to NICU, the Neonatal Intensive Care Unit. After a while I was wheeled up to see her. She looked so helpless, lying in the middle of a humidicrib; it was terrifying. Then they took me back downstairs for more treatment. Afterwards they told me that this time I'd haemorrhaged so badly that if I had gone out as planned, the chances were very high that both my baby and I would have died.

Shakylah, as we named her, had to stay in the NICU for her first three months. I went to the hospital every day to be with her, but it was a full four weeks after she was born that I got to hold her outside the humidicrib, and even then she was still wired up to a machine to help with her breathing. Being born so premature brought with it a whole heap of medical problems. She has chronic lung disease and severe asthma. She has a bicuspid aortic valve, meaning her heart hasn't developed normally. She's got thyroid and iron-level problems. She has severe gastric reflux. And she has a condition called haemangioma, which causes a tangle of blood vessels to build up on her liver, although fortunately this is benign, and she might grow out of it.

Finally, after three months, Shakylah was discharged and could come home, although she still only weighed 1.7 kilograms. But the very next day I had to rush her back to hospital because she stopped breathing and went blue. I stimulated her—which means I had to rub her body and breathe in her face to try to kick her system back into gear—as the NICU nurses, who'd treated her this way when she'd had episodes when her heart stopped, had taught me. Having been out for one day, she was readmitted and stayed in hospital for another six weeks. In her first six months home Shakylah stopped breathing about fifty times. We've been back to the hospital so many times I have literally lost count. There have been many times I thought Shakylah wouldn't make it. But I just have to keep thinking to myself, 'She's made it this far. She's here for a reason.'

Not long after her first birthday Shakylah had a gastric-peg feeding tube surgically fitted. Eating and drinking normally is hard for her, because she is liable to choke and aspirate into her lungs and stop breathing. When she first came home she had a nasal feeding tube, but she kept pulling it out and we had to go back to the hospital repeatedly to have it reinserted. She'll have the belly peg, which hooks up to a portable feeding machine, until she is at least five. Since it was inserted she's needed fewer hospital admissions, thank goodness.

It's been very hard on our family having a child with such serious health problems. John lost a job because I had to be at the hospital so much with Shakylah and he needed to be at home with the other girls. We worry about her so much. I get really tired, but what eats at me the most is the feeling that I'm neglecting my other kids. They definitely feel the lack of our time and attention. They try to understand, and they love their baby sister, but they're only kids after all and it can be hard for them to accept that their mum can't be there for them at an important sports match or school presentation day. Sometimes they look at me with tears in their eyes when I tell them I have to be with Shakylah in hospital instead and it breaks my heart.

This last couple of years has been my biggest challenge so far, even including the trials. It didn't help that in late 2011 Joseph Timbery lodged an appeal against his sentence, claiming it was unduly harsh. On 28 June 2012 the Court of Criminal Appeal handed down its decision: his case was rejected, his sentence stands.

With all the stresses pulling at us, my relationship with John got very rocky over this period. We were arguing all the time, just due to worry. My attendance at AA meetings dropped right off. I haven't been for my check-ups for the MCTD because there just isn't time to attend to my own needs.

I've never pretended to be perfect, and I'll freely admit that sometimes it's all too much. A while ago things came to a head when I had all the kids in the bus (as we call our old people-mover), heading home after their various netball games. They were bickering away with each other, as kids do, and nagging me about this and that, and I just lost it. I drove to Mum's, pulled the car into the driveway, said to her, 'I'm done, I can't cope any more. You look after them.' I handed her the keys and walked off. She called John, who was on his way home, and tried to calm the kids, who were freaking out. I just turned my phone off and walked.

They were madly trying to call me and I knew they'd be worried, but I was stressed to the max and I had to let off some steam. So I just walked for a couple of hours. It certainly wasn't how I'd planned to spend my Saturday evening, but here's what I didn't do: I didn't go and have a drink at one of the many nearby pubs. I didn't turn to drugs. I didn't fall back into the old habits that at one time would have been my immediate choice. I was stressed and miserable, but I got through it. And when I'd been out long enough I went home, back to the family I love.

JOHN DUCKETT: When the second verdict and the second sentence came down, we were just looking for closure. And we thought we had it. But then he appealed the sentence so it was still going. But the strength of Lani's character sees her through. Look at it, from her walk into that police station on her own to declare what happened to her, to going through the trials, having a baby on a Friday by caesarean then back on the stand on a Monday, that just shows her determination.

Domestic violence happens every day. People have got to put their hands up and say enough's enough, like Lani did. I grew up with it and most of my family grew up with it. It's not for me to judge anyone, but when you're in that situation you've got problems before you've even lived life. I had problems a long time before I even drank. I grew up with fear and still, today, that can affect me.

It's very important to Lani and me to protect our girls against that. I keep telling Lani, 'The reason you have six daughters is because of the life that you've lived. Those girls are going to carry on the fight.' They've got the fighting spirit in them already. The best we can do for them is to set a good example. I think that it's important that I work. My dad drank, my dad did drugs. I hold down a steady job, I provide. And they can see that. And I cook, I clean, I mop; everything is equal, we're all equal. And when Lani and I have problems, the girls can see we sort them out. Like my gambling. It was a problem and I had to deal with it. It was unacceptable. It was just an escape from reality. So I dealt with it.

Fifteen years ago, I never would have believed I could have the life I have today, happy with Lani and my girls, and sober. My main priority still today is that I'm sober, that comes before anyone. I'm very selfish. Because I'd lose everything I care about if I wasn't.

While I sometimes wish I had things easier, I know there are a lot of people worse off than me. I try to keep that sense of perspective and to remind myself how far I've come. Money is always tight for us, and it's easy to get envious when people say they're going off on this fantastic holiday or they've bought this or that. I'd love to be able to buy us a new bus or a better TV. And as for owning a home of our own ... But when I find myself thinking like that I try to look around at everything I do have—beautiful children, a loving man, and enough material possessions to keep us reasonably comfortable—and remind myself that when John and I started out together we had a mattress on the floor and not much else. I've come so far. I'm not well off, but I have the things that matter and my life has been a success story.

Joseph Timbery used to say to me, 'Every time you look in the mirror you'll see the marks I've left on you. No one else will ever want you because of that.' I do still carry those marks. I have chipped and missing teeth, a steel plate in my jaw, a broken cheekbone and nose, scars on my scalp and face that even all these years later itch and burn. I have scars all over my body, the worst of which is the huge scar on my leg from the broken plate. For years I didn't wear skirts, even in hot weather, because

I was so embarrassed about it and hated people asking me how I got it.

For all the healing I've done and the distance I've travelled, I do also still have emotional scars, and in a way they're even worse. Even now some odd little thing can set off a flashback. And I still have bad days when the voice in my head tells me I'm worthless and I sabotage myself by doing something like picking a fight with John, as if I still don't trust what we have or don't think I deserve it. I've spoken to a lot of other survivors who say they do exactly the same thing. When the words 'damaged goods' have been burned so deep into how you see yourself, it's not something that ever really leaves you—you just have to be aware of what's going on and try to be kind to yourself until you're feeling stronger.

I will never forget what that evil man did to me, but I decided not to hold onto any resentment, because the resentment that ate into me for years wasn't hurting him, it was hurting me. For a long time I regretted saving his life when he OD'd, but I came to realise that death would have been the easy way out for him. Having to live every day locked up in prison, knowing what he's done and what society thinks of him, that's a lot harder than death.

So while I do still bear scars, to me now they are like badges of courage. They don't just show the bad things I went through, they are testament to the fact that I survived it all. In a way, I shouldn't even be alive today. The life that I chose, the path that I went down, I was much more likely to die than to live. But I feel I've been put on this earth to achieve something, to help other people. Everything I've been through has made me stronger.

CAROL SIMON: Seeing Lani when she was drinking and out of control, I never would have thought she'd be the person she is today. I talk about her a lot to other people, because if a person can survive after the way she was living, to me that's a miracle. The drugs, the alcohol, the assaults, living with violent people, being violent—usually the only way for people like that is death or jail. But she pulled through.

KATHY BRENNAN: I think really highly of Lani. I have a lot of respect for her. She's incredibly determined. She's a good mother. She tries to help everybody—she's a people pleaser, always has been—she's got so many friends. But she needs to look at herself too.

RORY BRENNAN: Looking at Lani now, she's a legend. She's not a well girl herself, yet she's out doing what she's doing, having six kids, especially one of them sick, and she's out giving talks about DV around the place, involved in the community. She's just unbelievable.

I always say I'm damaged goods, I've got scars from the past. I'll never be a hundred per cent. It affects your daily living sometimes and your feeling of self-worth. The old you and the old thinking can come back when you least expect it. But Lani's survived it, too. If you survive that kind of thing you're doing well. If you survive it and go on to be someone living a good life and making a contribution then you're doing extremely well.

JOHN DUCKETT: Lani's come a long way since I met her. She's a good mother. You walk in my house and you wouldn't even think we've got kids, the house is so clean. She's a good listener. She's unique. She's got a lot of qualities, it'd take a long time to actually go through each one, but she's a strong lady. She reminds me a lot of my grandmother. Lani has a beautiful, beautiful nature; she's very happy, very bubbly. But she's honest and will tell you straight if you step out of line.

I guess if there's anything I'd change about Lani it's that she's loud! We go to the football and everyone knows her. She's a mad Lapa supporter and everyone knows her, I'm telling you, everyone can hear her. She stands on one side of the oval; I take the baby and go sit on the other. I say, 'See you later.' She goes, 'See ya, boy.' But that's just her.

Twenty years into the future I'd love to be living on a property with Lani, just the two of us. But that's not going to happen. Lani hates quiet. She thinks if there's no one in the house, it's boring. She likes having twenty kids around. Everyone's got to be loud, she can't operate if it's quiet. My dream would be living on a farm—I love Picton, it's beautiful. She doesn't love Picton, she loves La Perouse.

I'm here for a reason. I'm here to raise six strong girls who will go out into the world knowing a good man from a bad one. I'm here to try to stop kids from making the same mistakes I did. I work now as a youth support officer with Police Citizens Youth Clubs. It's a job I had to fight for because there were some people in the organisation who thought someone who'd been on the wrong side of the law, like I was when I was young, was the wrong person for the job. But who better than someone who's been through it and come out the other side?

I've tried to resign a couple of times when things got too much with Shakylah and all the rest, but my boss wouldn't let me. He said to me, 'Take whatever leave you need, but I don't want you to resign.' I was glad of that because I love the job. It's kept me going by giving me a bit of breathing space where I can think, 'I'm helping someone here.' So much of the time with Shakylah I feel helpless; it does me good to feel I'm making a difference at work.

I run programs through the youth centre for seven to eleven year olds, trying to get to them before they go off the rails, and I take out the late-night Boomerang Bus for the teenagers who are out on the streets, often drunk or off their faces on drugs. They can phone a free-call number and we come and pick them up and take them home safely, or find them some refuge accommodation. Those kids can't put anything over on me. I know what drugs they're on, I know when they're drinking, I know when they're fighting, I know their families. I know how to get through to them on their level. They know they can trust me. They can tell me honestly what's going on and I won't judge them. I won't take any bullshit from them. I'll just find a way to help them.

And, of course, I'm here to help women break free of domestic violence. I do that by going out and speaking to groups. As my grandmother, my beloved Wha Wha, always used to say, 'A problem shared is a problem halved', and that's how healing begins. I feel the truth of that every time I speak out about domestic violence—the more I talk, the more I heal.

But I also do it one-on-one. I often get calls or Facebook contact from people in the community or friends of friends who know of a woman who is being abused, or from the woman herself. I let them know I'm here for them, and if they're not ready to leave or if they leave and go back, I don't judge them. It's hard for women in DV to reach out, but if they do, you need to be there for them because that might be the day you save their life.

A few months ago, for instance, someone I know called and told me her cousin needed urgent help. She turned out to be a young woman with two babies who was being bashed and had been held hostage in her own home by her partner. She and the children had managed to escape when he briefly left the house and she called her cousin in the kind of panic I was in when I called Dad that Boxing Day thirteen years ago. My friend urgently needed a car to go pick her up, so she took mine and brought her cousin back to my place.

We talked with her, and she tried to play it all down. She was numb at first, talking about it as if it was all happening to someone else, unable to accept that there might really be a way out. I made some calls and we got her a place at a refuge. I talked to her again several times over the next few days and eventually she was ready for us to take her to the police station. Now she's got her own Housing Department place and she's going to court soon to testify against the perpetrator. She's happy and settled.

It feels good to help people out like that, but I do it because I feel like I need to. If I know there's something I can do that might just help, I've got to try. I get uncomfortable when other women who've survived DV tell me I'm an inspiration to them. I just say, 'I'm no different to anyone else. You're an inspiration to me.'

Someone recently asked me to do one of those mini psychology tests where you have to name your three best qualities and your three worst ones. I found it much easier to name the worst ones (too loud, too outspoken, my temper). But maybe that's true of a lot of us, regardless of our life experience. I guess if I really have to name the best parts of me they would be determination, resilience and persistence. Even when I felt I had no more strength left, somehow I just kept on going. Step by step, day by day, year by year I've made it through and I've found a happiness I once could never have believed possible.

My name is Lani and I'm a survivor.

'I didn't hit you—you fell down the stairs.'

Q&A with Karen Wilcox, Good Practice Officer for the Australian Domestic and Family Violence Clearinghouse

What is domestic violence?
Domestic violence is a relationship of power and control. It's characterised by fear and intimidation on the part of the victim and coercion and control on the part of the perpetrator. The way that it manifests itself is different for every perpetrator, who can tap into his victim's fear. The acts of abuse often differ. There can be physical violence, but something as seemingly small as a raised eyebrow or a few innocent-sounding words can be part of a pattern of domestic violence in context, because of the previous history of abuse which has led to this state of intimidation by the perpetrator of violence. Physical violence is usually the tip of the iceberg that we see, but so much is going on underneath to maintain the control and fear.

DV covers physical violence, psychological violence and emotional violence (which is different from psychological violence). It covers the exposure of children to violence, financial abuse—control of the purse strings—social isolation and social control in other ways, and sexual abuse.

What about younger women—are they at risk?
Definitely. They're at a stage in their lives where their identities are forming. Their vulnerability is so much greater. A young Victorian woman called Angela Barker has a horrendous story and has since become a campaigner for greater awareness of

domestic violence, particularly against young women. She was a vibrant, popular sixteen-year-old when an abusive ex-boyfriend brutally bashed her almost to death. She was in hospital and a nursing home for three years and has been left with permanent brain damage and paralysis. She is an inspirational figure who was named Victoria's Young Australian of the Year in 2011 in recognition of her advocacy work. Her attacker got a minimum jail term of just five years before it was increased to seven and a half years after the prosecution appealed against the sentence.

Whenever we do training using one of Anj's videos and people hear her story, there is always someone who says, 'Why didn't her parents keep her away from him right from the start? The guy was obviously a loser; if that was my daughter …' My response to that is, 'Anyone here have a sixteen-year-old daughter?' If your parents or teachers tell you to stay away from a boy at that age, the first thing you're going to do is go straight out the door to him. Those teenage years are all about rejecting your parents' values; that's normal. But it gives young women a particular vulnerability. The mere fact of being a teenager isolates you from the people who might support you.

Is there ever any excuse for domestic violence?
Never. Living free from violence and abuse and feeling safe in our homes is a fundamental right for us as human beings. That's it, end of story. Nobody deserves to be abused, nobody deserves to be assaulted, nobody deserves to be diminished to the point where they compare themselves to their partner and the rest of the universe and feel, 'I am a piece of crap. I am an ant, and you are like God.' Nobody deserves to be in that position. And nobody deserves to be blamed for being in that position, either.

It's often hard for women to be sure they're experiencing domestic violence, isn't it?
Yes, because the men perpetrating the violence commonly redefine everyday reality for their victims—in other words, they mess with their minds so that their victims think they're going crazy if they challenge what's happening to them. The man will say things like, 'I didn't hit you—you fell down the stairs. What's going on? You must be really tired.' Or, 'That wasn't a punch.' Or, 'I didn't rape you, we were just having a bit of sex. I know you said you didn't want it but then you enjoyed it.'

To someone outside the family, like the doctor, the perpetrator will say, 'Oh, she's under so much stress at the moment, you know. She's really struggling with the kids. I didn't want her to have more kids, but you know, she's the one that went and had them. And I'm trying my best but she's just not quite with it.' Or he'll tell her, 'You made me do this. You're the reason I did this. I've got no choice but to do this. This happened because you drove me to it, you didn't let me see the kids, you nagged me, you're stupid, you're hopeless, you're lazy.'

It's like an indoctrination camp, living with a perpetrator: deny, minimise, blame; deny, minimise, blame. If you're told over and over again that what is happening didn't really happen or that it's normal, or you are the one who is responsible, of course you're going to doubt yourself and think that the way you see the world must be wrong. We'd all react the same way in that situation. You can't underestimate what constant undermining like that does to your capacity to make a rational assessment of the relationship—which is why most women don't leave until they get some decent counselling.

Those men will also set out to make the women feel like they have no other choice, won't they?
Yes. They'll say, 'Look at yourself. Nobody else would want you.' Sleep deprivation is a really common technique used by perpetrators, and if you don't sleep properly, you don't look good and you can't think clearly. So, often, if the woman looks in the mirror she looks bad, and she thinks what he said must be right. And when she goes down the street people may treat her like dirt because she may be presenting like someone in crisis—as she is. Victims of domestic violence may not be able to work well. They don't present well. Their lives are often in chaos.

Can you give some other examples of the ways in which perpetrators control and threaten women?
The physical violence might be minimal, but the relationship is still all about power, control, coercion, fear, intimidation. So you might get a guy who just once puts his hands around his wife's throat and looks her in the eye with utter hatred and evil, and says, 'I will kill you if you ever do that again.' He might only have done it once, but for the rest of the twenty years of their married life she lives under that fear, and he reminds her of the power he has to actually kill her by other means, such as that same look, flexing his tanked muscles, etcetera.

Or there's stalking, and that doesn't necessarily mean looking out your window and seeing somebody standing out there. It can be him letting her know that he is aware of her every move: 'Where were you at 9.05 this morning after you dropped the kids off at school? You should have been home by then, but I rang and you weren't there.' Or, 'What were you doing down at the beach this morning?' 'I was just walking the dog.' 'Who was that bloke you were talking to?' 'Oh it's just some guy whose dog came up to me. It's nobody.' 'No it's not, you're lying ...' If this is what you're going through on a day-to-day basis, you become intimidated. You don't go for a walk down the beach with your dog for fear of what might happen afterwards.

It can literally be the movement of an eyebrow. One counsellor I know was at a divorce mediation where everything was going along fine when all of a sudden the woman just stopped. She said, 'Oh, I'll just sign it as it is.' Because this counsellor is very good, he picked up that something was wrong. He stopped the session, took her outside and said, 'What went on there? Why did you decide to consent to everything he said all of a sudden?' She said, 'Because he raised his eyebrow. I know when he raises that eyebrow if I don't do what he wants, that's it.' She was terrified. He had intimidated her so much that he could control her with just that tiny movement.

Something that's particularly distressing in some indigenous communities (and also with some non-indigenous women) is threats around children being used for sexual gratification. A perpetrator of violence with an indigenous woman can make what might seem veiled and vague references to taking the children with him to a mate's place but those words are designed to instil fear and terror in that woman.

Is there a simple test to show if the relationship is one of domestic violence? For instance, is it a question of whether the person you're with generally makes you feel more anxious or unhappy?

No, because lots of people are in relationships with jerks who make them feel anxious and unhappy. It doesn't mean those men are perpetrators of violence. They could just be jerks. What you're looking for is whether you feel fear, and intimidation in any form. You don't have to worry about what he does to cause that. If you feel it, it's real.

What part do drugs and alcohol play?

There's a strong correlation between drug and alcohol use and the severity of domestic violence, but it is not the cause. The more drunk a perpetrator is, or the more affected by a drug like ice, the more damage he's likely to do, but there are still many, many perpetrators of domestic violence who are teetotallers. And there are many, many alcoholics and drunks who don't engage in domestic violence.

The other way in which drugs and alcohol can be significant is that it can make it harder to leave if the victim also has drug and alcohol issues. There's often a dependency on the perpetrator to get them the stuff, which they need physically. So the perpetrator is the person who brings them whatever golden substance they are hanging out for. Perpetrators can also manipulate or exacerbate addictions in vulnerable victims—it becomes one of the control and submission tactics they use very 'cleverly'.

That's why the rehab pathway out of domestic violence is not atypical. You might not be at the point of addressing the relationship but you suddenly think, 'I want to get off this ship. I do not want to be in this point in my life in ten years' time.' In unwrapping themselves from the addiction, the victim suddenly realises how much the addiction and the perpetrator were entwined.

What is the research telling us about the effects of domestic violence on the brain?

There's been a whole lot of work done in neuroscience and brain science that shows us that experiencing domestic violence causes the same changes in the brain that you see in people who have been in serious trauma such as a terrorist event or a hostage-taking. In other words, we now have scientific proof that domestic violence victims are trauma victims.

We recognise that people who have been through a trauma like a bus crash or the September 11 attacks are going to be really disturbed. We understand that they will need counselling and we are happy to give them months off work if they need it. But many people don't understand that for a domestic violence victim the trauma is persistent. It's not a one-off event. In fact it's worse because it's ongoing and they see the cause of their trauma on a daily basis, which doesn't generally happen with those other sources of trauma.

What about the effect on children who are exposed to domestic violence?
When I first started working in this field, we all believed tiny babies would be okay because they were too young to realise what was going on. But neuroscience research has shown us that the younger the child, the more serious and long-lasting the damage. In fact, it starts before birth. If the developing brain stem of a baby in the uterus gets too much adrenal hormone (which happens when the mother is stressed) then the brain stem doesn't develop properly.

The next level is the emotional brain: the limbic brain, the amygdala. That develops in the first year of life, the attachment year. If there's exposure to domestic violence, that will be damaged. For the rest of their life, that child will not be able to regulate emotions in the way it should. They are hypervigilant to stress, or they may even dissociate in order to get away from the powerful fears and stresses they are experiencing.

The next level to grow developmentally speaking, simplified, includes the prefrontal cortex, the thinking brain. Trauma at this age results in the child being unable to lay down the neurological pathways that allow them to think logically and problem solve and respond rationally. What this means is that if a child is exposed to stress they are stuck in a 'freeze, fight, flight' response. This can be the pattern for the rest of their life. So if they're at school and Jimmy walks past and accidentally bumps them, they'll smash Jimmy in the face, or they'll freeze and not know how to respond, or they'll smash Jimmy in the face and then freeze. They may dissociate, because there have been trauma triggers in the playground that remind them, at an unconscious level, of the fear and trauma they experienced when they were little.

There's no point saying to them, 'Did you not think about what you were doing?' The child is incapable of thinking of what they're doing because they're not in a thinking part of their brain, they're in the emotional part of their brain. All of the punishments, all of the behaviour management plans in the world aren't going to work. They're also very much educationally disadvantaged, because you can't learn when your brain is constantly scanning for threats.

Finding this out often makes a huge difference to women with children when it comes to leaving domestic violence. Often women will have said, 'I don't want to leave because he's good with the kids,' or 'I don't want to disrupt the kids' lives.' But once they find out the way the violence is really affecting their children, when they realise the children are being damaged even if they're not being physically hurt, it's often the thing that spurs them to take action and leave. Because it's not just for themselves: they realise that by staying, their kids are far worse off.

It's hard to get out of a domestic violence situation, isn't it?
Yes, but it can be done. On an emotional level it's hard because of all the low self-esteem that's been created by the abuse, and because most perpetrators have a nice side that made the victim love them in the first place, and they show that nice side to the outside world.

Most of them are very good at behaving well with their boss or their best mate, even when they're angry. So women think, 'If I behave well like he says, if I do this and this and this, I won't trigger that change; he'll stay nice.' Of course he won't, but that's what he wants her to believe. And so she may still love him and that's normal. At some point in our lives all of us love people that we oughtn't to have loved. Attachment is a really strong, powerful, normal human drive.

Usually it takes the development of a trust relationship with a really good counsellor or friend before the victim can see the relationship for what it is, and that takes time. It might take many sessions with a domestic violence counsellor before they get to that point.

Financially it's hard to leave because women in that situation are often financially dependent. It's common for him to prevent her working, and our system is not geared to support women who leave abusive relationships. What's the Newstart Allowance now—$245 a week (plus maybe Family Tax Benefit and child support, which can be minimal)? If that's not a deterrent to leave a domestic violence relationship and start a new life, I don't know what is. You can't even pay rent on a flat for that.

And then there's the problem of simply being believed: women very often aren't believed at first when they reveal what's been happening. Even the legal system, which should be there to help, sometimes doesn't.

It can take women several attempts before they leave a relationship for good. The fact that they leave and then go back does not mean they cannot succeed in getting away in the end.

What are the first steps?

The first step involves talking to someone who is experienced and familiar with domestic and family violence, so they can provide immediate support and assess the level of risk. There might be real and immediate dangers that the victim is in too much of a fog to see. She might need to escape immediately and go to a refuge or shelter. On the following pages are the first points of contact across the country, and they can put women in touch with an appropriately qualified DV service. And if you are really scared, the first point of contact is always the police.

Once victims are at the point of doing post-crisis work, counselling and therapy can really help, if the counsellors understand the dynamics and effects of domestic violence. Referrals from other women or from a DV service can help women find the right counsellor or psychologist.

Australians who are Medicare card holders may be entitled to free or subsidised visits to a psychologist if they are suffering from mental health issues, and this includes the depression and anxiety that are normal responses to a situation of ongoing crisis and trauma. To do this, you go to your doctor (or to a new doctor, if you feel more secure doing that) and tell them what's happening. This can be as simple as saying to them, 'I'm finding it really hard because I'm in this really bad relationship, and I want to work through the issues that this relationship has caused me so that I can move on with my life.' The doctor might then do a mental health screen and provide a psychologist referral, if appropriate.

It's much harder for women in regional and rural areas, but there are internet services and phone counselling and support options (see the 'Where to Get Help' pages that follow), which can be a good place to start. They can cover the risks and the options to keep you safe, and they can look at your support needs and get things organised, whether it's crisis accommodation or liaising with the police to get an AVO or protection order.

What action can people take who are concerned that someone they love is experiencing domestic violence?
Don't say, 'If he really loved you he wouldn't treat you like that. You don't have to put up with this.' That's not why she's there and it just makes her feel worse, as though it's her fault for staying. Instead, try putting your arms around her and saying, 'I love you. You so don't deserve this. You're far too beautiful a person for this.' That's chipping away at the negative messages she's been getting. Say, 'Let's help you get out of this. What do I need to do to help you get out of this?'

If you think she's at risk of serious physical harm like Lani and Anj Barker were, or if there are children at risk, you just have to step in, even if you run this risk of escalating things. Perpetrators will often threaten victims, saying, 'If you tell anyone anything, you'll pay.' So the people who love her need to wrap her in some kind of safety blanket. That might mean moving her to a safe house or just bringing her into a home with an uncle or a brother who will stand up to the perpetrator, or moving her in with a girlfriend whose husband's a cop—these old-fashioned cultural protective mechanisms can work quite well and be a good start. The criminal justice system can also be called upon to provide an AVO, and you can let the police know the risk she's under. All of this creates a protective network around her.

What about helping younger women?
My view is that an adult has to step in. An adult just has to say, 'Teenagers aren't able to make those decisions. I'm going to step in for their safety, even if they hate me.' Suck it up, they will hate you. At the point when she called her dad to come and get her, Lani knew that she had to hand over to an adult. For young women, adults have to step in at some point, even though their daughters might be kicking and snarling and doing everything they can to push you away.

In the first trial of Lani's perpetrator, his defence barrister suggested that domestic violence was accepted within the indigenous community and questioned whether it was even a matter for the court. What's your response to that?
Of course domestic violence is vile and not a part of traditional culture. It's a crime, no matter who it happens to, no matter where it happens. We white people have a really funny view of law and discipline and child rearing, that it's just about the wrongdoings. As far as I understand it, as a non-Aboriginal person (and I don't like to speak as if I do know, as that is for Aboriginal people), Aboriginal laws and lores aren't just about punishing wrongdoing, it's about the right-doings. It seems to me to be about defining who you are, and giving you a sense of who you are. Punishing wrongdoing then is only a really, really small part of it. Speak to the grandmothers in indigenous communities, the ones who hold the whole society together, and they often say, 'We want to help our men grow into the men that we need them to be.'

Is it possible to rebuild your life after leaving a domestic violence situation?

Yes, definitely! While we now know that the brain is damaged by trauma, and that domestic violence is worse trauma than being in a bank robbery, we also know that damage can be healed by direct interventions with the brain. It's called 'Trauma-Informed Practice' and it's very new. With kids the results are phenomenal—they're healing and their mothers are healing. It's beautiful.

And the practical things can fall together as well with the right kinds of support—lives can definitely be rebuilt.

'Domestic and family violence is not acceptable in any culture.'

Q&A with Heather Nancarrow, Director of the Queensland Centre for Domestic and Family Violence Research and organiser of the annual Indigenous Family Violence Forum

The defence barrister in the first trial of Joseph Timbery said, 'This is clearly a trial that involves the Aboriginal race and their conduct to one another ... What persons in the general community might accept as reasonable and acceptable conduct ... might not necessarily be the accepted conduct of persons who fall within the earth people of this land. The accepted and proper tribunal may be, for these people, tribal councils and elders of the community.' What is your response to that?

We've had a number of cases where magistrates have reportedly said similar things, suggesting that these incidents don't have the same impact in indigenous communities—that they're 'used to it' so it's not as significant. But domestic and family violence is not acceptable in any culture.

There's very strong advocacy from indigenous men and women who say, 'This has never been accepted in our culture, and we need to stop it. We need strong sanctions opposing violence against women.' They are looking for alternative strategies, because the mainstream strategies haven't been effective and there are some barriers to indigenous women seeking mainstream justice. But that doesn't mean that they are in less need of protection from violence, or in less need of a justice response.

Another comment from the defence, pre-sentencing, was that the fact the offence occurred in the course of an ongoing relationship was a mitigating factor. Your comment?
Well, that's what domestic violence is! That's an outrageous comment and says something about the complete lack of understanding of the nature and dynamics of domestic violence.

One of the things that Lani had to overcome in order to seek justice was her mistrust of police. That's a significant issue for many indigenous women, isn't it?
This area of how the justice system responds to indigenous family violence, and the impact of that on women, has been my key area of research interest. In the year 2000 there were two Queensland investigations, one that I call 'the indigenous women's taskforce' and the other 'the non-indigenous women's taskforce'. They had opposite recommendations about the utility of restorative justice [an approach which focuses on repairing the harm done, rather than on punishment, and which brings together victims, offenders and community members to decide how that is best achieved]. Indigenous women were advocating for restorative justice, but there was strong opposition to it from non-indigenous women in the domestic and family violence area. So I set out to investigate.

My research revealed that indigenous women tend not to separate spousal violence from child abuse and sexual violence in the way that the mainstream society tends to compartmentalise them. That's one of the reasons they often prefer to use the term 'family violence' rather than 'domestic violence'. That ties in with the interest in restorative justice. Indigenous women are worried about the relationship of indigenous people to the criminal justice system, which is representative of the state.

In my research, women said they were worried that attempting to seek protection from violence against them by their male partners might lead to violence against the men if, for example, they were imprisoned. They were worried about appearing to be a traitor by turning a brother in to the cops. And a number of women talked about the ways in which going to the police resulted in more violence, not less. Sometimes they were further victimised by the original perpetrator, but sometimes they were victimised by other members of his family or even their own family, or by the broader community for 'betraying' him to the coppers.

In terms of that mistrust of the state, the stolen generations and the issue of deaths in custody are within very recent memory for a lot of indigenous people, aren't they?
Absolutely. I recently spoke with a youngish woman who is working in remote Aboriginal communities as a police prosecutor. She's been surprised by what the uniform still represents. She said, 'Time moves so slowly out there, it's like things that happened fifty years ago happened yesterday. Wearing that uniform, I'm representing those things that happened fifty years ago.' There's no longer the *Aboriginal Protection Act* and there's been the Apology [to the Stolen Generations, by (then) prime minister Kevin Rudd], but that history is still so present for a lot of those people.

So basically they want strategies to end violence against women that unite indigenous people rather than separate them through state intervention. Having said that, many women do call the cops because they want immediate help. But they want a different response than they get—they're suddenly embroiled in a whole criminal justice process when they just wanted immediate intervention for their own safety.

Given that fear and mistrust, but at the same time the need for some kind of safety and for some kind of external help, what can be done for indigenous women in that situation?
It's very complex, and I don't think that we can assume that indigenous women are all in the same circumstances or will have the same wish for the way their cases are dealt with. But certainly, a lot of the women I interviewed were saying, 'The mainstream justice that's applied isn't always effective for us. Even going to jail has no impact on some of these men.'

To give just one example, when I was deputy chair of the National Council to Reduce Violence against Women and their Children, I spent some time in the Cape communities, including Thursday Island. There was a story from there about a woman whose partner had been sent to prison on the mainland for three months after an extreme assault on her. She said to us there was nothing in jail to give him any insight into his behaviour or the issues affecting him; no program, no one helping him. And this is a common thing that women say. So he spent the entire three months working out in the gym. He came back not only bigger and stronger but also no longer afraid of going to jail. He just about killed her; she and her kids had to hide for three days on a remote island before they could get evacuated out to a shelter.

For those men, the women I spoke to said that it's got to be their own people holding them accountable, not just a reliance on the police and the external criminal justice system.

Tom Powell and Randal Ross have developed a program called Red Dust Healing. I don't think it's been rigorously evaluated yet, but people are finding it very valuable. It's hard to convey it in a few sentences, but it's based on traditional concepts. It's basically saying, 'We understand that there's a lot of violence in Aboriginal communities; we're tearing ourselves apart. It's largely a consequence of the harmful impacts of colonisation and the disruption to our traditional cultural practices, and our feelings of despair, and the whole context that we're living in. We need to heal. Here's a process to help us get in touch with our own pain and our own suffering, and to look at dealing with that as a way of healing ourselves and reinstating respect and appropriate behaviour towards others.' It's not an answer for everybody but it's a program that is in much demand.

With the research I'm currently doing, I went to a men's group out at Mount Isa. These are men who breached protection orders. There were about twenty men in the room, and most of them were indigenous. I told them about the research and asked if any of them would like to talk to me. I was surprised that four men immediately wanted to. I arranged to go out to where two of them were staying and they were waiting for me at the gate, they were so keen to tell their story. They weren't blaming or minimising particularly, although they didn't necessarily have the insight that you'd like to see. But they wanted someone to hear what was going on for them and hear about what shit lives they've had. Sometimes we can say, well, that's just them minimising or justifying or excusing. But those men have had pretty shit lives.

What Red Dust Healing does is an approach of challenging those men and holding them accountable, but in a way that also recognises their pain without justifying or excusing their behaviour. I think that's the power of the program, that it's able to get them to recognise that what they're doing is wrong, and they're responsible, they're making these choices, but to recognise they're making these choices from within the context of their experience and their pain. It's helping them to see they've got to deal with that and then move on so that they begin to feel good about themselves and not feel they have to batter other people down.

I don't think that we're ever going to have true reconciliation or healing for Aboriginal people until we've closed that gap so that they can get adequate and equal educational opportunities, employment opportunities and respect. It won't happen until the day comes when Aboriginal people can walk into a shop and not be looked at as if everyone's got to watch the till—because this is what Aboriginal people are still experiencing in urban communities as well as remote communities. I was speaking at an International Women's Conference in Cairns recently and I met up with an Aboriginal woman I know quite well. She said to me, 'We still warn our kids to be careful of you fellas.' She probably wouldn't say that to another white person because it's not what white people want to hear, but it's true. For a lot of Aboriginal people there isn't trust of white people in general, because they do continue to experience discrimination.

Alcohol and drug addiction were a really significant factor in the domestic violence Lani experienced. How common is that for indigenous women?
Very common. Indigenous women are suffering more homicide and hospitalisation than in the general community. Violence overall, including to men, is higher in indigenous communities. Within families, there's nearly always alcohol involved, and we see really quite serious attacks with weapons—seldom firearms,

but knives and bottles and star pickets; a heavy plastic milk crate was used in one incident I've just been reading about. There are all kinds of really terrible violence. You can't just deal with the violence, you have to deal with the broader context in which the violence is occurring, and that includes the alcohol and substance use.

Despite the many difficulties involved in seeking help, how important is it that women in that situation reach out to somebody?
I think it's critical. Because often they don't realise themselves just how much danger they're in.

We also know that the sooner women can get specialist help, with an appropriate response, the better. The longer it goes, the harder it is to get out, and the harder it is to get help.

There is routine screening for domestic violence in some settings, such as in antenatal clinics in Queensland, where they ask four questions: Are you ever afraid of your partner? In the last year has your partner hit, kicked, punched or otherwise hurt you? In the last year has your partner put you down, humiliated you or tried to control what you can do? And, in the last year has your partner threatened to hurt you? There are debates about whether routine screenings are appropriate because a woman might get an inappropriate response—if that woman feels she is being blamed in some way or doesn't get a response that is empathetic and helpful it might mean she never discloses again. So the people doing it must have the skills to respond appropriately.

Basically, there needs to be a wide range of responses to domestic and family violence. The system as a whole needs to be able to respond better to support victims of violence. We also need communities to be able to serve as ethical bystanders. To have family and strangers, neighbours and whoever else in the community stand beside the victim, stand with the victim, and report or challenge what's going on.

In your job you encounter so many incredibly grim stories. How do you keep going? What makes it all worthwhile for you?
I have been working in this area for thirty years and there's been such positive change in terms of programs and policy and services and awareness in that time. I think we are getting somewhere. We still have a major problem. This is a problem that's centuries old and we're not going to fix it in one generation or two generations, but we have to keep the momentum.

I see amazing people doing incredible work. I'm not only speaking about indigenous people, but in some ways I think they are the most inspiring because they tend to have the hardest jobs with the fewest resources, and for a lot of them this issue is very close to home. They have such passion and such commitment and such innovation.

I feel hope that we can address this. But it's much more complex than just addressing the individual: his violence against her. It's got to be a much more systemic response to the whole context in which that violence is occurring.

WHERE TO GET HELP

Getting help on domestic violence for yourself and others
If you or someone you know is in immediate danger, call 000 in Australia or 111 in New Zealand immediately.

Help is available from many services in Australia and New Zealand. The following DV lines are gateway services that can put you in touch with the best service for your needs, or can provide a listening ear.

AUSTRALIA, NATIONAL
Available twenty-four hours a day, seven days a week

1800RESPECT
(1800 737 732)
www.1800respect.org.au
The National Sexual Assault, Domestic Family Violence Counselling Service is a free and confidential telephone and online service for any Australian who is experiencing or has experienced domestic or family violence and/or sexual assault.

Translating and Interpreting Service: Call 13 14 50 and ask them to contact 1800RESPECT.

National Relay Service: for callers who are deaf or have a hearing or speech impairment:
- TTY/voice calls: phone 133 677 and ask them to contact 1800RESPECT (1800 737 732).
- Speak and Listen users: phone 1300 555 727 and ask them to contact 1800RESPECT (1800 737 732).
- Internet relay users: visit www.relayservice.com.au and ask them to contact 1800RESPECT (1800 737 732).

LIFELINE
13 11 44
www.lifeline.org.au/Get-Help/Facts---Information/Domestic-Abuse-and-Family-Violence
Among its crisis support services, Lifeline deals with domestic and family violence.

RECOMMENDED WEBSITES
www.lovegoodbadugly.com
www.burstingthebubble.com
These originate in Victoria but contain information on identifying and acting on domestic violence that is useful no matter where you are.

AUSTRALIA, STATES AND TERRITORIES
Available twenty-four hours a day, seven days a week

AUSTRALIAN CAPITAL TERRITORY
Domestic Violence Crisis Service ACT
02 6280 0900
www.dvcs.org.au

NEW SOUTH WALES
Domestic Violence Line
1800 65 64 63
www.domesticviolence.nsw.gov.au

NORTHERN TERRITORY
Dawn House
08 8945 1388
1800RESPECT (1800 737 732)

QUEENSLAND
DV Connect Women's DV Line
1800 811 811
www.dvconnect.org/dvline

SOUTH AUSTRALIA
Domestic Violence Crisis Service
1300 782 200
Domestic Violence and Aboriginal Family Violence Gateway Service (including DV Help Line)
1800 800 098

TASMANIA
Family Violence Response and Referral line
1800 633 937
www.safeathome.tas.gov.au/services

VICTORIA
Women's Domestic Violence Crisis Service
1800 015 188 or 03 9322 3555
www.wdvcs.org.au

WESTERN AUSTRALIA
Women's Domestic Violence Helpline
08 9223 1188 or 1800 007 339

NEW ZEALAND

WOMEN'S REFUGE NATIONAL CRISISLINE
0800 REFUGE (0800 733 843)
Available twenty-four hours a day, seven days a week; call toll free from anywhere in NZ. (If you're in Auckland you can also call 09 378 1893.)
www.womensrefuge.org.nz
Provides information, advice and support about domestic violence as well as help in a crisis.

SHINE
0508 744 633
9 am to 11 pm, seven days a week.
www.2shine.org.nz

Domestic Abuse Helpline for anyone living with abuse. The website includes information on how to stop someone knowing you have been seeking information online about domestic violence.

FAMILY VIOLENCE INFORMATION LINE
0800 456 450
9 am to 11 pm, seven days a week, with an after-hours message redirecting callers in an emergency.
www.areyouok.org.nz
Provides self-help information and connection to appropriate services.

OTHER RECOMMENDED WEBSITES
www.familyservices.govt.nz
The Family and Community Services site has a directory of social services in each community.

www.justice.govt.nz
The Ministry of Justice site has information about protection orders.

www.nnsvs.org.nz
The National Network of Stopping Violence site has a directory of local services.

For those working in the domestic violence area (Australia)

DV-ALERT
A free, accredited domestic violence response training program run by Lifeline and available nationally to health, allied health and frontline workers helping those who have experienced domestic and family violence.
www.dvalert.org.au/
02 6215 9418

EDUCATION CENTRE AGAINST VIOLENCE
A NSW Health-run service, its brief is to improve services for people whose lives have been affected by interpersonal violence. It does this by providing state-wide training and development for people who provide services to children and adults who have experienced sexual assault, domestic or Aboriginal family violence and/or physical and emotional abuse and neglect.
www.ecav.health.nsw.gov.au
02 9840 3737

Getting Help and Information on Drugs and Alcohol

AUSTRALIA, NATIONAL
Cannabis Information and Helpline
1800 30 40 50

AUSTRALIA, STATES AND TERRITORIES

AUSTRALIAN CAPITAL TERRITORY
24 Hour Alcohol and Drug Helpline
02 6207 9977

NEW SOUTH WALES
Alcohol and Drug Information Service
02 9361 8000 (Sydney); 1800 422 599 (free call)
www.yourroom.com.au

NORTHERN TERRITORY
Alcohol and Drug Information Service
1800 131 350 (statewide free call)

QUEENSLAND
Alcohol and Drug Information Service
1800 177 833 (statewide free call)

SOUTH AUSTRALIA
Alcohol and Drug Information Service
1300 131 340 (statewide, local call fee)

TASMANIA
Alcohol and Drug Information Service
1800 811 994 (statewide free call)

VICTORIA
DirectLine
1800 888 236 (statewide free call)

WESTERN AUSTRALIA
Alcohol and Drug Information Service
08 9442 5000 (Perth); 1800 198 024 (free call)
Parent Drug Information Service
08 9442 5050 (Perth); 1800 653 203 (free call)

To check on any updated numbers, go to the National Drugs Sector Information Service website, http://ndsis.adca.org.au/ndsis_publications.php, and see the *Tips and Tricks for New Players* publication.

NEW ZEALAND

ALCOHOL DRUG HELPLINE
0800 787 797
10 am to 10 pm, seven days a week.
www.addictionshelp.org.nz
Alcohol Drug Association New Zealand provides free, confidential information, help and support through its helpline.

The website includes an online directory with a searchable list of alcohol and drug treatment and advice services available throughout New Zealand.

ALCOHOLICS ANONYMOUS
0800 AA WORKS or 0800 229 675
www.aa.org.nz
General help, information and support on alcohol issues as well as details for AA meetings in your area.

NARCOTICS ANONYMOUS
0800 NA TODAY or 0800 628 632
General help, information and support on drug issues, as well as details for NA meetings in your area.

NEW ZEALAND DRUG FOUNDATION
www.drughelp.org.nz
Shared stories from people whose lives have been affected by drugs and practical information on how to help yourself or a friend with drug issues.

Acknowledgements

There are so many people who have helped me along the journey. Without their love and support I wouldn't be here today. John, you showed me what real love is and you helped me heal. You're my rock and I'm so proud of you and our beautiful girls, Tymekqwa, Iesha, Lateia, Kiani, Kirrawahn and Shakylah. Mum, we have an unbreakable bond, even if I haven't always been able to see it. Dad, you're my hero, not just for coming to my rescue but for stepping up and speaking out about male violence, and for showing there is another way. My beloved late nan, Wha Wha, my sisters Koorine and Shalitta and my brothers Darryl, Garri and Carlos are the other points on my heart's compass—they never gave up on me, even when things were at their worst. Aunty Carol, Symone and Guyleen went so far above and beyond, putting my needs above their own. I'll always be grateful. Anna, Bianca, Naomi and Allira were always there for me, along with too many other friends to mention—you know who you are.

I couldn't imagine navigating my way through the justice system without Josephine Cashman, Scott Johnson and Samantha Smith by my side. Patsy Gray's kindness helped me open up for the first time and she spoke out for me later. Gujaga Child Care Centre made it possible for me to leave my babies and go to court knowing they were in loving hands. The La Perouse community have seen too much pain, but they, too, are staunch survivors who were there for me.

Genevieve Grieves, Lisa Kitching and the team at Blackfella Films, and SBS helped me to take the first steps in sharing my story with the world via television documentary. Tara Wynne at Curtis Brown, Fiona Henderson, Catherine Milne and Amanda O'Connell at HarperCollins helped me to take the next step and write this book. Hazel Flynn got to know me inside and out and helped me find the words.

My thanks, too, to Anna Cooper at the DPP and Karen Wilcox, Heather Nancarrow and the other experts and organisations who helped us with the information at the end of the book and who work every day to turn lives around.

www.ingramcontent.com/pod-product-compliance
Lightning Source LLC
Chambersburg PA
CBHW022034290426
44109CB00014B/858